W9-BVS-008

Château
Cuisine

ANNE WILLAN

CHÂTEAU CUISINE

PHOTOGRAPHY BY
CHRISTOPHER BAKER

IN ASSOCIATION WITH
FRIENDS OF VIEILLES MAISONS FRANÇAISES

MACMILLAN PUBLISHING COMPANY
NEW YORK

MAXWELL MACMILLAN INTERNATIONAL
NEW YORK   OXFORD   SINGAPORE   SYDNEY

NOTE

Basic recipes included in the glossary are cross-referenced with page numbers, whereas glossary tips and techniques are indicated with an asterisk.

First published in 1992 by
Conran Octopus Limited
37 Shelton Street
London WC2H 9HN

U.S. edition published by
Macmillan Publishing Company
866 Third Avenue
New York, NY 10022

Macmillan Publishing Company
is part of the Maxwell
Communication Group of Companies

Text copyright © 1992 by Anne Willan Inc
Photography copyright © 1992 by Christopher Baker

All rights reserved. No part of this book may be
reproduced or transmitted in any form or by any means,
electronic or mechanical, including photocopying, recording,
or by any information storage and retrieval system,
without permission in writing from the Publisher.

Designer – Paul Welti
Project Editors – Louise Simpson and Denise Bates
Editor – Norma MacMillan
Editorial Assistant – Josephine Mead
Production – Julia Golding
Food Photography Stylist – Caroline Champenois
Map Artist – Rodney Paull

Library of Congress Cataloging-in-Publication Data
Willan, Anne.
    Château cuisine / Anne Willan: photography by Christopher Baker.
        p.   cm.
    "In association with Friends of Vieilles Maisons françaises."
    Includes index.
    ISBN 0–02–629955–0
    1. Cookery, French. 2. Castles—France. I. Title.
TX719.W5673   1993   92–41797   CIP
641.5944—dc20

Macmillan books are available at special
discounts for bulk purchases for sales
promotions, premiums, fund-raising, or
educational use. For details, contact:

Special Sales Director
Macmillan Publishing Company
866 Third Avenue
New York, NY 10022

10 9 8 7 6 5 4 3 2 1
Printed in Hong Kong

CONTENTS

FOREWORD

Château d'Ainay-le-Vieil, a magnificent fortress with nine imposing turrets, is owned by Princesse Georges-Henri de la Tour d'Auvergne and her five brothers and sisters (right).

The elegant drawing room at Château du Feÿ, home of La Varenne cooking school (title page).

Anne Willan takes full advantage of the glorious produce at her local market in Burgundy (copyright page).

It is often said that the history of a society can be traced through the recipes of its people. In France, a country renowned for its crops and livestock as well as its fish and wild game, it was often the kitchens of the *châteaux* that gathered and retained the traditional recipes of the region. Here these recipes were influenced by the exotic spices and methods that came from the East and the strange fruits and vegetables from the New World. These imports enhanced the produce of the great *châteaux*, bringing out the full flavors of their native fish, meat, and game.

In a land of such indisputable gourmands and gourmets, history and gastronomy have developed hand in hand. Henri IV owes his popularity to his Sunday Chicken, which he promised to all his people, and the *grand chef* Vatel is best remembered for committing suicide when the dinner he had prepared for Louis XIV was not ready on time. Many other celebrities have given their names to delicious recipes and are still commemorated on our menus today.

Gastronomy and the fine arts are more closely linked in France than in any other country. Paintings, porcelain, glassware, sculpture, and even interior design all bear witness to the historic importance of food in our culture. Even the word *cuisine* refers not only to the kitchen as a workplace, but signifies the entire art of cooking for the French. Right from the beginning, the kitchen was a hallowed area of the château, often carefully planned and equipped, as today, with mechanical wonders, not to mention a battery of copper pots and earthenware. The recipes that our cooks created have always been a subtle synthesis of different tastes, influenced by geography and climate, by fashion, religious belief, and folklore.

I myself spent a privileged childhood in a medieval château, which has been in my family for more than 500 years. I had a happy time there, living in step with the seasons among a continuous throng of cousins, playing under the canopy of the trees or up in the huge old lofts. Like so many other old families, we knew how to live in the present, but the house acted as a touchstone with the past, withstanding the hustle and bustle of the outside world.

The hold of such houses on our lives and our emotions is also keenly felt by everyone who has so kindly opened their doors to us. And it is to those people that I would like to express my sincere thanks for their warm welcome and the generous sharing of their personal recipes and family traditions.

The mission of Friends of Vieilles Maisons Françaises is to help preserve the architectural heritage of France. We at FVMF have joined enthusiastically in creating this very special book, which brings you a personal glimpse of more than thirty *châteaux* and country houses, of the families who live in them, and of their cooking. Through *Château Cuisine* we hope you will enjoy not just the richness of French cooking, but also the splendid architecture, which bridges the centuries from the Middle Ages through the Renaissance and right up to the present day.

[signature]

Princesse Georges-Henri de la Tour d'Auvergne
President, Friends of Vieilles Maisons Françaises
Château d'Ainay, February, 1992.

Château Cuisine has been published in collaboration with Friends of Vieilles Maisons Françaises, an international nonprofit association dedicated to preserving France's architectural heritage, notably through mobilizing international support for the restoration of historic monuments. If you would like more information about FVMF, please contact Friends of Vieilles Maisons Françaises

91 rue du Faubourg Saint-Honoré
Suite 31
75008 Paris, France.

INTRODUCTION

Château d'Anjony with its gracious interiors and beautiful antiques is also a family home (right).

Surely no two words are more evocative of the civilization and culture of France than *château* and *cuisine*. Both are universal terms, needing no translation. And for me, working on *Château Cuisine* has proved to be a double pleasure, involving two of my favorite subjects: history and fine food.

Early on, my husband and I had the good fortune to meet Friends of Vieilles Maisons Françaises, the international foundation based in New York. Through Burks Hamner, Vice Chairman of FVMF's Southern California chapter, we met Princesse Georges-Henri de la Tour d'Auvergne, President of FVMF, and her associate, Simone Monneron, in Paris. From start to finish, this book has depended on their joint dedication and great enthusiasm more than I can say.

The four of us rapidly agreed on the ground rules for *Château Cuisine*: Each château, whether large or small, great monument, or family *manoir*, must be privately owned and inhabited. The properties would cover a wide range of styles and geographical settings. And most importantly, the owners must share our own love of good food. We defined five regions – the Île de France and the Loire valley, with their great palaces of leisure; the romantic north, land of mist and sea; the heart of France – Burgundy and the Berry in particular; *châteaux*, often fortresses, with a mountain background; and, of course, *châteaux* in the sun.

Missing from our grand design was a photographer. The imaginative pictures of Christopher Baker speak for themselves – his creative eye and camera are a château's best friend. Jane Sigal's contribution as roving researcher, recipe editor, and project coordinator is less visible, yet has also been vital to the progress of this book. My associates at FVMF join me in expressing our deep appreciation to them both.

What has emerged is a personal portrait of thirty-four *châteaux*. Times change, and we now live in a world where owners must be highly inventive to make their properties habitable and economic. Talking to the châtelains who have so generously given of their time, I've been constantly delighted by the diverse ways great old buildings are being brought to life, whether by opening to the public, by accepting overnight guests, or by launching a restaurant in the out-buildings. Few *châteaux* now depend in the old way on the surrounding land, though some are vineyard properties, particularly in the south. For every owner, a château is a way of life; in the words of the Duchesse de Chevreuse at Dampierre, "to leave is unimaginable."

What a pleasure, too, the hundred recipes in *Château Cuisine* have been. No sign of dreary old classics, but plenty of surprises with dishes which transfer extraordinarily well from page to plate – reassuring proof, if any were needed, of continuing French expertise in the kitchen. Appropriately, it was a niece of that great gourmet Talleyrand, the Princesse de Poix, who declared that "*Le signe distinctif d'une femme bien née, c'est de se connaître en cuisine*" ("The distinguishing mark of every well-bred woman is to know her way in cuisine"). Two Empires, five Republics, and several foreign occupations later, this lapidary judgment still stands. As Henrik de Monpezat, the French-born Prince Consort of Denmark, told me, "I take pride in keeping a good table." Now I've come to appreciate that he was speaking for all his fellow châtelains.

Anne Willan

Anne Willan

Château du Feÿ, 89300 Villecien, February, 1992.

CHÂTEAUX

OF LEISURE

CHÂTEAU DU MARAIS

THE CONCEPT OF THE COUNTRY RETREAT, OR *"RÉSIDENCE SECONDAIRE,"* IS BY NO MEANS A NEW ONE. PARIS IS RINGED WITH *CHÂTEAUX* BUILT FOR THE LEISURE OF THEIR METROPOLITAN OWNERS. VERSAILLES BEGAN AS A HUNTING LODGE, AND HENRI II DESIGNED ANET FOR THE ENJOYMENT OF HIS MISTRESS, DIANE DE POITIERS. THE CHÂTEAU DU MARAIS IS A LATECOMER AS A PLEASURE DOME, HAVING BEEN CONSTRUCTED AS RECENTLY AS 1778 BY A WEALTHY GOVERNMENT TREASURER-GENERAL CALLED LE MAISTRE. IT WAS CLEARLY HIS INTENT TO ENTERTAIN ON A GRAND SCALE — HENCE THE STATELY PILLARS AND VAST *COUR D'HONNEUR* FOR THE RECEPTION OF CARRIAGES. THE ARTIFICIAL LAKE, OVER 550 YARDS LONG, REFLECTS ITS SURROUNDINGS SO PERFECTLY IT IS KNOWN AS "THE MIRROR."

THE PROPERTY QUICKLY PASSED FROM LE MAISTRE TO A YOUNG WIDOW, MADAME DE LA BRICHE, WHO ORGANIZED COUNTRY FESTIVALS FOR THE PEASANTRY. "WE SET LARGE TABLES IN THE PARKLAND ALLEYS," SHE RECORDED IN HER DIARY. "THE ONLY EXPENSES FOR A CHARMING DAY, FULL OF GAIETY AND GOODWILL, WERE THE CAKES AND SPICE BREADS, THE WINE, AND THE VIOLINISTS FOR DANCING." HER GENEROSITY WAS HAPPILY REWARDED; LE MARAIS WAS LEFT UNTOUCHED DURING THE REVOLUTION.

The magnificent gardens of Château du Marais, with their spring cloak of daffodils (right), stretch down to the imposing "Mirror" lake (previous page).

In the early 19th century, Château du Marais was a favorite meeting place of the French literary and political establishment. The restoration of the property began in earnest under Anna Gould, the American railroad heiress who married the Duc de Talleyrand-Périgord in 1908.

Happily, the tradition of receptions and literary salons at Le Marais lasted another 50 years, so much so that in the 1830s the château was called "the most solid structure of the monarchy." Guests included statesmen such as Talleyrand and the novelists Madame de Staël and Prosper Mérimée. Another literary giant of the age, François-René de Chateaubriand, described Madame de la Briche as "an excellent woman, never short of good luck."

Since the time of Madame de la Briche, Le Marais has been a château owned and appreciated by women. It passed to her daughter and granddaughter, and then at the end of the century to the most famous châtelaine of all, the American railroad heiress Anna Gould, who started a program of restoration. In 1908, she married Hélie de Talleyrand-Périgord, who was a duke not once but three times over – Duc de Talleyrand, Duc de Dino, and Duc de Sagan. The first person to hold all three titles was a colorful personality, Dorothea of Courland, who was Talleyrand's niece by marriage and also one of his many mistresses.

Under the American duchess, the Château du Marais again became an exclusive haven for Europe's nobility. Her granddaughter, known as the Duchesse de Sagan, is the present owner. She shares with her three children the task of maintaining the château and its outbuildings, which include an orangery, a museum devoted to family history, and a functioning water mill, besides more than 60 acres of parkland. "It is so hard to preserve," laments Comtesse Guy de Bagneux, the Duchesse's daughter. "We are only 25 miles from Paris. Highways and power lines encroach all the time." For Comtesse Guy the menace seems all the more threatening – her most nostalgic childhood memories are of intimate afternoon tea in the park with her legendary American grandmother. "The chef prepared special cakes, but what we all loved best was cinnamon toast."

Majestic balustrades and exquisite classical lines are softened and broken in the limpid reflections of the lake below the château.

PERDREAUX EN CHARTREUSE

MOLDED PARTRIDGE WITH CABBAGE

This ancient recipe has featured at Le Marais for years. It apparently originated with Catherine de Thouars, who in the 1430s was thrown into a dungeon by her husband, Gilles de Thouars, otherwise known as Bluebeard. While imprisoned, Catherine is said to have amused herself by cooking. This elaborate recipe would certainly have whiled away her time!

6 servings

2 MEDIUM HEADS SAVOY CABBAGE (ABOUT
3½ pounds EACH)

1 pound CARROTS

1½ pounds TURNIPS

1 tbsp VEGETABLE OIL

¼ pound SLAB BACON, CUT INTO *LARDONS**

3 PARTRIDGES (ABOUT 1 pound EACH),
GIBLETS REMOVED
AND TRUSSED*

2 tbsp BUTTER, AT ROOM TEMPERATURE

SALT AND PEPPER

1½ cups CHICKEN STOCK (see page 221)

9-inch SHALLOW ROUND BAKING DISH

Discard any damaged outer leaves from the cabbages. Immerse 8 large green leaves from each head in a large pan of boiling salted water, then remove them with a slotted spoon as they soften. Refresh the leaves with cold water*. Cut the heart of each cabbage into 8 wedges. Blanch the wedges in the boiling water* until tender, 10 to 15 minutes, then remove with a slotted spoon and refresh them. Shred the cabbage wedges, discarding the core. Keep the water boiling.

Preheat the oven to 450°F.

Peel the carrots and turnips and cut them lengthwise into ⅛-inch-thick slices. Cook the carrots and turnips separately in the boiling water until just tender, 8 to 10 minutes for the

carrots and 5 to 7 minutes for the turnips. Drain them and then refresh with cold water. Using a 1¼-inch cookie cutter, cut out rounds from one-third of the carrot and turnip slices. Cut the remaining slices into rectangles, trimming them to the height of the baking dish and to a width of about ½ inch.

Heat the oil in a frying pan. Add the bacon and cook over low heat until golden, about 5 minutes. Drain on paper towels.

Rub the partridges with the butter and sprinkle them with salt and pepper. Set them in a roasting pan and roast in the heated oven until the juice runs pink when a bird is lifted with a two-pronged fork, 20 to 30 minutes. Baste them often during cooking. When the birds are cooked, remove them to a carving board. Discard the string; cut the legs from the birds and reserve them. Cut off the breast meat and carve each piece into two or three slices on the diagonal. Reserve the carcasses. Reduce the oven temperature to 350°F.

Pour the stock into the roasting pan and bring to a boil on top of the stove, stirring to dissolve the roasting juices. Add the reserved carcasses and simmer the stock until reduced by two-thirds, 10 to 15 minutes, then strain it and taste for seasoning.

To assemble the *chartreuse*, first butter the baking dish and line the bottom and sides with waxed paper; also butter the paper. Arrange a ring of alternating carrot and turnip rounds, slightly overlapping, around the bottom of the dish. Arrange a smaller but similar ring of vegetable rounds in the center. Stand the vegetable rectangles upright around the sides, alternating the carrots and turnips and spacing them slightly apart. Line the dish with the cabbage leaves, saving 2 or 3 leaves for the top. Combine the shredded cabbage and bacon. Taste the cabbage mixture and adjust the seasoning. Spread one-third of the cabbage mixture in the dish and pour one-third of the reduced stock over it. Arrange half the partridge slices on top. Cover with half the remaining cabbage mixture, pour in half the remaining reduced stock, and then add the rest of the partridge slices. Pack the remaining cabbage mixture in the dish, add the

LIQUEUR A L'ESTRAGON

TARRAGON LIQUEUR

One of the villagers who worked at Le Marais left this recipe with the Bagneux family. French markets sell neutral spirits for conserving fruits in alcohol, but vodka also works well. Other herbs such as rosemary and thyme, or spices such as juniper, can be substituted for the tarragon. Tarragon liqueur adds an unusual flavor to strawberries and to cantaloupe.

Makes 3 cups liqueur

A LARGE BUNCH OF FRESH TARRAGON
(ABOUT 1 ounce)
3 cups NEUTRAL *EAU-DE-VIE*
OR VODKA
1½ cups SUGAR
2 VANILLA BEANS, SPLIT

1-quart PRESERVING JAR

Perdreaux en Chartreuse, molded partridge with cabbage, is a dish that dates back to the 15th century. It is still made at Le Marais with local partridge and homegrown vegetables.

rest of the stock, and set the partridge legs on top. Press the reserved cabbage leaves over the surface, trimming them to fit.

Cover the dish with buttered waxed paper or aluminum foil and set a heatproof plate that fits inside the dish on top to compress the *chartreuse*. Set the dish in a water bath* and bring the water to a boil on top of the stove. Transfer the dish to the heated oven and bake until a skewer inserted in the center for 30 seconds is hot to the touch when withdrawn, about 1 hour. Remove from the oven and let it stand in the water bath at least 2 hours to firm up.

Remove the plate and paper or foil and unmold the *chartreuse* onto a warmed platter. Peel off the lining paper and adjust the decoration if needed. Serve the *chartreuse* cut into wedges.

The *chartreuse* can be kept in the refrigerator overnight; remove it from the water bath and let it come to room temperature first. Before serving, reheat the *chartreuse* in a water bath in a preheated 350°F oven, if necessary.

Reserve 2 tarragon sprigs for decoration. Coarsely chop the remaining tarragon, including the stems. Combine the chopped tarragon in a saucepan with the *eau-de-vie* or vodka, sugar, and vanilla beans. Cook over low heat, stirring from time to time, until the sugar dissolves. Remove the pan from the heat, cover, and let cool. Taste the liqueur and add more sugar to taste.

Sterilize the preserving jar*. Pour in the liqueur and seal it. Leave it in a cool place 2 or 3 days, shaking the jar occasionally.

Strain the liqueur through cheesecloth into a pitcher. Put the reserved tarragon in the preserving jar and pour in the strained liqueur. Seal the jar and store it in a cool place at least 1 month before drinking.

A glimpse across the pillared dining room.

BISCUIT GLACÉ CARÊME

STRAWBERRY AND VANILLA ICE CREAM CAKE

At the Congress of Vienna, Marie-Antonin Carême acted as chef to Charles-Maurice de Talleyrand-Périgord, the "architect of Europe." No chef could have had a better assignment because Talleyrand always maintained that the success of political negotiations depended on "receiving with magnificence and offering the finest cuisine." The memory of Carême has been preserved in the Talleyrand-Périgord family by this recipe above all others – a typically elegant creation of the greatest of chefs. This cake is also delicious made with raspberry ice cream.

8 to 10 servings

1 pint VANILLA ICE CREAM
(see page 220)
1 pint STRAWBERRY ICE CREAM
(see page 220)
1 STRAWBERRY, SLICED

For the sponge cake
⅔ cup ALL-PURPOSE FLOUR
PINCH OF SALT
3 LARGE EGGS, SEPARATED
7 tbsp SUGAR
¾ tsp VANILLA EXTRACT OR
GRATED ZEST OF 1 LEMON
¼ cup COGNAC OR BRANDY

For the Chantilly cream
½ cup HEAVY CREAM
2 tsp CONFECTIONERS' SUGAR, SIFTED
¼ tsp VANILLA EXTRACT

8-inch SQUARE CAKE PAN; PASTRY BAG AND MEDIUM STAR TUBE; ICE CREAM MAKER (OPTIONAL)

For the sponge cake, butter the cake pan and line the bottom with waxed paper. Butter the paper and coat the pan with flour, discarding the excess. Preheat the oven to 350°F.

Sift the flour with the salt. Whisk the egg yolks with half the sugar and the vanilla extract or lemon zest in a bowl by hand or with an electric mixer until the mixture falls from the whisk in a thick ribbon and holds a slowly dissolving trail, about 5 minutes. In another bowl, whisk the egg whites until stiff. Add the remaining sugar and whisk until glossy to make a light meringue, about 30 seconds longer. Gently fold the meringue into the egg yolk mixture with the flour, adding it in three batches.

Pour the batter into the prepared pan and bake in the heated oven until the cake shrinks slightly and the top springs back when lightly pressed with a fingertip, 20 to 30 minutes. Run a knife around the cake and unmold onto a rack to cool. Peel off the lining paper. (The cake can be kept 1 or 2 days in an airtight container. It freezes well, too.)

About 1 to 1½ hours before serving the cake, transfer the vanilla and the strawberry ice cream to the refrigerator to soften just until spreadable. Make the Chantilly cream (see page 220) and refrigerate it.

Trim the crusty brown sides from the cake, then cut the cake in half horizontally with a long serrated knife to make two layers. Brush each layer with Cognac or brandy to moisten it.

To assemble the cake, spread one layer with the softened vanilla ice cream using a metal spatula. Cover it with the second cake layer and press lightly to flatten it. Spread the top with the softened strawberry ice cream. Freeze the cake until firm, about 20 minutes.

Scoop the Chantilly cream into the pastry bag. Pipe a rosette of Chantilly cream in the center of the cake and top with the sliced strawberry. Pipe rosettes of Chantilly cream in rows around the edge of the cake. (The cake can be kept in the freezer up to 30 minutes, but is best served as soon as possible after decorating so the Chantilly cream does not freeze.)

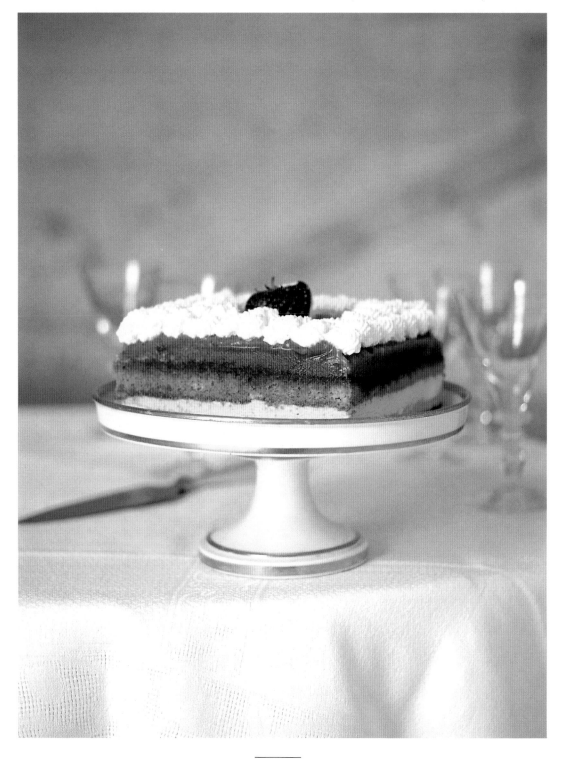

Biscuit Glacé Carême, a sublime dessert created by Marie-Antonin Carême, the famous 19th-century French chef still regarded by many as the greatest of all time.

CHÂTEAU DE COURANCES

Louis XIV much appreciated the fresh water of Courances — 12 springs feed the ornamental gardens. Today the gardens attract visitors from all over the world, who come to see one of the best-preserved examples of Le Nôtre landscaping in France.

WHEN I ASKED THE MARQUISE DE GANAY THE NUMBER OF ROOMS AT COURANCES, SHE SOUNDED AMUSED. "IMPOSSIBLE TO COUNT!" SHE REPLIED. "THERE ARE, IN ANY CASE, SIX KITCHENS — ONE FOR OURSELVES, ONE FOR THE STAFF, ONE FOR PARTIES, AND ONE FOR EACH OF MY THREE DAUGHTERS WHO HAVE A HOME HERE." COURANCES IS ONE OF THE GREAT *CHÂTEAUX* OF THE ÎLE-DE-FRANCE, BUILT IN THE MID-16TH CENTURY FOR COSME CLAUSSE, MINISTER OF FINANCE TO HENRI II. ITS NAME SUGGESTS RUNNING WATER — A REFERENCE TO THE MANY STREAMS THAT TRAVERSED THE PROPERTY BEFORE THEY WERE TAMED IN THE 17TH CENTURY BY THE GREAT LANDSCAPIST, ANDRÉ LE NÔTRE. HE ENDOWED COURANCES WITH AN ORNAMENTAL LAKE AND A SERIES OF CASCADES AND VISTAS WHICH ALMOST RIVAL THOSE OF VERSAILLES.

AFTER 250 YEARS OF CONSPICUOUS PRESENCE, COURANCES PROVED TOO TEMPTING A TARGET FOR REVOLUTIONARY FRANCE. IN 1791, THE CHÂTEAU WAS INVADED BY TROOPS LOOKING FOR NONEXISTENT WEAPONS. TWO YEARS LATER THE OWNER, MARQUIS "LE GRAND NICOLAY" AND HIS SON WERE IMPRISONED AND EXECUTED. HIS WIDOW CLUNG BRAVELY TO THE FAMILY HOME, BUT BY 1830 THE CHÂTEAU HAD BEEN ABANDONED. IN FEBRUARY 1866, ARTIST JULES COEUR NOTED: "RENOIR, SISLEY, AND I . . . LEFT BY CARRIAGE FOR COURANCES AND ITS BEAUTIFUL CHÂTEAU. ABANDONED AND SURROUNDED BY WATER, IT IS CRUMBLING LITTLE BY LITTLE LIKE A PIECE OF SUGAR IN A DAMP CORNER."

Courances is full of ghosts, like that of the young Huguenot, Agrippa d'Aubigné, who at the age of 12 danced with such grace that he was spared an imminent death sentence and lived to become a noted 16th-century poet. The diarist Madame de Sévigné spent a rather uncomfortable night here in 1676, complaining of a very damp bed.

In 1870, the Baron de Gaber, great-grandfather of the current Marquis de Ganay, arrived on the scene. He restored what was left of the château and its grounds with the help of another great gardener, Achille Duchène. But the renaissance was short-lived. In World War II Courances became headquarters of the Luftwaffe, which exploded a munitions dump while making a hasty retreat in 1944. Then Courances became an American military prison, and was again badly shaken by an explosion, this time accidental. It was Field Marshal Montgomery who put the property to rights when he chose it as his base during his NATO command after the war.

Today this troubled past is invisible. After ten years of arduous restoration, Marquis and Marquise de Ganay were satisfied with the state of the gardens. Today Marie-Rose de Ganay leaves them in the charge of an Englishman, whose other vocation is music. The château is lively with friends, visitors from abroad, garden openings in spring, and hunting in the fall.

All the daughters have their own living areas in the château, and they bring their families and spend what time they can at Courances. Anne-Marie de Ganay-Meyer runs an international decorating business under the name *"Juste Mauve."* Valentine is a feature writer on literature and gardens, while in the 1970s, Lauraine ran a catering business in Paris. "My hobby became my *métier*," she says. "Everyone thought there must be a chef behind the scenes, but it was actually me peeling the potatoes. I cooked as I would at home. My food was homemade and certainly looked it. There were no lobsters in starched napkins and coatings of aspic, the typical caterer's signature."

Lauraine was certainly untypical in the world of Parisian cuisine, monopolized as it is by macho chefs. For her parents' anniversary, Lauraine cooked a dinner for 50 of Moroccan-style *bstila* filled with skate, spinach, and mushrooms, and a *snob au chocolat*, a molded specialty of their old Polish cook, with a texture that is half cream, half chocolate truffle. Lauraine had told me, "We are all multilingual at Courances," and I couldn't help thinking that this was equally true of the cooking!

BAVAROIS A LA TOMATE

TOMATO RING FILLED WITH GOAT CHEESE AND BASIL

An array of cheeses from the Barthélemy dairy in Fontainebleau, including (clockwise from top right) brie de Meaux, brie de Melun, Coulommiers, and fromage de Fontainebleau (right). Guardian geese survey their terrain under a fine canopy of old sycamores (below).

We may think of molded salads as somewhat old-fashioned, but they have never gone out of style in French households. Lauraine de Ganay updates this fifties' classic by filling the ring with a mixture of tangy goat cheese, olive oil, and fresh chopped basil – a wonderful way to enjoy the wealth of local dairy produce. One of the delights of this dish is its convenience. "Like most of my recipes," she says, "it can be prepared well ahead."

8 servings

3 pounds TOMATOES, PEELED
AND SEEDED*
2 STALKS CELERY,
FINELY CHOPPED
SALT AND PEPPER
6 DROPS OF TABASCO SAUCE,
MORE IF NEEDED
2 tbsp UNFLAVORED GELATIN
6 tbsp BROWN STOCK (see page 221)
½ pound FIRM GOAT CHEESE,
CUT INTO ⅜-inch PIECES
¼ cup OLIVE OIL
2 tbsp CHOPPED FRESH BASIL
FRESH BASIL LEAVES TO DECORATE
(OPTIONAL)

1-quart RING MOLD

Process the tomatoes and celery in a food processor or blender until smooth. Season the purée to taste with salt, pepper, and Tabasco sauce.

Sprinkle the gelatin over the stock in a small saucepan and set aside until it swells to a spongy consistency, about 5 minutes. Melt the gelatin over low heat, then let it cool until tepid, stirring occasionally.

Stir the gelatin smoothly into the tomato purée. Sprinkle the mold with cold water. Pour the tomato purée into the mold, cover it, and refrigerate until set, at least 6 hours. The tomato *bavarois* can be stored up to a day in the refrigerator, provided it is not in a metal mold.

To finish, toss the cheese with the oil, chopped basil, and pepper to taste. Unmold the *bavarois* onto a platter. Pile the cheese in the center. Decorate the *bavarois* with basil leaves if you like.

CARRÉ DE PORC AUX GROSEILLES

PORK LOIN FILLED WITH RED CURRANTS

Fresh red currants from the garden at Courances make an unusual stuffing for pork, as well as flavoring the sauce. At other times of year, tart fruits such as cherries, plums, and cranberries can be substituted for the red currants. Pit the fruit when necessary and cut it into chunks. A crisp potato cake is an excellent accompaniment.

8 servings

1 PORK LOIN ROAST, CONSISTING OF 8
CHOPS, RIBS SCRAPED CLEAN
1½ pounds RED CURRANTS
SALT AND PEPPER
2 tbsp VEGETABLE OIL
1 cup DRY WHITE WINE

Preheat the oven to 425°F.

Set the meat on a carving board, scraped ribs upward. Cut down between each chop, leaving the base joined, to form pockets for stuffing. Or have the butcher do this for you.

Pull the currants off the stems with the tines of a fork. Sprinkle the fruit with salt and pepper and push half of them into the pockets between the chops. Tie the roast lengthwise tightly with string. Brush the oil over the meat. Put the loin in a roasting pan and roast it in the heated oven, basting often, until a skewer inserted in the center of the meat feels hot to the touch when it is withdrawn after 30 seconds, 50 to 60 minutes. A meat thermometer should register 170°F.

Transfer the roast to a carving board with a juice catcher, cover it loosely with aluminum foil, and let it rest while preparing the sauce.

Skim all the fat from the roasting pan, leaving the cooking juices. Add the wine and remaining currants to the pan and bring to a boil, scraping to dissolve the browned roasting juices. Boil until the liquid is reduced by half and the currants are tender, 5 to 7 minutes. Taste the sauce for seasoning.

Remove the string from the roast and carve it, cutting down between each chop. Arrange the chops on a warmed platter. Stir the carving juices into the sauce. Spoon some of the sauce around the chops. Serve the remainder separately in a warm sauceboat.

Carré de Porc aux Groseilles. Home-grown red currants marry well with pork in this surprisingly simple dish.

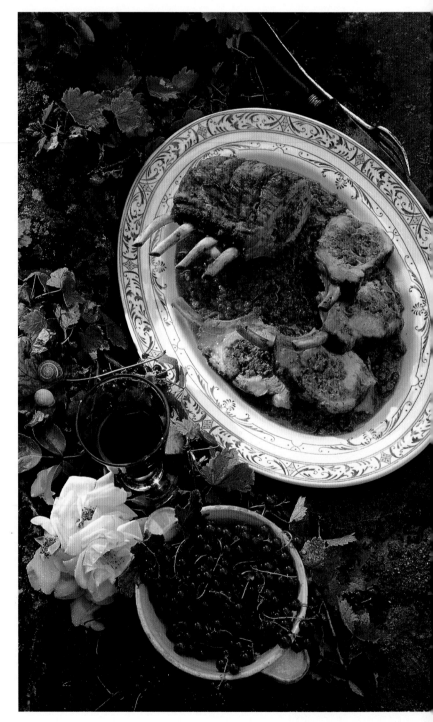

NOUGAT GLACÉ

FROZEN NOUGAT

"This dessert is impressive," says Lauraine de Ganay with authority. *"It can be varied to your liking with different dried and candied fruits."*

8 to 10 servings

¼ cup WHOLE UNBLANCHED ALMONDS
3 tbsp ORANGE JUICE
⅓ cup MIXED CANDIED FRUITS
⅓ cup RAISINS
1¼ cups HEAVY CREAM
3 LARGE EGG WHITES
2 tbsp SUGAR
3 tbsp HONEY
PRALINE MADE FROM ¼ cup WHOLE UNBLANCHED ALMONDS AND ¼ cup SUGAR
(see page 221)

For the sauce
6 KIWIS, PEELED
6 tbsp SUGAR, MORE IF NEEDED

9-×5-×4-inch LOAF PAN

Preheat the oven to 350°F.

Line the loaf pan with waxed paper. Spread the almonds in a single layer in a shallow pan. Bake them, shaking the pan occasionally, until they are toasted inside, 5 to 7 minutes. Let cool.

Combine the orange juice, candied fruits, and raisins and set aside to soak.

Whip the cream until stiff. Beat the egg whites with an electric mixer until stiff. Add half the sugar and continue beating to make a light meringue, about 30 seconds. Set aside.

Combine the honey with the remaining sugar in a small heavy saucepan. Cook over low heat until the honey and sugar melt, stirring occasionally, then boil 1 minute.

Beating the meringue with the electric mixer, gradually add the hot honey mixture. Continue beating until the meringue is cool and stiff, about 5 minutes.

Gently fold the whipped cream into the meringue. Then fold in the toasted almonds, praline, and drained fruits. Spoon the mixture into the lined pan. Cover and freeze until firm, at least 5 hours. (It will keep for a month in the freezer.)

An hour or so before serving, make the sauce: Process the kiwis with the sugar in a food processor or blender until smooth.

Unmold the *nougat* onto a chilled platter and peel off the lining paper. Cut it into ¾-inch slices and place on dessert plates. Pour a little sauce around the edge of each slice and serve the rest separately.

Nougat Glacé made with candied fruits and raisins and served with fresh kiwi sauce.

CHÂTEAU DE SAINT-JEAN-DE-BEAUREGARD

I THINK OF THE VEGETABLE GARDEN AT SAINT-JEAN-DE-BEAUREGARD AS A CELEBRATION OF THE FRUITS OF THE EARTH. HARVEST CULMINATES ON ARMISTICE DAY,

NOVEMBER 11, WITH A GREAT FESTIVAL OF "VEGETABLES OLD AND NEW" — A SHOP WINDOW FOR THE AMAZING VARIETY OF APPLES, PEARS, GRAPES, PUMPKIN AND SQUASH, ROOTS, AND HERBS THAT COME TO THE TABLE IN THE FALL FROM A WELL-TENDED GARDEN. ITS 40 ACRES ARE THE PRIDE AND THE OBSESSION OF MURIEL DE CUREL. IN LESS THAN A DECADE, SHE HAS BROUGHT THE GARDEN FROM A STATE OF NEGLECT TO ONE OF JOYFUL ABUNDANCE.

SINCE CHILDHOOD, THE VICOMTESSE DE CUREL HAS ALWAYS LOVED GARDENS. WHEN SHE AND HER HUSBAND INHERITED SAINT-JEAN-DE-BEAUREGARD, THE HANDSOME LOUIS XIII CHÂTEAU CAME WITH ONE OF THE EARLIEST *POTAGERS* IN FRANCE, DATING FROM THE MID-1600S AND THEREFORE CONTEMPORARY WITH THE KITCHEN GARDEN AT VERSAILLES. THE CHANCE WAS TOO GOOD TO MISS. SOON THE BORDERS OF THE SQUARE VEGETABLE BEDS WERE REPLANTED WITH FLOWERS SET OFF BY MULTICOLORED CABBAGE, ODDITIES LIKE GOURDS, AND SUCH HALF-FORGOTTEN ROOTS AS HAMBURG PARSLEY, CROSNES OR JAPANESE ARTICHOKES, AND SALSIFY. THE FRUIT TREES ESPALIERED ALONG THE GARDEN WALLS TO CATCH THE SUN WERE RETRIMMED WITH PRECISION. THE NEGLECTED 17TH-CENTURY HERB GARDEN, ONCE SO IMPORTANT FOR MEDICAL REMEDIES BUT NOW AN ESSENTIAL COMPLEMENT TO THE TABLE, WAS BROUGHT BACK TO LIFE.

It was in the village of Thoméry, near Fontainebleau, that a system was developed almost 150 years ago for preserving grapes as long as six months. Bunches are picked a week before they are fully ripe, with an extra-long stem. This is inserted into a glass phial filled with spring water purified with charcoal. The grapes are then left to hang in a dry constant temperature of 42°F; any withered fruit is trimmed regularly from the main bunch (far left).

The annual garden festival "La Fête des Fruits et Légumes," held in November, is renowned for its many unusual varieties. Colorful squashes, pumpkins, and yew berries (in the "Dangerous Fruits" category) are just some of the local fruits on display.

Now all is ordered with logic, a checkerboard of grass paths and beds guarded by bristling cardoons, a member of the thistle family. "We have neglected so many plants that used to be popular," laments Muriel de Curel. "For example, chestnuts, fava beans, and chervis (related to cumin) used to flourish here. They were displaced long ago by potatoes, tomatoes, and other vegetables brought from the New World."

November is by no means the end of the produce season at Saint-Jean-de-Beauregard because traditional methods of storage are followed to the letter. Apples and pears, picked scarcely ripe so they do not rot, are ranged on wooden slats, each one separated from the next to allow the free circulation of air. Roots are stocked in the old way, layered with dry sand in a "pie." In the cool, dim grapery, Chasselas table grapes are preserved for up to six months.

All this is not just for show. "We supply our own table," says Muriel de Curel, "with plenty left over for charity." She is unusual in liking to cook as well as to cultivate the food she grows. "Jams and preserves are a specialty of mine," she declares, "and sauces, too. The copper pots we have at Saint-Jean are put to good use!"

SALADE DU POTAGER

KITCHEN GARDEN SALAD

In late summer and fall, when the ripening vegetables and ornamental flowers at the Château de Saint-Jean-de-Beauregard are in their prime, salads practically make themselves. For her vinaigrette, Muriel de Curel likes to use one part olive oil to two parts vegetable oil so as to give a hint of the south to this northern salad. For the perfect accompaniment, serve a bowl of iced red radishes with plenty of fresh baguette and unsalted butter.

6 to 8 servings

¼ pound SMALL TENDER GREEN
BEANS, TRIMMED
¼ pound SNOW PEAS, CUT INTO 1½-inch
PIECES ON THE DIAGONAL
1 cup SMALL BROCCOLI FLORETS
1 cup SMALL CAULIFLOWER FLORETS
¼ pound MUSHROOMS,
THINLY SLICED
½ cup SHREDDED RED CABBAGE
½ pound MIXED GARDEN LETTUCE,
SUCH AS SWEET BUTTERCRUNCH,
OAKLEAF, RUBY LETTUCE,
AND ARUGULA
1 SMALL RED ONION, THINLY SLICED AND
SEPARATED INTO RINGS
½ SMALL CUCUMBER, THINLY SLICED
½ cup PEELED AND SHREDDED BLACK
RADISH OR DAIKON
1 FRESH YELLOW OR RED HOT PEPPER OR
½ YELLOW BELL PEPPER, SEEDED AND
CUT INTO THIN STRIPS

For the vinaigrette
2 tbsp VINEGAR
SALT AND PEPPER
2 tbsp OLIVE OIL
¼ cup VEGETABLE OIL

Cook the green beans, snow peas, broccoli, and cauliflower separately in boiling salted water until just tender, 5 to 7 minutes. Drain and refresh* each with cold water.

Make the vinaigrette (see page 222). Toss the mushrooms and cabbage separately with a little of the vinaigrette and let them marinate up to 1 hour.

Trim the lettuce, wash, and tear into bite-size pieces. Dry thoroughly and put in a bowl. (The beans, snow peas, broccoli, cauliflower, mushrooms, cabbage, and lettuce can all be prepared several hours ahead, but add the vinaigrette to the mushrooms and cabbage not more than an hour before serving. Refrigerate the lettuce to keep it crisp.)

To finish, arrange the beans, snow peas, broccoli, cauliflower, mushrooms, cabbage, onion, cucumber, and black radish in small piles on the lettuce. Scatter the pepper strips over the top. To serve, add the remaining vinaigrette and toss the salad until the ingredients are evenly coated.

Salade du Potager, with a delicious selection of salad vegetables grown on the estate.

FRICASSÉE DE LAPIN AUX TROIS RACINES

RABBIT STEW WITH ROOT VEGETABLES

The potager, or vegetable garden, is the pride of St-Jean-de-Beauregard and replete with unusual and old-fashioned vegetables, including Japanese artichokes, black salsify, and huge squashes and pumpkins (below). Visitors stroll around the extensive grounds, admiring the espaliered fruit trees and the glorious produce (above right).

Over 2,000 varieties of plants grow in the garden of Saint-Jean-de-Beauregard, and Muriel de Curel is constantly adding new ones. In this recipe, created by the young chef Pascal Pineau for the château's fall fruit and vegetable festival, the hard-to-find roots – root chervil and Hamburg (root) parsley – can be replaced by carrot, turnip, and celery root.

4 to 6 servings

3 tbsp VEGETABLE OIL
3- to 3½-pound RABBIT, CUT INTO SERVING PIECES*
1 CARROT, CHOPPED
I ONION, CHOPPED
1 STALK CELERY, CHOPPED
2 CLOVES GARLIC, CHOPPED
2 TOMATOES, PEELED, SEEDED, AND CHOPPED*
SALT AND PEPPER
3 tbsp ALL-PURPOSE FLOUR
½ cup DRY WHITE WINE
1 quart CHICKEN STOCK (see page 221) OR WATER
A BOUQUET GARNI*
1 WHOLE CLOVE
5 ounces ROOT CHERVIL, CUT INTO 1-inch CHUNKS
5 ounces HAMBURG (ROOT) PARSLEY, CUT INTO 1-inch CHUNKS
5 ounces PARSNIP, CUT INTO 1-inch CHUNKS
3 tbsp BUTTER
FRESH CHERVIL SPRIGS TO DECORATE

Heat the oil in a sauté pan or flameproof casserole. Brown the rabbit pieces a few at a time over medium heat. Add the carrot, onion, celery, garlic, tomatoes, and a little salt and pepper to the pan. Sprinkle the flour over the rabbit and vegetables and cook until foaming, 2 or 3 minutes. Stir in the wine and stock, add the bouquet garni and clove, and bring to a boil. Reduce the heat to low and simmer, covered, until the rabbit is tender, about 40 minutes. (The rabbit can be cooked up to 2 days ahead and refrigerated in the cooking liquid.)

Remove the rabbit pieces from the pan. Discard the bouquet garni and clove. Process the vegetables with the cooking liquid in a food processor or blender until smooth. Return the purée to the pan and bring it to a boil. Add the vegetable chunks and simmer until tender, 15 to 20 minutes. Using a slotted spoon, transfer to a warmed serving dish and keep warm.

The sauce should be thick enough to coat a spoon lightly; if necessary, boil it to the desired consistency. Reheat the rabbit pieces in the sauce, then transfer them to the serving dish and keep warm.

Reduce the heat under the sauce to very low and gradually whisk in the butter in small pieces. Taste for seasoning. Spoon the sauce over the rabbit and vegetables, decorate with chervil sprigs, and serve.

FONDANT AUX POMMES

OLD-FASHIONED APPLE CAKE

"Just an old family recipe," insists the Vicomtesse de Curel. *"But it's the best!"* This is a very good way to use the aged, slightly dry apples that have been stored in *clayettes*, or wooden drying racks.

8 servings

2 LARGE EGGS
½ cup SUGAR
1 cup ALL-PURPOSE FLOUR
1 tbsp BAKING POWDER
1 VANILLA BEAN, SPLIT
7 tbsp UNSALTED BUTTER,
AT ROOM TEMPERATURE
3 APPLES (ABOUT 1¼ pounds TOTAL
WEIGHT), PEELED, CORED, AND CUT INTO
SMALL CUBES
CONFECTIONERS' SUGAR FOR SPRINKLING
(OPTIONAL)

9-inch ROUND CAKE PAN OR SPRINGFORM PAN

Butter the pan and line the bottom with waxed paper. Butter the paper. Coat the pan with flour and sugar, discarding the excess. Preheat the oven to 375°F.

Whisk the eggs with the sugar until thick and light. Sift the flour and baking powder into the bowl, then stir them in. Scrape the seeds from the vanilla bean into the mixture. Cream the butter and stir it in, then stir in the apples. Spoon the batter into the prepared pan.

Bake the cake in the heated oven until it shrinks from the sides of the pan and a wooden toothpick inserted into the center comes out clean, 40 to 45 minutes. Let the cake cool slightly in the pan, about 5 minutes, then turn it out onto a rack to cool completely, discarding the lining paper. (The cake keeps up to 3 days in an airtight container.)

Sprinkle the cake with sifted confectioners' sugar just before serving, if you like.

Apples, quince, and pears are stored in the capacious cellars, ranged on wooden slats to prevent rotting. Darkness is essential for storage, otherwise the fruit will spoil.

CHÂTEAU D'ANET

HUNTING WAS THE PASSION OF DIANE DE POITIERS, MISTRESS OF HENRI II (KING OF FRANCE FROM 1547 TO 1559) AND BUILDER OF THE CHÂTEAU D'ANET. DIANA, GODDESS OF THE HUNT, IS FEATURED IN THE STATUARY, WHILE OVER THE MAIN GATEWAY OF ANET STANDS A STAG AT BAY, FLANKED BY HOUNDS. ONLY AN HOUR FROM PARIS, THE FOREST OF ANET IS STILL PRIME HUNTING GROUND, AND THE SPORT REMAINS A LOVE OF THE CURRENT CHÂTELAINE, LAURETTE DE YTURBE. "I USED TO RIDE IN A 'PILLBOX.'" SHE SAYS, "A HORSEDRAWN CARRIAGE WITH HIGH WHEELS AND EXTRA SPRINGS FOR THE BUMPS, BUT MOST PEOPLE FOLLOW THE HUNT ON HORSEBACK OR EVEN BICYCLE. ON FOOT IS TOO SLOW."

RULES FOR THE TRADITIONAL *CHASSE À COURRE* DATE BACK HUNDREDS OF YEARS, AS DO THE HUGE CIRCULAR HORNS AND COSTUMES OF THE HUNTSMEN. "THE STRUGGLE BETWEEN STAG AND HOUNDS IS DRAMATIC AND CAREFULLY STAGED." MADAME DE YTURBE TOLD ME. "EARLY IN THE DAY, THE MASTER OF THE HUNT SELECTS THE QUARRY. ONLY THAT PARTICULAR ANIMAL IS PURSUED. WHEN THE CHASE BEGINS, SELECTED HUNTSMEN USE A COMPLEX SYSTEM OF CALLS ON THE HORN AS SIGNALS FOR THE HOUNDS AND HUNTERS PATROLING THE FOREST ALLEYS IN SEARCH OF THE STAG. IF THE ANIMAL ESCAPES, THEN THE HUNT IS ABANDONED FOR THE DAY. THIS HAPPENS OFTEN. ONCE IN MY FATHER'S TIME WE RECOGNIZED A STAG WE HAD ALREADY HUNTED THREE TIMES. ITS COURAGE COULD BE ACKNOWLEDGED ONLY BY LETTING IT GO FREE."

Most châteaux have character, but Anet's sense of identity, stemming from a gay and sophisticated past, is stronger than most. "A charming valley, haven of peace, of greening trees and murmuring streams," wrote an enamored 18th-century visitor. "Your pride, Anet, rests on thee. You alone possess the gifts of this world: love, glory, spirit, and virtue."

The inscription on the entrance portal reads: "This ample dwelling was consecrated by Phoebus to the good Diana who in return is grateful for everything she has received." Diana was, of course, Diane de Poitiers, and Phoebus, Henri II (right).

The eastern façade of Anet, the only surviving wing of the original château.

Such chivalry harks back to another age when Anet was very much on center stage. The original château, built in the 1540s, was recognized even then as a landmark of French Renaissance architecture, the ultimate hunting lodge and *château de plaisance*, on a par with the grandest of the Loire. Famous artists, including the Florentine silversmith and sculptor Benvenuto Cellini, decorated the Italianate buildings of architect Philibert de l'Orme. The beautiful Diane reigned supreme in France – she was 20 years older than her lover the King, who had grown tired of his wife, Catherine de Medicis. When the King was killed in a joust, Diane retired to Anet and passed her time in its embellishment until her death in 1566.

The 17th and 18th centuries brought the social and literary world to the château, including celebrities like La Fontaine and Saint-Simon. Voltaire took advantage of a stay at Anet not only to write a play, but also to act in it with other guests. When the Duc de Vendôme, owner of the day, received the Grand Dauphin (the King's putative heir), Jean-Baptiste Lully presented a new opera, and the Duc organized a grand banquet. The menu included 30 soups, 132 hors d'oeuvres, and a huge spread of game birds including pheasant, pigeon, woodcock, gray and red partridge, and plover, not to mention 334 game roasts and four whole wild boar. In the style of the times this would have been served in two or three "removes," or courses, in which hundreds of dishes were arranged in careful geometric patterns on huge tables for maximum show. Ostentatious display was the name of the game.

As so often, the French Revolution brought a sad change in fortune. Anet was sold piece by piece as public property; paneling was torn out, tiles stripped off, and the walls demolished for use elsewhere. Of the main château, only a wing has survived, along with the chapel, entrance gate, and flanking pavilions. Happily, after nearly two centuries of work by devoted owners, all these structures have been fully restored, though what was lost in the Revolution has gone forever. In 1929, Madame de Yturbe's father was one of the first to open a privately owned château to the public. "He felt that history should be shared," she explains. "We open Anet only in the afternoons, so that for at least half the day we can lead a normal life with our children and grandchildren. The château is self-supporting, and we cannot ask for more."

The blessing of the hounds on the feast of St. Hubert takes place in a village chapel near Anet. Huntsmen, hunters, and spectators gather at the shrine, not to mention the eager hounds, who were originally allowed inside the chapel as well.

CUISSOT DE CHEVREUIL, SAUCE POIVRADE

MARINATED ROAST LEG OF VENISON WITH A PEPPERY SAUCE

Cuissot de Chevreuil is now reserved for special occasions at Anet, and is served with tart red berries called airelles.

The hunting season at Anet lasts from October until "you can smell the violets," says Madame de Yturbe, but venison is less common on the château table than you might think. "We never eat the mature stags hunted on the property; they would be far too tough," she says. "And we leave the females and young males to keep up the breeding stock." However, she much enjoys this marinated leg of venison, served with the classic piquant sauce poivrade, braised chestnuts, and a purée of celery root. As a condiment, the tart French berries called airelles *are suggested. Cranberry sauce is a good alternative.*

8 servings

6-pound LEG OF VENISON
2 tbsp BUTTER, AT ROOM TEMPERATURE
SALT AND PEPPER

For the marinade
3 PARSLEY STEMS
A SPRIG OF FRESH THYME
1 BAY LEAF
1 tsp PEPPERCORNS
2 WHOLE CLOVES
2 BOTTLES (750 ml EACH)
FULL-BODIED WHITE WINE
1¼ cups WHITE WINE VINEGAR
½ cup VEGETABLE OIL
2 CARROTS, THINLY SLICED
2 ONIONS, THINLY SLICED
2 SHALLOTS, THINLY SLICED
1 STALK CELERY, THINLY SLICED
2 CLOVES GARLIC

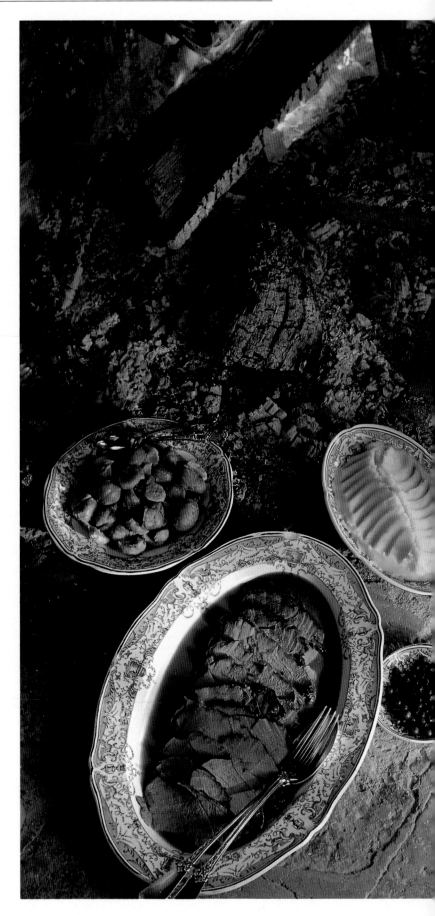

For the sauce
½ cup WHITE WINE VINEGAR
¾ cup FULL-BODIED WHITE WINE
2 quarts BROWN VEAL OR
BEEF STOCK (see page 221)
4 PEPPERCORNS, CRUSHED
5 tbsp BUTTER, CUT INTO SMALL PIECES

For the marinade, combine the herbs, peppercorns, cloves, wine, and vinegar in a large saucepan and bring just to a boil. Reduce the heat and simmer 30 minutes. Heat 2 tablespoons of the oil in a frying pan. Add the carrots, onions, shallots, celery, and garlic and sauté, stirring often, until they begin to color, 7 to 10 minutes. Add the sautéed vegetables and remaining oil to the marinade and let cool.

Put the venison in a deep nonreactive bowl and pour over the cooled marinade. Cover and refrigerate 2 or 3 days, turning the meat occasionally.

Lift the venison out of the marinade and reserve it. For the sauce, boil the marinade in a heavy saucepan until reduced to 5 cups, then strain it and return to the pan. Add the white wine vinegar, wine, and stock. Simmer until reduced to 3 cups, about 2 hours. Add the peppercorns 10 minutes before the end of cooking. Strain again and season to taste. (The sauce and venison can be prepared to this point 12 hours ahead and refrigerated.)

Preheat the oven to 400°F.

Pat the venison dry with paper towels. Lay it in a large roasting pan, rub the surface with the butter, and season. Roast, basting often, until the meat is rare, ¾ to 1 hour: The juices should run slightly pink when the meat is pierced, or a meat thermometer should register 125°F. For well-done meat, the juices should run clear, or the temperature on a meat thermometer should be 140°F. Transfer the meat to a carving board, cover it with aluminum foil, and let it rest 15 minutes.

Reheat the sauce, if necessary. Whisk in the butter over low heat, but do not boil.

Carve the venison and arrange it on a warmed platter. Pour a little of the sauce around the venison and serve the rest separately.

LA POMME CHÂTEAU D'ANET

BAKED APPLE SLICES WITH CINNAMON AND RAISINS

In case weekend visitors from Paris are delayed, Madame de Yturbe likes to serve country dishes that reheat well, such as blanquette de veau (see page 129) and boeuf bourguignon. Desserts are equally simple – in summer strawberries with fresh cheese or a tart of figs from the garden, and in winter this baked apple dish. Since Anet borders on Normandy, the land of apples and Calvados, it's not surprising that Madame de Yturbe adds a generous glass of apple brandy to her baked apples just before serving. Serve the baked apple slices very hot, with chilled vanilla custard sauce (see page 222) or crème fraîche (see page 220) as an accompaniment.

4 servings

3 tbsp RAISINS
¼ cup CALVADOS OR APPLE BRANDY,
MORE IF LIKED
4 BAKING APPLES (ABOUT 1½ pounds TOTAL
WEIGHT), PEELED, CORED, AND CUT INTO
⅛-inch SLICES
¼ cup SUGAR
1 tsp GROUND CINNAMON
3 tbsp UNSALTED BUTTER

1-quart BAKING DISH

Preheat the oven to 350°F and butter the baking dish. Soak the raisins in the Calvados or apple brandy to plump them.

Arrange the apple slices, overlapping, in layers in a neat pattern in the baking dish. Sprinkle them with the sugar, cinnamon, and drained raisins (reserve the Calvados). Dot the top with the butter and bake in the heated oven until the apples are tender, about 35 minutes. Sprinkle with the reserved Calvados and serve very hot.

CHÂTEAU DE DAMPIERRE

The elegant Château de Dampierre was built between 1675 and 1683 by one of the greatest of French architects – Jules Hardouin Mansart. Today visitors are attracted not only by the classical architecture but by the impressive restaurant, Les Écuries du Château, housed in the old stables and set up by the present Duc de Chevreuse.

EVEN BEFORE THE PRESENT CHÂTEAU WAS BUILT, DAMPIERRE — A PROPERTY ASSOCIATED FOR CENTURIES WITH THE DUCAL TITLES OF LUYNES AND CHEVREUSE — WAS A HAVEN FOR CELEBRATED GUESTS. ANNE OF AUSTRIA SPENT SEVERAL DAYS THERE IN 1661 WITH HER DAUGHTER-IN-LAW, HENRIETTA OF ENGLAND. ONLY A FEW YEARS LATER THE PROPERTY WAS DESCRIBED AS "BIG, VERY OLD, AND BY NOW COMPLETELY RUN DOWN." BUT NOT FOR LONG, BECAUSE THE NEW DUC DE CHEVREUSE HAD MADE A STRATEGIC MARRIAGE WITH THE DAUGHTER OF FRANCE'S MINISTER OF FINANCE, JEAN-BAPTISTE COLBERT.

THIS GAVE THE YOUNG DUC THE MEANS TO REBUILD AND REDESIGN HIS DOMAIN, USING THE SERVICES OF THE GREAT ARCHITECTS OF THE TIME — MANSART FOR THE CHÂTEAU AND LE NÔTRE FOR THE GARDEN. BOTH THE CHÂTEAU ITSELF — IN GRACEFUL PINK BRICK AND GOLDEN STONE — AND THE HUGE LAKES AND LAWNS THAT SURROUND IT HAVE CHANGED LITTLE SINCE THESE TWO MASTER CRAFTSMEN LAID OUT DAMPIERRE. INSIDE, THE ROYAL APARTMENTS WHERE LOUIS XIV, LOUIS XV, AND LOUIS XVI ALL STAYED AT ONE TIME OR ANOTHER REMAIN UNTOUCHED, ECHOING THE GRANDEUR OF VERSAILLES.

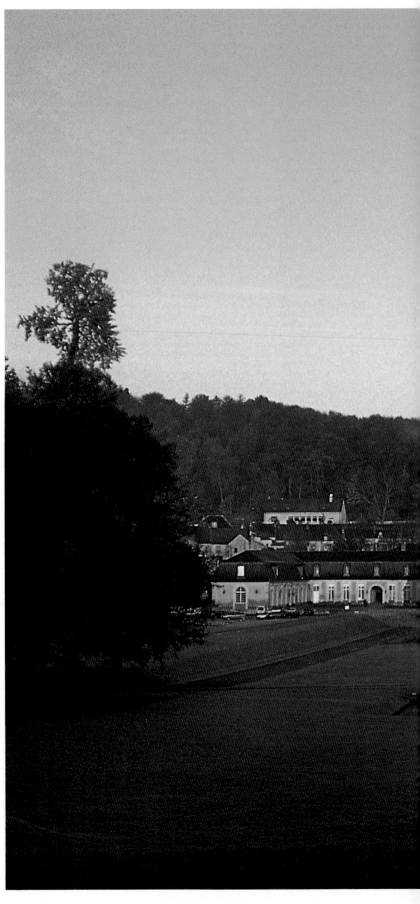

One of the more notorious occupants of Dampierre, Marie de Rohan-Montbazon, pretended to spend hot summer nights in the summerhouse by the lake, when really it was a cover for her illicit liaisons in Paris.

The link between Dampierre and the Ducs de Luynes and Chevreuse remains extraordinarily close (the two titles are separate, being held by father and son in alternating succession). The family survived the Revolution thanks to the affection in which they were held by the local community. When the Duc and Duchesse were arrested with their daughter in 1794, villagers hid the heir to the dukedom, young Honoré. What is more, each day they sent a carriage-load of meat and vegetables to the prison because the Duc was a gourmand of renown. It is said that the provisions were equally appreciated by the prison governor, who eventually arranged for the release of his noble detainees.

A love of good food runs in the family and can be traced back to the Duc de Chevreuse who built Dampierre. For all his distinction as tutor to the King's grandson (and would-be heir), he was a true eccentric: "He once poisoned his stomach with chicory water throughout the entire course of the meal, just for the sake of drinking a bumper of wine with sugar and nutmeg at the end," the diarist Saint-Simon reported. "He never appeared at meals until the second course was served; then he would hastily devour a shoulder of rabbit or a grill, whatever was least acid, and for dessert, a few sweetmeats, which he thought were good for the digestion, with a weighed portion of bread from which the crust had been removed . . . toward midnight he would eat some kind of an egg dish or fish cooked in water and oil."

The present family's favorites are a bit different. "Philippe is so lucky," sighs the Duchesse de Chevreuse of her teenage son. "He is tall and thin and loves to try everything – another Gargantua. He'll take a double helping just to test the difference between the common gray partridge and the Savoy red partridge, found mainly in the Midi."

His father is an equal enthusiast, not hesitating to wander into famous kitchens for a chat with the resident chef. He insists that all of the fruit and vegetables on the family table be grown at Dampierre and "would never go out and buy a chicken from a shop," says the Duchesse. "It must be raised at home."

Both the Duc and Duchesse like to cook. "I act as *marmiton* (the lowest rung in French kitchen hierarchy)," she laughs. "I'm more fussy about food than Jean, though I'm crazy about chocolate. He is a true gourmand; he enjoys everything." "Nothing beats a *rable de lièvre à la royale*," interjects the Duc, more tempted than some by marinated saddle of hare served in a dark red wine sauce thickened with the blood of the animal.

In spending a good deal of time at Dampierre and working hard to give it life, the Duc is inspired by his father, the Duc de Luynes, who has been a moving force behind Demeure Historique, the action group for *châteaux* proprietors. The Duc de Chevreuse surprised some of his clan by installing a charming restaurant, Les Écuries du Château, in the stables. Few if any historic monuments offer notable food, but the cuisine of chef Christian Deluchey, based on modern classics such as *ragoût de boeuf aux morilles et pâtes fraîches* and *gratin de mandarines*, has already achieved recognition in the gastronomic guides. For her part, the Duchesse oversees the flower garden and coordinates visiting groups. She is president of the local tourist office. "A big property like this is demanding," she admits. "But we would never think of giving it up. That is unimaginable."

BÉCASSES EN SALMIS

PAN-ROASTED WOODCOCK ON CROÛTES

Diminutive woodcock, with distinctive, straight beaks, are prized as much for their earthy insides as their tasty meat, for they are the only birds traditionally cooked with the innards left intact. Since their sale has been outlawed in France, you would have to befriend a generous hunter to taste one – quail is not quite the same thing, although delicious prepared en cocotte *as here. If cooking quail, substitute 2 or 3 chicken livers (about 2 ounces) for the woodcock innards.*

4 servings as a first course

4 WOODCOCK OR QUAIL (ABOUT ¼ pound EACH), WITH
THE INNARDS
SALT AND PEPPER
¼ cup CLARIFIED BUTTER (see page 220)
⅔ cup COGNAC
2 SHALLOTS, FINELY CHOPPED
1 CLOVE GARLIC
1 SMALL CARROT, VERY THINLY SLICED
1 BAY LEAF
A SPRIG OF FRESH THYME
⅓ cup PORT WINE
2 cups CHICKEN STOCK (see page 221)
¼ pound *PÂTÉ DE FOIE GRAS*

4 SQUARE *CROÛTES*, FRIED IN OIL AND BUTTER (see page 220)

Sprinkle the birds inside and out with salt and pepper. Tie them into shape with string. Heat 3 tablespoons of the clarified butter in a sauté pan or flameproof casserole and brown the birds over medium heat, 6 to 7 minutes.

Add half the Cognac, bring it to a boil, and set it alight. (Stand back from the flame.) Simmer the Cognac about 30 seconds, basting the birds until the flame dies. Add the shallots, garlic, carrot, bay leaf, and thyme. Cover the pan and continue cooking the birds until they are barely done, 10 to 15 minutes: The juice from the cavity should run pink when a bird is lifted with a two-pronged fork.

Transfer the birds to a carving board, cover loosely with aluminum foil, and let rest.

Skim all the fat from the pan, leaving the cooking juices. Stir in the port, remaining Cognac, and the stock and bring to a boil, scraping to dissolve the browned pan juices. Season. Reduce the heat and simmer the sauce until it lightly coats a spoon, 10 to 15 minutes.

Strain the sauce into a saucepan, set it over very low heat, and gradually whisk in half the *pâté de foie gras*. Move the pan on and off the heat, so the *pâté* softens creamily to form a smooth sauce. Do not heat it too much or it will melt to oil. Taste the sauce for seasoning.

Cut the birds into quarters – 2 legs and 2 half breasts; discard the back. Scoop out the innards. Heat the remaining clarified butter in a small frying pan. Add the innards (or chicken livers if using quail) and sauté them, stirring often, until brown on the outside but still pink in the center, about 1 minute. Mash together the remaining *pâté de foie gras* and the innards or livers.

Spread this mixture on the *croûtes*. Set a piece of bird on top of each *croûte*, arrange on warmed plates, spoon on the sauce, and serve.

Pheasant hunting in the forest begins in the fall, and feathered game features regularly in family meals (above).

Bécasses en Salmis – woodcock was traditionally used for this dish, but quails make a perfectly suitable alternative, as used here (left).

SOLE COLBERT

GOLDEN SOLE WITH HERB BUTTER

This old family recipe must be served at once so the cold herb butter is firm inside the crisp hot fish. If you like, garnish it with deep-fried parsley.

4 servings

4 SOLE (ABOUT 10 ounces EACH), CLEANED AND TRIMMED
½ cup CLARIFIED BUTTER (see page 220)

For the parsley butter
½ cup BUTTER, AT ROOM TEMPERATURE
2 tbsp FINELY CHOPPED FRESH PARSLEY
1 tbsp LEMON JUICE
SALT AND PEPPER

For the coating
½ cup ALL-PURPOSE FLOUR SEASONED WITH SALT AND PEPPER
2 LARGE EGGS, BEATEN WITH 1 tbsp DIJON-STYLE MUSTARD AND 1 tbsp VEGETABLE OIL
1 cup DRY WHITE BREAD CRUMBS

PASTRY BAG AND MEDIUM STAR TUBE (OPTIONAL)

For the parsley butter, cream the butter, then beat in the parsley and lemon juice. Season. (This can be prepared 2 or 3 days ahead and refrigerated, but let the butter soften again by the time the fish are done.)

Prepare the fish or have it done by the fishmonger as follows: Remove top and bottom skin. Set each fish flat on a work surface. Using a flexible knife, cut along the edge of the right fillet. Holding the knife almost parallel to the bones, slice between the fillet and the bones. Continue cutting over and beyond the backbone until the whole fillet is loosened in one piece. Cut to the edge of the traverse bones, but do not remove the fillet completely. Turn the fish over and again loosen the fillet from the bones, taking care to work from the same cut

The grand stone staircase dominates the front of the château and affords a marvelous vantage point over the Le Nôtre parterres below.

side. With scissors, snip the backbone at head and tail. Cut all around the traverse bones so they are easy to remove after cooking. Fold the fillet back in place. Repeat for all the fish.

Coat the fish first with the seasoned flour, then the eggs, and finally with bread crumbs.

Heat the clarified butter in a large frying pan. Add 2 fish and brown them over medium heat, 2 to 3 minutes on each side. Continue cooking over fairly low heat until the fillets are opaque next to the bone, 5 to 7 minutes. Transfer the fish to paper towels to drain, then keep warm on a platter while you cook the remaining fish.

Pull out the backbone from the open side of each fish so the fillets remain intact, attached at the head and tail. Spoon or pipe the parsley butter into the backbone cavity. Serve at once.

TERRINE DE CANARD

WILD DUCK TERRINE WITH PISTACHIOS

The Duc de Chevreuse enjoys organizing hunting parties for his friends in the walled forest of Dampierre. Of course you can use domestic duck in this recipe, too.

16 to 18 servings

3 MALLARD DUCKS (ABOUT 1½ pounds EACH)
2 tbsp BUTTER
⅓ cup SHELLED PISTACHIOS, BLANCHED AND SKINNED*
1¼ pounds GROUND PORK
2 tbsp SALT, MORE IF NEEDED
1 tbsp PEPPER, MORE IF NEEDED
3 SHALLOTS, FINELY CHOPPED
⅓ cup DRY WHITE WINE
¼ cup COGNAC
¼ pound BARDING FAT*
A SPRIG OF FRESH THYME
2 BAY LEAVES

1½-quart TERRINE MOLD WITH LID

Ask the butcher to bone the duck breasts, or do it yourself: Place each duck, breast up, on a board and cut out the wishbone. Cut the breast meat away from the bone on one side until you reach the ridge of the breastbone, where the skin and bones meet. Turn the bird around and repeat on the other side. Pull to separate the breastbone and carcass from the meat. Discard the skin from the meat. Repeat the process with the remaining ducks.

Cut 3 duck breast halves lengthwise into 4 or 5 strips each. Heat the butter in a frying pan, add the strips of duck breast, and sauté them on all sides over low heat, stirring constantly, until they are lightly browned but still pink in the center, 1 to 2 minutes. Remove them. Cut the remaining breasts into pieces.

Scrape the meat off the legs, discarding the skin and any tendons and sinew. Work the leg and breast meat with the giblets through a meat grinder fitted with a medium blade. Or, purée them a little at a time in a food processor.

Mix together the pistachios, $1\frac{1}{4}$ pounds of the ground duck, the pork, salt, pepper, shallots, wine, and Cognac. Beat with a wooden spoon until this forcemeat holds together. Sauté a small piece in a frying pan and taste it, then adjust the seasoning of the remaining forcemeat.

Preheat the oven to 350°F.

Line the terrine mold with the barding fat, reserving some for the top. Spread half the forcemeat in the lined mold. Top with the strips of duck breast, laying them lengthwise. Spread the remaining forcemeat on top and cover with the reserved barding fat. Add the thyme and bay leaves and put the lid on the mold.

Set the mold in a water bath* and bring the water to a boil on top of the stove. Transfer to the heated oven and cook until a skewer inserted in the center of the terrine for 30 seconds is hot to the touch when withdrawn, about $1\frac{1}{2}$ hours. Let the terrine cool until tepid. Remove the lid and set a 1-pound weight on top so the mixture will compress (this ensures it will slice well). Keep the terrine in the refrigerator at least 3 days or up to a week before serving to allow the flavor to mellow. Serve the terrine directly from the mold.

Terrine de Canard. The forest of Dampierre is enclosed by almost 9 miles of wall and is well stocked with a wide variety of game birds including wild duck.

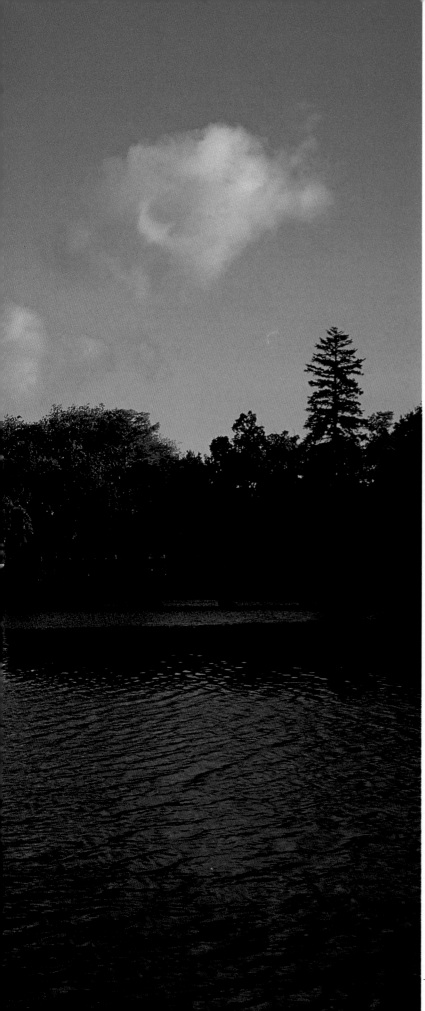

CHÂTEAU DE LA FERTÉ-SAINT-AUBIN

JACQUES GUYOT BOUGHT LA FERTÉ-SAINT-AUBIN IN 1987 AS A CALCULATED BUSINESS RISK. HE FIRST HEARD ABOUT THE PROPERTY BY THE CLASSIC COUNTRY METHOD, WORD OF MOUTH, AND WAS ATTRACTED AT ONCE. LA FERTÉ IS IN SOLOGNE, A FLAT BUT DISTINCTIVE REGION OF PINE FOREST AND HEATHER, DOTTED WITH LAKES AND WELL STOCKED WITH GAME, WHICH JACQUES GUYOT KNEW FROM CHILDHOOD. TO ALL APPEARANCES, HOWEVER, LA FERTÉ WAS UNSALEABLE, HAVING CRUMBLED OVER THE YEARS IN THE HANDS OF AN ELDERLY OWNER. BUT MONSIEUR GUYOT KNEW BETTER BECAUSE HE HAD ALREADY BEEN PARTNER WITH HIS BROTHER IN THE RESTORATION OF THE NOW-FAMOUS CHÂTEAU DE SAINT-FARGEAU. "OLD PLACES MUST LIVE AGAIN," HE INSISTS. THE BANKERS WERE LESS ENTHUSIASTIC. "I HAD TO WORK LIKE THE DEVIL TO CONVINCE THEM," HE LAUGHS.

SINCE THEN HE HAS INVESTED AN ADDITIONAL SIX MILLION FRANCS, ALMOST ALL OF IT EARNED BY THE CHÂTEAU ITSELF, WITH A MINIMUM OF GOVERNMENT HELP. A MASTER OF PUBLIC RELATIONS, JACQUES GUYOT TELLS VISITORS THAT EACH 35-FRANC ENTRANCE FEE BUYS THREE NEW SLATES FOR THE ROOF, WHICH COVERS ABOUT TWO ACRES. THE FIRST AREA TO BE RESTORED AT LA FERTÉ WAS THE STABLES — TWO SETS OF THEM — BECAUSE JACQUES GUYOT WAS ONCE A RIDING INSTRUCTOR. "THE CHÂTEAU BELONGED TO TWO MARSHALS OF FRANCE, SO OF COURSE HORSES WERE IMPORTANT," HE EXPLAINS. RIDING AND CARRIAGE DISPLAYS ARE HELD EVERY WEEKEND, WITH REGULAR DRESSAGE COMPETITIONS.

The imposing Château de La Ferté-Saint-Aubin is surrounded by over 17 acres of water. After years of neglect, it is now being restored by its energetic owner, Jacques Guyot.

La Ferté is covered with over 9,500 square yards of roofing – a considerable area when so many of the slates need repairing or replacing. In fact, the châtelain, Monsieur Guyot, delights in telling visitors how each entrance fee pays for 3 new slates precisely.

From horses, the transition to other animals was easy. The park now houses deer, mountain sheep, and goats, as well as a model farm with poultry, ponies, and miniature goats. An *Île Enchantée* for children has been created, where they can visit Snow White and other fairytale characters. The orangery has recently been restored for receptions and banquets, while within the château, visitors may tour 25 rooms from attic to cellar, including a magnificent period kitchen with old worktables, cast-iron pots, and an open fireplace with a working spit. It was to this kitchen that a 19th-century owner, a retired chef and hotelkeeper, would descend in the morning to sniff the air for clues to the day's fare. "Leopold," he would cry, "your ragoût is not *à point.*" It lacks this, or there is too much of that, he would say – with which the nervous chef always concurred, mindful that a gourmet's nose must not be contradicted.

In the midst of all his activity, Jacques Guyot still finds time to cook. He holds clear views about this, too, dividing responsibility with his wife. He likes to roast game birds with a whole onion inside to keep them moist, and he sautés *trompettes de la mort*, or "trumpets of death," (a species of wild mushroom that he gathers in the park) in butter with salt, pepper, and a whole garlic clove, which is discarded before serving. Crushed garlic, he believes, is too strong. A few spoons of cream are added at the end of cooking: "I like to cook with cream, though I'm not Norman," he remarks.

Meanwhile, business goes from strength to strength. "We try to offer a whole day of country entertainment," explains Jacques Guyot, "tempting people to come back again and again, particularly with children." His success can be measured in attendance figures, which have grown from 25,000 in 1987 to over 60,000 in 1990. "We were so pleased to jump the 40,000 mark, the average for *châteaux* open to the public," he says. His crowning achievement came in 1990, with the award for the restoration of the orangery – listed as a *chef d'oeuvre en péril* – which had been ruined by fire in 1944. For Jacques Guyot, it was a public recognition of his personal belief that "like nature, stones can talk."

DAIM LOWENDAL

VENISON SIMMERED IN LOIRE VALLEY WINE

La Ferté is known as "Château des Maréchaux" because it was built by Henri de Saint-Nectaire, Duc de La Ferté and a marshal of France, then later bought by one of Napoleon's marshals, the famous André Masséna. Jacques Guyot recommends a fruity red Loire wine such as a Bourgueil for this recipe, in which venison is marinated and then simmered very slowly.

4 servings

1½ pounds BONELESS STEWING VENISON,
CUT INTO 1-inch CUBES
1 cup BUTTER
1 ONION, SLICED
⅓ cup ALL-PURPOSE FLOUR
SALT AND PEPPER

For the marinade
1 ONION, HALVED
2 BAY LEAVES
1 tsp PEPPERCORNS
1 BOTTLE (750 ml) RED WINE, PREFERABLY
FROM THE LOIRE VALLEY

Combine the meat with the marinade ingredients in a large nonreactive bowl. Cover and refrigerate 2 days.

Lift the meat out of the marinade and drain it in a strainer, then pat dry with paper towels. Clarify ¼ cup of the butter (see page 220). Heat the clarified butter in a flameproof casserole. Add the onion and sauté it over medium heat, stirring often, until it browns, about 5 minutes. Remove it. Coat the pieces of meat with half the flour, tossing to discard the excess. Brown the pieces of meat, a few at a time, in the casserole over very high heat, stirring constantly. Return them all to the casserole with the onion.

Preheat the oven to 325°F.

Strain the marinade into a saucepan and bring it to a simmer. Cream the remaining butter and, with a whisk, work in the remaining flour to make a smooth paste. Drop pieces of this kneaded butter into the simmering marinade, whisking rapidly until smooth and thickened. Stir into the casserole containing the meat and season with salt and pepper. Cover and bring just to a boil, then transfer to the heated oven and cook until the meat is very tender, about 4 hours. Stir occasionally and add a little water if the meat gets too dry.

Taste the stew for seasoning before serving. (It can be cooked up to 3 days ahead and the flavor will improve.)

In restoring La Ferté, Jacques Guyot was keen to preserve as much of the elegance and character of the property as he could. He and his wife try to use all the rooms at different times of the year in order to keep the château looking and feeling like a real home.

FAISAN A LA MASSÉNA

ROAST PHEASANT STUFFED WITH WILD MUSHROOMS

Out of game season, this recipe can be made with chicken or guinea hen and cultivated button mushrooms. If you would like a more generous serving of mushrooms than fits comfortably inside the birds, sauté more separately.

4 servings

⅓ cup BUTTER, MORE IF NEEDED
1 CLOVE GARLIC, PEELED
1 pound FRESH WILD MUSHROOMS, SUCH
AS IVORY AND BLACK VARIETIES OF
CHANTERELLES AND OYSTER
MUSHROOMS, CLEANED* AND CUT INTO
⅜-inch SLICES IF LARGE
SALT AND PEPPER
3 to 4 tbsp CHOPPED FRESH PARSLEY
2 tbsp CRÈME FRAÎCHE (see page 220)
OR HEAVY CREAM
2 YOUNG PHEASANTS (ABOUT 2 pounds
EACH)
2 STRIPS BARDING FAT* (OPTIONAL)
1 cup CHICKEN STOCK (see page 221)
4 SMALL FIRM APPLES, SUCH AS GOLDEN
DELICIOUS, PEELED, CORED, THICKLY
SLICED INTO RINGS, AND HALVED
1 tbsp SUGAR
¼ cup ARMAGNAC OR BRANDY

TRUSSING NEEDLE AND STRING

Preheat the oven to 375°F.

Melt half the butter in a frying pan. Add the garlic clove and cook, stirring, until fragrant, then add the mushrooms with salt and pepper. Toss the mushrooms over medium-high heat until they lose most of their moisture, about 5 minutes, then pour off any liquid. Add the parsley, cover, and cook over low heat until the mushrooms are tender, about 10 minutes. Stir in the crème fraîche or cream and adjust the seasoning. Discard the garlic clove.

Season the cavities of the birds. Stuff them with the mushrooms and truss the birds*. If using barding fat, drape it over the breasts and tie it in place with string. Otherwise, spread about 1 tablespoon of softened butter over each breast. Set the birds in a roasting pan and roast them in the oven until just done, about 30 minutes. The juice from the breast should run slightly pink when pierced with a fork, if you like meat pink at the bone. For well-done birds, continue roasting 5 to 10 minutes longer.

Transfer the birds to a carving board, cover them with aluminum foil, and let rest while finishing the dish. Skim off the fat from the roasting pan, leaving the cooking juices. Add the stock to the pan and boil, stirring to dissolve the juices. Simmer until it reduces by half, 10 to 15 minutes. Strain, and taste for seasoning.

Wipe out the frying pan used to cook the mushrooms and in it melt the remaining butter. Add the apples, sugar, salt, and pepper and sauté, turning the apples so they cook evenly, until tender, 10 to 12 minutes. Add the Armagnac or brandy to the pan, and set it alight. (Stand back from the flame.) Continue cooking, shaking the pan, until the flame subsides, about 30 seconds. The apples should taste peppery.

Remove the string and barding fat, if used, from the birds and carve them. Arrange the meat on a platter or plates with the mushrooms and apples. Pour a little of the cooking juices over the meat and serve the rest separately.

Faisan à la Masséna (left). Named after André Masséna (a previous owner of La Ferté), who was one of Napoleon's marshals, this dish is prepared in the fall when pheasant, apples, and wild mushrooms are all in season.

TARTE TATIN

CARAMELIZED UPSIDE-DOWN APPLE TART

Tarte Tatin – succulent baked apples with a caramel topping. The tart is baked in the oven with a pastry lid, then unmolded upside down just before serving.

Tarte Tatin *originated in Lamotte-Beuvron, a small town only a few miles from Château de La Ferté. The story goes that the Tatin sisters, left penniless when their father died, started selling a rustic apple tart topped with caramel that their father had much enjoyed. With the railway age, Lamotte became an important junction and the sisters' baking flourished. There is still a Hotel Tatin near the station.*

The secret of Tarte Tatin *is to cook the apple halves so the butter-flavored caramel penetrates deep inside them.*

8 to 10 servings

¾ cup UNSALTED BUTTER

1½ cups SUGAR

5 to 6 pounds FIRM APPLES, SUCH AS
GOLDEN DELICIOUS

For the sweet pie pastry
1½ cups ALL-PURPOSE FLOUR

6 tbsp UNSALTED BUTTER

½ tsp SALT

7 tbsp SUGAR

3 LARGE EGG YOLKS

12-inch ROUND HEAVY PAN

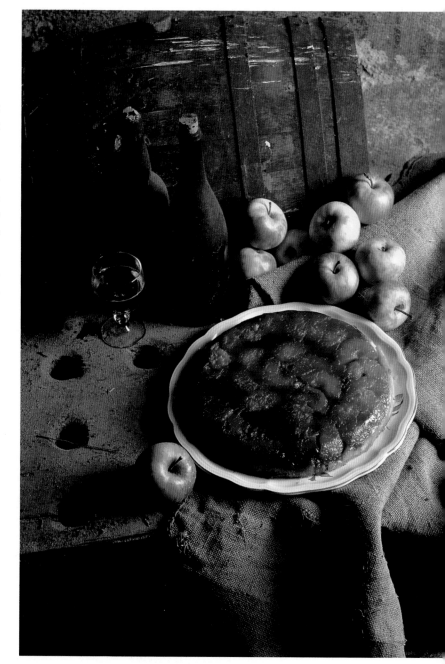

Make the pastry dough (see page 221) and chill.

Melt the butter in the pan and sprinkle with the sugar. Cook over medium heat, stirring occasionally, until the sugar caramelizes to a deep golden. Let the pan cool.

Peel the apples, cut them in half, and core them. Arrange them upright in concentric rings to fill the pan, packing them tightly. Cook the apples in the caramel until they are a dark brown and the juice they have rendered has evaporated, 15 to 20 minutes. Let cool.

Preheat the oven to 375°F.

Roll out the pastry dough on a floured surface to a 12-inch round. Lay the round over the apples so they are completely covered. Chill until the dough is firm, 10 to 15 minutes.

Bake the tart in the heated oven until the crust is golden, about 15 minutes. Let the tart cool to tepid, then unmold it onto a large platter. (Do this carefully because the caramel juice from the bottom of the apples may splash.) Serve the tart warm, with crème fraîche (see page 220) or vanilla ice cream (see page 220).

(*Tarte Tatin* can be cooked up to 8 hours ahead and left in the pan, provided it is not made of uncoated cast iron or aluminum. Warm it over low heat before unmolding.)

CHÂTEAU DE BEAUREGARD

Elegant Château de Beauregard, dating from the 16th century, is a superb and rare example of a prominent Loire château that is still a family home.

THE GREAT ROYAL *CHÂTEAUX* OF THE LOIRE ARE WITHOUT EQUAL. BUT FOR ALL THEIR GRANDEUR AND BEAUTY, THEY SEEM TO LACK A SOUL, STANDING EMPTY AND LIVING OUT THEIR YEARS IN THE CARE OF THE STATE. I GET SO MUCH MORE PLEASURE OUT OF VISITING A CHÂTEAU LIKE BEAUREGARD. "THE BUILDING IS NOT LARGE," THE ARCHITECT ANDROUËT DU CERCEAU NOTED IN HIS INVENTORY OF 1576, "BUT IT IS CHARMING AND FITTED OUT IN IMPECCABLE STYLE." THE AMBIANCE HAS SURVIVED ALMOST UNTOUCHED, FROM THE PAINTED CEILINGS TO THE 17TH-CENTURY FLOOR OF HAND-PAINTED TILES FROM HOLLAND, NO ONE ALIKE. THE GREATEST TREASURES ARE THE 327 PORTRAITS OF THE KINGS AND NOTABLES OF FRANCE SPANNING 300 YEARS, FROM THE 14TH-CENTURY PHILIPPE VI DE VALOIS TO LOUIS XIII OF FRANCE.

THE CHÂTEAU WAS BUILT IN THE 1550S BY JEAN DU THIER, CONTROLLER GENERAL OF FINANCE FOR HENRI II, AND A MAN OF IMMENSE WEALTH, KNOWN FOR HIS LOVE OF ART, MUSIC, HUNTING, AND OUTDOOR GAMES. PAINTINGS CELEBRATING THESE DIVERSIONS ADORN BEAUREGARD'S MAGNIFICENT *CABINET DES GRELOTS*, SO NAMED BECAUSE ITS CARVED PANELING FEATURES SLEIGH-BELLS. DU THIER WAS ALSO A LOVER OF GARDENS; THE GROUND PLANS FOR BEAUREGARD SHOW THAT HE ADOPTED ITALIAN PRINCIPLES THERE, WITH THE KNOTS OF BOX HEDGE SO ARRANGED THAT A GARDENER COULD REACH OUT TO ANY PLANT WITHOUT TREADING ON THE SURROUNDING SOIL. DOWN RIVER FROM BEAUREGARD, AT VILLANDRY, A SIMILAR VEGETABLE GARDEN HAS BEEN REPLANTED AND UNDOUBTEDLY IS ONE OF THE GREAT SIGHTS OF THE LOIRE.

(Top) The old kitchen, equipped with an impressive range of copper pots, was used by the family until a decade ago, when the antiquated cast-iron range was removed and the two immense open chimneys were restored to their original state (right).

When today's owners of Beauregard, Comte and Comtesse Alain du Pavillon, inherited the château in 1968, they were determined that it should not just be a "*monument historique*" but a family home as well. In practice this meant dividing the château into two parts. The public rooms are open to visitors most of the year, with exhibitions and concerts held in the summer.

On the family side, Comtesse du Pavillon talked to me animatedly about the gatherings in her dining room: "We may be two, we may be twenty-five," she says. Many classic recipes have been handed down in the family – the Comtesse was born Anne-Marie Suchet d'Albuféra and can claim title to *sole à la Suchet*, with carrots in a wine sauce, and *poularde Albuféra*, a poached chicken stuffed with rice, truffles, and *foie gras*. But such outmoded fare is not for the Pavillon family. "My cooking is simple, with plenty of fish and vegetables, salads, and fruit tarts," says Anne-Marie du Pavillon.

I was especially pleased to hear this comment because to my mind this is what the cooking of the Loire is all about. There are almost as many fruit tarts as there are fruit trees in the region – open-faced tarts of sweet pastry brushed with jam and filled with fresh berries; rhubarb or plum tarts with the fruit cooked first with sugar as a compote and then baked in a double crust, or packed under a single crust as in an English-style pie. In winter Anne-Marie du Pavillon makes a spectacular *tarte demi-deuil* (half-mourning) filled with whipped Chantilly cream which camouflages prunes soaked in tea.

For a first course, the Pavillons often serve the delicious asparagus of the Loire with a walnut vinaigrette dressing and chopped hard-boiled egg for color. An alternative starter (or some-times a light main dish) is a *feuilleté* of goat cheese wrapped in puff pastry – hot and golden brown – served with a green salad. Dozens of goat cheeses are found along the Loire: From the Beauregard area come Selles-sur-Cher, a disk rolled in powdered charcoal, as well as the taller, narrower Cornilly, and little cheese rounds sold specifically for baking.

The portrait gallery at Beauregard testifies to the history of France, with 327 portraits from Philippe VI of Valois up to Louis XIII. Family portraits rub shoulders with royal figures and the colorful mosaic-like composition complements the regularity of the tiled Delft floor (above). The famous "Cabinet des Grelots" is a lavish oak-paneled room decorated with paintings depicting various human pleasures and pastimes. The "grelots," or bells, are embossed decorations carved out of the paneling.

TOMATES CAMBACÉRÈS

TOMATOES STUFFED WITH ARTICHOKES

Jean-Jacques Régis de Cambacérès, a famous forbear of the Comtesse du Pavillon, was consul and then High Chancellor of France under Napoleon. He also made his mark as a gourmet, leaving this

4 servings

4 LARGE RIPE TOMATOES
SALT AND PEPPER
4 ARTICHOKE BOTTOMS, COOKED AND
COOLED (see page 220)
½ cup MAYONNAISE (see page 221)
4 LETTUCE LEAVES

For the toasts
2 HARD-BOILED EGGS
1 tbsp SMALL CAPERS
¼ cup MAYONNAISE (see page 221)
8 THIN SLICES RYE BREAD, OR
4 LARGE SLICES CUT IN HALF
2 SMALL RIPE TOMATOES, THINLY SLICED
8 ANCHOVY FILLETS IN OIL, DRAINED
AND HALVED

Cut off the top of each tomato about one-quarter of the way down and discard. Cut out the core and seeds, and cut a thin slice from the base of each tomato so it will sit flat. Sprinkle the inside of the shells with salt and pepper, turn them upside down, and set aside to drain.

Dice the artichoke bottoms and stir them into the mayonnaise. Taste for seasoning.

For the toasts, slice the hard-boiled eggs. Chop the capers, reserving 8 whole ones to decorate. Stir the chopped capers into the mayonnaise. (The stuffed tomatoes and toasts can be prepared to this point up to 2 hours ahead. Cover and refrigerate the mayonnaise.)

Tomates Cambacérès. Fresh, perfectly ripe tomatoes are essential for this simple but eye-catching dish.

To finish, toast the rye bread. Spread each slice of toast with caper mayonnaise. On each, arrange one slice of tomato sprinkled with salt and pepper, one slice of egg, and 2 anchovy halves crossed on top. Top with a whole caper.

Carefully spoon the artichoke and mayonnaise mixture into the tomato shells. Arrange a lettuce leaf, a stuffed tomato, and 2 decorated toasts on each plate.

SAUMON AU BEURRE BLANC

ROASTED SALMON WITH WHITE BUTTER SAUCE

"No one tolerates fish bones nowadays," remarks the Comtesse du Pavillon. So she opts for salmon or sea trout rather than the bonier pike, which is also native to the Loire. White butter sauce originated in the western reaches of the Loire where Poitou-Charentes, home of fine butter, meets the Pays Nantais, land of Muscadet wine.

8 servings

5½-pound WHOLE SALMON, FILLETED WITH SKIN AND CUT INTO 8 PIECES
1 tbsp VEGETABLE OIL
SEA SALT AND PEPPER

For the white butter sauce
¼ cup WHITE WINE VINEGAR
¼ cup DRY WHITE WINE
2 SHALLOTS, FINELY CHOPPED
1 tsp CRUSHED WHITE PEPPERCORNS
SALT
1 cup CHILLED UNSALTED BUTTER, CUT INTO SMALL PIECES
½ LEMON

Preheat the oven to 450°F.

Brush the skin side of the fish with the oil, and sprinkle with salt and pepper. Brush a large baking sheet with oil and place the pieces of fish on it, skin-side up. Roast the fish until the skin is crisp and slightly blackened and the flesh just flakes easily, 8 to 12 minutes. When ready, transfer the fish to a warmed platter and keep warm.

While the fish is roasting, make the white butter sauce: Boil the vinegar and wine with the shallots, peppercorns, and a little salt in a heavy saucepan until the liquid is reduced to 1 tablespoon, 5 to 10 minutes. Reduce the heat to very low and gradually add the butter, whisking vigorously so the sauce foams. Move the pan on and off the heat so the butter softens creamily to form a smooth sauce. Do not heat it too much or it will melt to oil. Strain the sauce. Squeeze a teaspoon of juice from the lemon and stir it in. Taste for seasoning. Serve as soon as possible.

Roasted Saumon au Beurre Blanc, with its distinctive blackened and crispy skin.

CHÂTEAUX OF

MIST AND SEA

CHÂTEAU DE CREULLET

Château de Creullet was a key command post for the allied liberating forces in 1944 and the headquarters for Field Marshal Montgomery.

FROM BAYEUX, SEAT OF THE DUKES OF NORMANDY, LUSH MEADOWS STRETCH WITHOUT INTERRUPTION TO THE SEA. THIS FERTILE REGION CAUGHT THE EYE OF THE VIKINGS JUST AS IT DID THAT OF LOUIS XIV, BUT HIS INTENT WAS RATHER DIFFERENT. THE KING WANTED TO CREATE A JEWEL, IN THE STYLE OF THE PETIT TRIANON AT VERSAILLES, AS A RETREAT FOR A YOUNG MISTRESS. REPUTEDLY SHE DID NOT ENJOY THE FAVORS OF THE KING LONG ENOUGH TO EARN HER REWARD. SINCE THEN, THE CHARMING CHÂTEAU DE CREULLET, WITH ITS BALUSTRADED GARDENS AND ORNAMENTAL LAKE INSPIRED BY LE NÔTRE, HAS BEEN PASSED FROM HAND TO HAND, DOWN TO ITS CURRENT OWNERS, THE MARQUIS AND MARQUISE DE CANCHY.

MAINTAINING CREULLET FROM A BASE IN PARIS IS A STRUGGLE FOR A GROWING FAMILY — THE CANCHYS HAVE FIVE YOUNG CHILDREN — BUT NORMAN TRADITIONS ARE MAINTAINED ON WEEKENDS AND DURING VACATIONS. WHAT A FINE DOMAIN THIS IS FOR EVERYONE, YOUNG AND OLD — TWO ACRES OF WALLED VEGETABLE GARDEN, A GREENHOUSE SHELTERING SPECIAL PINK MUSCAT GRAPES WITH A FLAVOR OF RASPBERRY, A THRIVING HERB GARDEN, AND AN APPLE ORCHARD WITH 100-YEAR-OLD TREES ESPALIERED TO CATCH THE SUN. A DOZEN OR MORE VARIETIES CAN BE COUNTED, SOME RIPENING EARLY, SOME LATE, SOME FOR COOKING, OTHERS FOR THE TABLE, AND STILL OTHER SMALL BITTER CIDER APPLES, DESTINED FOR PRESERVES AND FOR JUICE. "IN SUMMER WE LIVE OFF THE GARDEN," SAYS HÉLÈNE DE CANCHY. "WE HAVE OUR OWN CHICKENS AND SALT-MARSH LAMB — WE ARE ONLY THREE MILES FROM THE SEA — AND THE SOLE AND SCALLOPS FROM THE LITTLE VILLAGES ON THE COAST ARE OUTSTANDING."

The Château de Creullet lies in Calvados, the Normandy region famous for apple brandy. Once a year the cider press arrives at the farmhouse, a venerable truck fitted out with clanking machinery.

A famous stretch of ground! On June 5, 1944, the first invasion beachhead was established here, and Field Marshal Montgomery made Creullet his headquarters during the Normandy landings. Distinguished visitors included Général de Gaulle, General Eisenhower, and King George VI, who held an impromptu inspection of troops in the garden. After the war, Montgomery returned several times: "My Normandy home," he called the château.

Apples naturally find their way into the cooking at Creullet. Roast chicken is basted with cider, and crêpes are filled with sautéed apples and flamed with Calvados. This is Creullet's very own Calvados, for Jean-François de Canchy holds the right to distill his own cider under a personal license, which is now quite rare in France. At one time all of this happened furtively. In the château cellars you will still find an old fireplace which was used as an escape route for the telltale apple-scented vapors produced during distillation. It was then bricked up from season to season in case an excise inspector passed by!

The vintages stored in the scarred oak barrels in the cellars at Creullet are identified with chalk.

FONDS D'ARTICHAUTS FARCIS MORNAY

STUFFED ARTICHOKE BOTTOMS WITH CHEESE SAUCE

Artichokes flourish in the garden at Creullet and are at their best with this mushroom stuffing.

6 servings

¼ pound *PÂTÉ DE FOIE GRAS* OR
CHICKEN LIVER *PÂTÉ*
1 cup FRESH BREAD CRUMBS
½ cup FINELY CHOPPED MUSHROOMS
2 tbsp MADEIRA WINE, MORE IF NEEDED
SALT AND PEPPER
6 ARTICHOKE BOTTOMS, COOKED AND
DRAINED (see page 220)
2 tbsp BUTTER

For the sauce
1 cup MILK
A SLICE OF ONION
1 BAY LEAF
2 tbsp BUTTER
2 tbsp ALL-PURPOSE FLOUR
GRATED NUTMEG
SALT AND WHITE PEPPER
¼ cup GRATED GRUYÈRE CHEESE

Preheat the oven to 375°F.

Mash together the *pâté*, bread crumbs, and mushrooms with a fork until fairly smooth. Add enough of the Madeira to make a spreadable mixture. Adjust the seasoning if necessary.

Mound the mixture on the artichoke bottoms, spreading it to the edges. Dot the top with the butter. Arrange in a buttered baking dish, cover with buttered aluminum foil, and bake until the stuffing is very hot, about 15 minutes.

Meanwhile, prepare the white sauce (see page 222); it will be thick enough to spread. Off the heat, beat in the cheese. Taste the sauce and adjust the seasoning if necessary.

Heat the broiler. Cover the artichoke stuffing with the sauce using a metal spatula. (The artichokes can be prepared to this point a day ahead and refrigerated; reheat them in a 300°F oven before finishing.) Broil several seconds until the top is golden, watching carefully so they do not burn. Serve immediately.

Haricots blancs, white kidney beans, are hung up to dry in an airy attic to catch the breeze.

As for all such preserves, the way to keep rose-petal and apple jelly clear is not to press on the fruit in the jelly bag.

CONFITURE DE ROSE

ROSE-PETAL JELLY

Creullet is famous for its roses. In September, the second flowering of the rose garden comes hand in hand with the appearance of apples. Hélène de Canchy's rose-petal jelly is the happy result of this accidental convergence.

Makes about 1 quart

13 cups JUST-PICKED, UNBLEMISHED
ROSE PETALS
1⅔ cups BOILING WATER
APPLE JELLY (see right)
1¼ cups SUGAR
JUICE OF 2 SMALL LEMONS

4 PRESERVING JARS (½ pint EACH)

In a covered heatproof bowl, steep the petals in the boiling water 3 or 4 hours.

Melt the jelly in a preserving kettle over low heat. Stir in the petals with their steeping water, the sugar, and lemon juice and boil as fast as possible to the jell point, 220°F on a candy thermometer (see below).

Let the jelly cool slightly, then pour it into sterilized jars*. Seal the jars. Store them in a cool place.

GELÉE DE POMMES

APPLE JELLY

This pure apple jelly is delicious on its own but is perfect as a base for other flavors.

Makes about 1 pint

2 pounds CRAB APPLES
ABOUT 1½ cups SUGAR

2 PRESERVING JARS (½ pint EACH)

Scrub the apples, especially at the blossom ends, and discard the stems. Cut the ·fruit into quarters (skins and cores are left to add flavor and pectin). Put the fruit in a pan with water barely to cover. Simmer, stirring occasionally, until they are very soft, about 20 minutes.

Remove the pan from the heat and let cool slightly, then spoon the fruit and juice into a jelly bag, or a colander lined with several layers of cheesecloth, set over a bowl. Leave the bag or colander in place overnight so the juice can drip slowly into the bowl.

Measure the juice. Bring the juice to a boil and stir in ¾ cup sugar for each 1 cup juice. Boil as fast as possible to the jell point, 220°F on a candy thermometer. At this temperature, the jelly falls from a spoon in a characteristic "sheet" of drips. Alternatively, remove the pan from the heat, pour a few drops of jelly onto a cold saucer, and wait a moment to see if the drops begin to set. Push them with your finger — if jell point has been reached, the surface of the jelly will wrinkle.

Let the jelly cool slightly, then pour it into sterilized jars*. Seal the jars. Store them in a cool place.

As well as the elegant Le Nôtre gardens, Creullet boasts a walled vegetable garden, a greenhouse sheltering pink muscat grapes, and an apple orchard with 100-year-old trees espaliered to catch the sun. The young de Canchys help out with the annual ritual of apple picking.

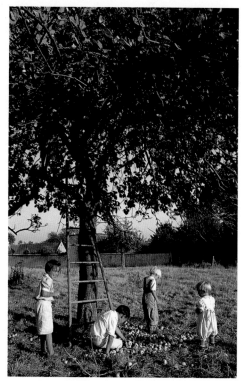

Le Pain Farci, a savory ham and olive loaf taken on beach picnics by the family.

LE PAIN FARCI

HAM AND OLIVE LOAF FOR A PICNIC

A regular event at Château de Creullet is a sea-side picnic, held on the nearby beaches, site of the Normandy invasion. This unusual savory bread raised with baking powder is a popular part of the feast.

Makes 1 loaf

3 cups ALL-PURPOSE FLOUR

1 tbsp BAKING POWDER

½ tsp SALT

⅓ pound BACON, CHOPPED

1 cup BUTTER, AT
ROOM TEMPERATURE

5 LARGE EGGS

⅓ pound COOKED HAM, CHOPPED

⅓ cup OIL-CURED BLACK OLIVES, PITTED
AND CHOPPED

9-×5-×4-inch LOAF PAN

Preheat the oven to 350°F.

Butter the loaf pan. Combine the flour, baking powder, and salt in a bowl. Fry the chopped bacon in a frying pan over low heat, then cook it until golden, about 5 minutes. Drain on paper towels.

In a large bowl, cream the butter. Beat in the eggs, one by one, adding a little of the flour mixture with the first egg. Sift the remaining flour mixture over the butter mixture in three batches, stirring until smooth after each addition. Stir in the bacon, ham, and olives.

Transfer the dough to the prepared loaf pan and smooth the top. Bake in the heated oven until the bread is golden brown and shrinks slightly from the sides of the pan, 1¼ to 1½ hours. It should sound hollow when tapped on the base. Transfer the loaf to a rack to cool.

The bread is best eaten the day of baking, although it freezes well. It's also good toasted the following day.

DOUILLONS NORMANDS

APPLES BAKED IN PASTRY

Firm apples such as Golden Delicious, which hold their shape during cooking, are essential to a good apple dumpling. Serve the douillons *with apricot sauce (see page 174) or vanilla custard sauce (see page 222) if you like.*

6 servings

1 pound PUFF PASTRY DOUGH (see page 221)

6 tbsp UNSALTED BUTTER,
AT ROOM TEMPERATURE

½ cup SUGAR

6 SMALL APPLES (ABOUT 2 pounds TOTAL
WEIGHT), PEELED AND CORED

1 LARGE EGG, BEATEN TO MIX WITH
¼ tsp WATER TO GLAZE

Sprinkle a baking sheet with water. Roll out the dough to a 21- ×14-inch rectangle. Cut out six 7-inch rounds. Transfer them to the baking sheet and chill until firm, about 15 minutes. Save the trimmings for decoration.

Cream the butter and beat in the sugar. Set an apple on each dough round. Spoon some of the butter mixture into the core cavity of each apple. Brush the dough with the egg glaze*, then bring up the dough around the apples, pleating it at the top to seal tightly. Brush the dumplings with the egg glaze and chill them until firm, about 30 minutes.

Preheat the oven to 425°F.

Roll out the reserved puff pastry dough and cut out six 2-inch rounds. Press a round over the seam on each apple dumpling and brush it with a little egg glaze. Bake the dumplings in the heated oven until the pastry begins to brown, about 15 minutes. Reduce the oven temperature to 350°F and continue baking until the pastry is brown and crisp and the apples are very tender when pierced with a knife, ¾ to 1 hour. Let the dumplings cool for 10 minutes before serving.

*Canon-les-Bonnes-
Gens – a dream of
18th-century Arcadia
(top).*

*An ancient apple press
stands in an out-
building (middle).*

*Bulbs and branches
are dried out in the
abandoned orangery
(below).*

*Old gardening tools
suspended in time and
space (right).*

CHÂTEAU DE CANON-LES-BONNES-GENS

"WE LIVE IN THE 18TH CENTURY," EXCLAIMS FRANÇOIS DE MÉZERAC. "HOW LUCKY WE ARE!" HE IS REFERRING NOT ONLY TO THE PROPERTY ITSELF, WITH ITS EXTENSIVE GARDENS, LAKES, AVENUES, AND CAREFULLY LANDSCAPED VIEWS, BUT ALSO TO HIS ANCESTOR WHO CREATED THE ENSEMBLE. THIS WAS JEAN-BAPTISTE ELIE DE BEAUMONT, FAMOUS AS A PARIS ADVOCATE WHO CAMPAIGNED WITH VOLTAIRE FOR HUMAN RIGHTS AND JUSTICE UNDER THE *ANCIEN RÉGIME*. THE ARCHIVES AT CANON RECORD HOW ELIE DE BEAUMONT TRAVELED TO ENGLAND BEFORE PLANNING THE TRANSFORMATION OF THE PROPERTY IN THE 1770S SO THAT IT WOULD EXPRESS, THROUGH NATURE, LIBERTARIAN IDEALS OF BEAUTY AND HARMONY.

WERE HE TO RETURN TODAY, ELIE DE BEAUMONT WOULD APPROVE: PARTS OF CANON ARE WILDERNESS, OTHER PARTS ARE MANICURED PATHS LEADING ONE TO ANOTHER AND OFFERING HERE A VISTA OF GRAZING SHEEP, THERE A FOLLY LACQUERED IN BRILLIANT CHINESE RED. MOST ENTERTAINING OF ALL ARE THE *CHARTREUSES* — A CORRIDOR OF 13 WALLED GARDENS, LIKE A SERIES OF SQUARE HOUSES WITHOUT ROOFS, THE WALLS ANGLED TO TRAP MAXIMUM SUN. PROTECTED FROM WINTER FROST, NOT TO MENTION NORMAN MISTS AND BREEZES, ESPALIERED PEARS, PLUMS, APPLES, PEACHES, AND EVEN KIWIS BASK IN THE WARMTH RETAINED BY THE STONE WALLS EVEN AFTER SUNSET. APRICOTS RIPEN IN MAY AND JUNE, FIGS IN AUGUST, A GOOD MONTH AHEAD OF THE LOCAL AVERAGE. APPLES MAY BE TYPICAL OF NORMANDY, BUT AT CANON-LES-BONNES-GENS THEY TAKE A BACK SEAT.

When in Paris, Elie de Beaumont supplied his table from Canon. "Be sure," he instructed his bailiff, "to include a hare, several game birds, two ducks so we have an old one to braise with turnips and the other to roast on the spit, two fat chickens . . . and if you can add a couple of pigeons, all the better." The delivery, by express coach in a wicker hamper, was expensive but "my health is more important than my pocket," wrote Canon's proud owner.

Today, François de Mézerac runs the farm attached to the property, while his brother and sister live in the château itself, overseeing and often personally guiding summer visitors. His wife, Marie-Josèphe, laughs when told her cooking is "the admiration of everyone." "No, no," she says, "it is simply that we have big dishes for big appetites." (The Mézeracs have six children, as well as a dozen nieces and nephews for whom Canon is home.)

Evening meals usually begin with *le potage du potager* – a soup supplied from the vegetable garden – followed perhaps by a roast leg of home-raised lamb basted with local cider and served with white kidney beans, or a whole fish baked in cider, or simply an open tart filled with cheese in a cream sauce. Dessert is mandatory, and equally simple: sponge cake, a vanilla cream, or Madame de Mézerac's favorite *tarte Alsacienne* – sweet pastry topped with rhubarb,

baked so the juice combines with the crisp pastry. "I like to cook everything slowly, so it simmers but never burns," she says. "In winter we have a big wood-fired stove and that's ideal."

Canon has seen some troubled times. German soldiers were billeted there for four years during the war. "At least we did not have to feed them," says Monsieur de Mézerac, alluding to 1815 and the aftermath of Waterloo, when 24 Prussians and their horses arrived at the château. "I rounded up chickens and hens," the bailiff of the day recorded distractedly. "I had two rabbits killed but it worries me that the meat smells. The women were put to work with the men setting the tables . . . but all went well. They departed at five in the morning, after a breakfast of three bottles of *eau-de-vie*, coffee, *soupe au lait*, meat, and butter, taking with them all the *eau-de-vie* that was left."

The Château de Canon survives scarcely touched by time. "This is a happy place, always sunny, always gay," declares François de Mézerac. Its 18th-century park and gardens, full of *fabriques* (statues and ornamental fantasies) and bold perspectives, are an unusual marriage of the English and French styles. A sign, perhaps, that these two battling nations could find common ground in landscaping long before they edged toward an *entente cordiale* in more worldly realms.

The first apple blossom of early summer (top).

A fully-stocked cider cellar (below).

The name Canon-les-Bonnes-Gens dates from 1776, when owner Elie de Beaumont launched an annual fête to choose the best villager of the year. First it was for the Best Young Girl. Next year it was the turn of the Best Old Man, followed by the Best Mother. The custom was eventually dropped; however, the name stuck.

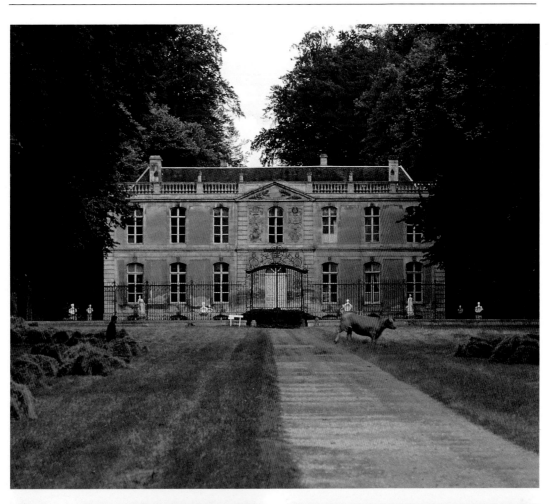

Hay drying in the summer sun (below left).

Stone arches lead into the 13 chartreuses, a series of walled gardens angled to trap the sun and protect tender plants from winter blasts (middle).

One of several follies in the park, designed to delight 18th-century strollers (right).

LE BON JEUNE HOMME

RICH CHOCOLATE CREAMS

The curious name in French for this recipe, "the nice young man," recalls a bit of parental mischief. Whenever a suitor came to dinner in Madame de Mézerac's family, her mother always served this dessert. At the appropriate moment, everyone turned to look at the mystified guest as she announced, "And now let's eat up le bon jeune homme!" Madame de Mézerac serves it in the traditional "pots" used for petits pots de crème; ramekins or espresso cups are quite suitable though.

4 to 6 servings

⅓ pound BITTERSWEET CHOCOLATE,
CHOPPED
10 tbsp SUGAR
2¼ cups MILK

*4 OR 6 POT-DE-CRÈME CONTAINERS
OR RAMEKINS*

Combine the chocolate, sugar, and milk in a heavy saucepan over low heat. Stir often until the chocolate melts and the sugar dissolves. Raise the heat and simmer the mixture, stirring occasionally, until it coats a spoon thickly, about 45 minutes.

Pour the mixture into the chosen containers and let cool completely, at least 2 hours. (The creams can be prepared up to 2 days ahead and refrigerated.)

TEURGOULE

CREAMY BAKED RICE PUDDING

Le Bon Jeune Homme, rich chocolate creams (right).

Genuine rice pudding, baked with milk for hours until creamy, never falls from favor. "When we were children at Canon," says Monsieur de

Mézerac, "we were served this pudding on Saturday nights." The family was especially fond of this homey dish during the war, when they best appreciated its nourishing qualities. Serve it straight from the oven in its glazed earthenware dish or let it cool to room temperature first.

6 to 8 servings

2 quarts MILK, MORE IF NEEDED
10 tbsp SUGAR
SCANT ⅔ cup SHORT-GRAIN RICE
PINCH OF SALT
PINCH OF GROUND CINNAMON

2½-quart DEEP EARTHENWARE BAKING DISH

Preheat the oven to 300°F.

Mix all the ingredients together in the baking dish and bake in the heated oven for 1 hour. If all the milk has been absorbed after this time, stir in more to make the mixture soupy. Continue baking until the rice is very soft, 1 to 2 hours longer. At the end of cooking, a golden crust will have formed and the pudding will be lightly set when the baking dish is shaken.

GÂTEAU NINITE

COFFEE LAYER CAKE WITH CHOCOLATE GLAZE

According to family tradition, this recipe was invented by Ninite, trusted old cook to François de Mézerac's great-aunt. It was and still remains the traditional dessert at Christmas dinner, which unites this large, far-flung family. Many French families seem to have a version of this cake in their repertoire. It's one of the first recipes mothers allow their children to make on their own; grown-ups love it, too.

8 to 10 servings

1 cup BUTTER, AT
ROOM TEMPERATURE
½ cup SUGAR

4 LARGE EGGS, SEPARATED
60 BUTTER COOKIES
1 cup STRONG BLACK COFFEE, CHILLED,
MORE IF NEEDED
½ pound BITTERSWEET CHOCOLATE,
CHOPPED

9-×5-×4-inch LOAF PAN

Set aside 2 tablespoons of butter, and cream the remainder with half the sugar. Beat in the egg yolks. Whisk the whites with the remaining sugar until the mixture stiffens and forms a long peak when the whisk is lifted, about 5 minutes. Mix this meringue into the butter mixture. (If the butter separates, whisk the mixture over a pan of hot water until smooth.)

Butter the loaf pan. Moisten about 7 of the cookies in the coffee. Arrange them in a layer on the bottom of the pan, trimming them to fit as needed. Cover with a layer of the butter mixture. Moisten more cookies in the coffee as you use them, layering them with the butter mixture until all the ingredients are used, finishing with a layer of cookies. Cover and refrigerate until firm, at least 4 hours and up to 2 days.

To finish, unmold the cake onto a platter. Melt the chocolate on a heatproof plate set over a pan of hot water. Stir in the reserved butter until the mixture is smooth. Let it cool slightly, then spread it evenly over the top and sides of the cake, using a metal spatula. Refrigerate the cake until the chocolate is set.

Norman cows, the wealth of this ancient province.

CHÂTEAU DE MIROMESNIL

The walled kitchen garden at Miromesnil burgeons with cottage flowers, vegetables, and soft fruit.

"GOOD COOKING STARTS IN THE GARDEN," WAS COMTESSE BERTRAND DE VOGÜÉ'S REPLY TO MY QUESTION ABOUT HER CUISINE. SO WHEN SHE AND HER LATE HUSBAND BOUGHT THE CHÂTEAU DE MIROMESNIL IN 1938, HER FIRST THOUGHT WAS TO RESTORE THE VEGETABLE GARDEN. THEY HAD TO WAIT TEN YEARS UNTIL THE PROPERTY RECOVERED FROM THE AFTERMATH OF THE OCCUPATION BY GERMAN AND ALLIED TROOPS. AND IT WAS MANY YEARS, TONS OF COMPOST, AND INNUMERABLE PACKETS OF SEEDS LATER THAT THE GARDEN BEGAN TO APPROACH ITS CURRENT GLORY.

NOW CABBAGES BURGEON BENEATH MIROMESNIL'S WINDOWS AND THE WALLED *POTAGER* IS ABLOOM WITH FLOWERS AS WELL AS VEGETABLES. THE COMTESSE IS ALSO AN AVID COLLECTOR OF NEW VARIETIES, BRINGING PLANTS FROM ENGLAND, AND EVEN FROM NORTH AMERICA WHERE HER SON LIVES. "FLOWERS ARE SO MUCH BETTER IN ENGLAND," SHE SAYS. "THEY ARE SELECTED AND BRED MORE CAREFULLY. BUT, EXCEPT FOR A FEW EXOTICA, FRANCE IS BEST FOR VEGETABLES." HOWEVER, HER CHOICE IS LIMITED BY THE CLIMATE. "HERE IN NORMANDY WE ARE TOO FAR NORTH FOR TOMATOES, FOR INSTANCE. AFTER AUGUST 15 IT'S FALL HERE AROUND DIEPPE. PEARS ARE A LOT OF WORK — THEY NEED INDIVIDUAL PROTECTIVE BAGS — AND EVEN APPLES DO LESS WELL THAN 50 KILOMETERS (30 MILES) SOUTH ALONG THE SEINE VALLEY."

Tall stems of eremurus from the kitchen garden decorate the cool stone staircase of the hallway.

Built in 1589, after an earlier mansion had been ruined by the English army at the battle of Arques, the château presents two faces to the world. To the south, the pink brickwork is unadorned, a friendly country mansion open to the sun. The north façade is severely classical in the style of Louis XIII, though its sobriety is relieved with carved stone dormer windows and whimsical tall chimneys. Miromesnil's beech trees, like those of the forest of Eawy nearby, are famous – and afford much-needed protection from the strong coastal winds.

Set just behind Dieppe near the old highway to Paris, Miromesnil used to be within earshot of the *chasse marée*, or tidal express – an infernal clatter of horse carts racing the 70 miles to Paris, day and night, to deliver the fish catch to the markets on the northern side of the city. (The faubourg Poissonière remains as a reminder.) Today, Dieppe still has a bustling Saturday market but, for the rest, it's a town of memories: The commercial port is moribund, the colony of famous artists and fashionable sea-bathers has disappeared, and the Channel tunnel further north will put the town even further off the map. For the Comtesse de Vogüé, who remembers the halcyon prewar days, this decline occasions much sadness.

The old map of the original château is carefully protected with a sheet of glass.

The 17th-century house still contains several items belonging to the writer Guy de Maupassant, who was born at Miromesnil and lived there from 1849 to 1853.

The Comtesse de Vogüé has tended Miromesnil's gardens for over 50 years and she takes great pride in showing visitors around the vegetable plots, lined with daffodils, delphiniums, clematis, and roses, and encircled by ancient brick walls.

Miromesnil was the birthplace of the writer Guy de Maupassant, who was brought up just along the coast at Fécamp. Many of his short stories portray the tough life in the Pays de Caux (land of chalk) – the jealousies and cunning of the peasantry and the rough justice meted out by the local dignitaries. Appropriately for a Norman, Maupassant was succinct when it came to eating: "Only an imbecile could fail to be a gourmand," he wrote.

SOLE A LA ROSALIE

BAKED SOLE WITH SORREL SAUCE

Rosalie was the first wife of Chancellor Hue de Miromesnil, the builder of the château, and she is remembered by the de Vogüé family in this namesake recipe. It's an easy and elegant dish. Serve it with steamed rice for a main course. Fish fillets cooked by this simple method are excellent with other sauces, too. Try them with hollandaise, white butter sauce (see pages 55 and 88), or even a vinaigrette (see page 222).

6 servings as a main course,
8 to 10 as a first course

1½ pounds SOLE FILLETS
SALT AND PEPPER
2 tbsp DRY WHITE WINE
2 tbsp BUTTER
¾ pound SORREL, RINSED
AND STEMS REMOVED
1 cup CRÈME FRAÎCHE (see page 220) OR
HEAVY CREAM, MORE IF NEEDED

A lighthouse off the Norman coast near Dieppe (above).

Preheat the oven to 350°F. Butter two large baking dishes.

Put the fish in the prepared dishes and sprinkle with salt and pepper and the wine. Bake in the heated oven until the fish is firm and opaque, 10 to 12 minutes. Take the dishes from the oven and keep the fish warm.

Meanwhile, melt the butter in a large saucepan. Add the sorrel and cook over medium heat, stirring often, until the leaves wilt and have given up most of their liquid, 3 to 5 minutes. Add the crème fraîche or cream and boil, stirring often, until the sauce thickens, 3 to 5 minutes, then briskly whisk until smooth. If the sorrel is very acid, add more cream and continue cooking 2 or 3 minutes. Season.

Spread the sorrel sauce on warmed dinner plates. Lay the fish on top of the sauce using a slotted spatula and serve.

A local fishing boat heads out to sea (right).

CHAPEAU DU MARQUIS A LA FRAISE

FROZEN STRAWBERRY SOUFFLÉ

Named for the Marquis Thomas-Hue de Miromesnil, Keeper of the Seals for Louis XIV, this cool and airy "top hat" dessert should rise above the rim of its dish like a traditional hot soufflé. The strawberries for this recipe are picked in Miromesnil's thriving kitchen garden, but it can also be made very successfully with fresh raspberries. The large proportion of fruit purée gives the soufflé an incomparable flavor and a texture similar to that of a granité.

10 servings

2 pounds STRAWBERRIES, HULLED
6 LARGE EGGS, SEPARATED
JUICE OF 1 LEMON
JUICE OF 2 ORANGES
¾ cup SUGAR
PINCH OF SALT

For the Chantilly cream
1 cup HEAVY CREAM
1 tbsp CONFECTIONERS' SUGAR
½ tsp VANILLA EXTRACT

For the decoration (optional)
CONFECTIONERS' SUGAR FOR SPRINKLING
10 SMALL STRAWBERRIES WITH HULLS

1-quart SOUFFLÉ DISH

To prepare the soufflé dish, cut a piece of waxed paper about 2 inches longer than the circumference of the soufflé dish. Fold the paper in half lengthwise to make it sturdier and wrap it around the dish; it should extend about 2 inches above the rim. Secure the paper tightly with adhesive tape.

Process the strawberries in a food processor or blender until smooth. There should be 3 cups of strawberry purée. Make the Chantilly cream (see page 220).

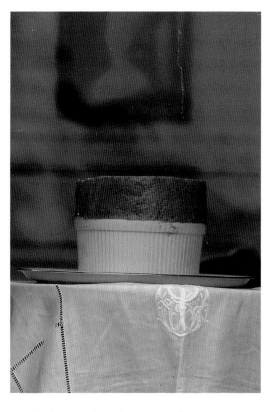

This glorious dessert is delightfully named after the top hat of the Marquis de Miromesnil.

Whisk together the egg yolks, juices, and two-thirds of the sugar by hand in a heatproof bowl until mixed. Set the bowl over a pan of hot, not boiling, water and continue whisking until the mixture falls from the whisk in a thick ribbon and holds a slowly dissolving trail, about 5 minutes. Take the bowl from the hot water and continue whisking until cool.

In another bowl, whisk 4 of the egg whites with the salt until stiff (save remaining egg whites for another use). Add the remaining sugar and whisk until glossy to make a light meringue, about 30 seconds. Gently fold the meringue into the egg yolk mixture. Then fold in the Chantilly cream and fruit purée.

Pour the soufflé mixture into the prepared dish; it should extend at least 1½ inches above the rim of the dish. Freeze it until firm, at least 6 hours. (The soufflé can be stored up to 2 weeks in the freezer.)

About ½ to 1 hour before serving, transfer the soufflé to the refrigerator to soften slightly. Just before serving, if you like, sprinkle the soufflé very generously with sifted confectioners' sugar. Remove the waxed paper and decorate the soufflé with strawberries if you like.

MALOUINIÈRE DU BOS

At Le Bos the paneling is remarkable, deeply carved in solid wood by Breton carpenters released from their usual occupation of building ships. The doors, on the left, were given an asymmetrical design to ease the passage of trays to and from the kitchen.

THE PICARD FAMILY ACQUIRED THE MALOUINIÈRE DU BOS IN 1976 WITH THE EXPRESS INTENTION OF RESTORING AN HISTORIC HOUSE FOR THEIR SIX CHILDREN. "IF WE WERE TO TAKE THE ROAD TO RUIN, WE DECIDED TO DO IT WITH PANACHE!" SAYS RENÉ PICARD. THE MALOUINIÈRE DU BOS IS AN OUTSTANDING EXAMPLE OF THE TYPE OF COUNTRY MANSIONS BUILT BY MALOUIN CORSAIRS — LICENSED PIRATES IF YOU WILL — WHO MADE THEIR FORTUNE IN THE BUSY PORT OF SAINT-MALO BOTH BY ORDINARY TRADE AND BY ATTACKING ENEMY SHIPS FROM THE CHANNEL DOWN TO THE MEDITERRANEAN, THEN SELLING THE BOOTY. THE 50 OR SO EXAMPLES OF THESE HOUSES THAT CLUSTER AROUND THE TOWN ARE UNIQUE, BUILT IN THE 17TH AND 18TH CENTURIES ON THE PROCEEDS OF THIS PRIVATEER TRADE. BUT WHAT TRADE!

SHIPS FROM SAINT-MALO PLIED THE ROUTE FROM BRITTANY'S NORTHERN COAST TO SOUTH AMERICA, THE INDIES, AND THE FAR EAST, CULMINATING IN TEN GOLDEN YEARS AT THE TURN OF THE 17TH CENTURY WHEN LOUIS XIV GAVE THE MALOUIN CORSAIRS EXCLUSIVE TRADING RIGHTS WITH THE FRENCH EAST INDIA COMPANY. IN RETURN, THE CROWN TOOK A FIFTH OF THE PROFITS. BY 1712, THE MALOUINS HAD TAKEN CONTROL OF THE COMPAGNIE DES INDES. FOR A SHORT WHILE SAINT-MALO WAS RENOWNED AS ONE OF THE RICHEST TOWNS IN FRANCE. HOWEVER, IT WAS FAR FROM SALUBRIOUS, BUILT IN A COASTAL HOLLOW AND SURROUNDED BY MASSIVE FORTIFICATIONS. SOON THE CORSAIRS DECIDED TO LIVE MORE COMFORTABLY OUTSIDE THE CITY WALLS AND BUILT COUNTRY HOUSES KNOWN AS *MALOUINIÈRES*.

This stone crucifix is part of the simple decoration of the chapel at Le Bos.

Saint-Malo's most famous son, the writer François-René de Chateaubriand, was born there in 1768. In his memoirs, he described the *malouinières* as "extremely luxurious. Bonnaban, the château of Monsieur and Madame de la Saudre, is partly built of marble brought from Genoa, and has a magnificence of which we have no idea in Paris. La Briantais, Le Bos, Le Montmarin, La Balue, and Le Colombier are or were adorned with orangeries, fountains, and statues. Some of the gardens slope down to the water through arcades of lime trees, and through colonnades of pines. Seen across beds of tulips, the sea displays its ships, its calms, and its storms."

So wealthy were the Magon de la Lande family, who built Le Bos in 1717, that a saying ran "Paris for the Bourbons, Saint-Malo for the Magons." The handsome house, with its decorative features picked out in local granite, is an archetypal *malouinière*, positioned so that the windows could overlook traffic on the River Rance. Only a cluster of tall chimneys is visible over the high wall sheltering the property – the Magons were discreet about their wealth and preferred a small estate of little more than twenty acres. "A *malouinière* was in essence a town house in the country," explains René Picard.

Le Bos attracted the Picards not only because it lived up to their expectations of beauty – the name is pronounced *"beau"* – but also because the property had changed little since 1763, when a younger Magon took over his inheritance. The process was reported to have taken 12 hours, for the new owner ceremoniously opened and closed every window, and lit a fire in each chimney. The doors of the chapel and sacristy were also opened and closed, and the altar panels unfolded. In the garden the young Magon planted a tree, then promptly uprooted it, presumably to remind the gazing crowd that the Magons always called the shots.

Such vignettes of times past provide much pleasure for René Picard as he combs the archives at Le Bos for insights into its history and the people who lived there. "Notice how the curve of the façade is repeated in the lawn," he points out. As for the marble statues, "they represent the four seasons, brought back from Italy in the hold of Malouin ships which had taken salt cod to Genoa."

The garden is another of René Picard's pleasures – he was called in from picking green beans to talk to me. "When the children come, I often do the cooking," he says. "Lots of simple food – baked ham, chocolate mousse, and our own potatoes to feed a multitude." His wife, Jacqueline, inclines toward fish, perhaps monkfish in a cream sauce, or salmon *en papillote*. Both are lovers of artichokes, a symbol of Breton agriculture. "We grow them to eat and for their splendid blue flowers," says Madame Picard warmly.

The Picard children and grandchildren surely enjoy a happier table than Chateaubriand remembered: "I had an intense dislike for certain dishes, but I was forced to eat them. I used to look imploringly at my nurse so that she could nimbly remove my plate when my father was looking the other way."

Old wooden beehives.

LA MORUE JACQUES CARTIER

SALT COD WITH POTATOES, ARTICHOKES, AND BELL PEPPER

"When we eat salt cod," says Madame Picard, "we always think of past centuries and the grande pêche off the coast of the New World." The Bishop of Rennes would bless the fleet when it sailed from Saint-Malo, then the boats (or "galleons of the fog," as they were called) disappeared for months at a time, some never to return. The fishermen swore that they would never go back to sea, yet when the time came, they could never resist another adventure.

It is a good idea to start preparing the cod well ahead as it may need soaking as long as 2 days if it is very salty. Salt cod is particularly good in broth soups and stews with vegetables that need salt, such as potatoes or turnips.

6 servings

1½ pounds SALT COD
BLACK PEPPER
¾ cup MILK
¾ cup ALL-PURPOSE FLOUR
½ cup VEGETABLE OIL
¼ cup BUTTER
JUICE OF ½ LEMON

For the garnish
3 tbsp VEGETABLE OIL
1 ONION, FINELY CHOPPED
4 CLOVES GARLIC, FINELY CHOPPED
3 RED BELL PEPPERS, CORED, SEEDED, AND SLICED
SALT AND BLACK PEPPER
GROUND CAYENNE PEPPER
3 ARTICHOKE BOTTOMS, COOKED AND DRAINED (see page 220)
¼ cup BUTTER
1 pound SMALL NEW POTATOES, WASHED AND PEELED
2 tbsp CHOPPED FRESH PARSLEY

Put the cod in a large bowl of cold water, cover it, and leave it in the refrigerator to soak at least 12 hours and up to 2 days, depending on the saltiness. Change the water three or four times during this time to remove excess salt. Drain and rinse the fish, then pat it dry with paper towels.

To prepare the garnish, heat the oil in a frying pan. Add the onion and cook over medium heat, stirring often, until soft, 3 to 5 minutes. Stir in the garlic and cook 1 minute. Reduce the heat to low and add the bell peppers, salt, black pepper, and cayenne pepper. Cover and cook until tender, stirring occasionally, 20 to 30 minutes. Taste for seasoning and add more salt and pepper if necessary.

Meanwhile, quarter the artichoke bottoms and set them aside. Melt the butter in a sauté pan or frying pan and add the potatoes – each one should touch the bottom of the pan. Cover tightly and cook over medium heat, shaking the pan occasionally, until the potatoes are tender and golden, 15 to 20 minutes. Sprinkle with salt and pepper. (The garnish can be prepared 3 or 4 hours ahead and reheated.)

Sprinkle the fish with pepper, dip it in the milk, and coat it with flour, patting to discard the excess. Heat the oil and half the butter in a frying pan. Brown the fish in batches over medium heat, 2 to 3 minutes on each side, adding more oil if necessary so the fish is half covered.

Reduce the heat to low and return all the fish to the pan. Cook, basting it often, until it flakes, 12 to 20 minutes, depending on the age of the fish.

Transfer the cod to paper towels to drain and keep the fish warm.

Reheat the garnish if necessary. Arrange the bell pepper mixture in a layer on a warmed platter. Set the fish on top and sprinkle it with the lemon juice. Surround the fish with the potatoes and artichokes and sprinkle them with the chopped parsley.

Melt the remaining butter in a small saucepan and cook until it is a hazelnut color, about 2 minutes, then pour it over the fish and serve immediately.

Artichokes and potatoes are staple vegetables of the region. They are cooked with salt cod in the typically Breton dish "Morue Jacques Cartier," named after the famous French explorer who discovered Canada.

POULET EN GELÉE DE CIDRE

CHICKEN IN CIDER JELLY

"The Bretons have long been great drinkers of cider in cups called bolées*," recounts René Picard. "After several* bolées *downed in Saint-Malo's rue de la Soif (Street of Thirst), the corsairs would heat piastre coins and throw them from the windows to the crowd, who would burn their fingers as they fought to catch them."*

Most Breton cider is cidre bouché, *or corked cider, the dry, fermented drink popular for cooking as well as sipping. Here, a chicken poaches in stock made with cider and vegetables, then the meat is layered with the strained cooking liquid in a terrine mold. The calf's feet add natural gelatin to the stock, ensuring that it sets.*

12 servings

2 CALF'S FEET, SPLIT IN HALF

2 quarts DRY HARD CIDER

2 quarts WATER

2 CARROTS, THINLY SLICED

2 ONIONS, THINLY SLICED

2 LEEKS (WHITE PART ONLY),
THINLY SLICED

1 STALK CELERY, THINLY SLICED

A BOUQUET GARNI*

3 CLOVES GARLIC

5-pound CHICKEN, TRUSSED*

SALT AND PEPPER

A BUNCH OF FRESH PARSLEY

CORNICHONS OR GHERKINS

PICKLED ONIONS

*TRUSSING NEEDLE AND STRING;
2-quart TERRINE MOLD*

Blanch the calf's feet* by putting them in a pan of cold water, bringing to a boil, and boiling 5 minutes; drain and rinse them. Put the calf's feet, cider, water, carrots, onions, leeks, celery, bouquet garni, and garlic in a flameproof casserole and bring slowly to a boil, skimming often. Simmer over low heat for 1½ hours, skimming occasionally.

Add the chicken to the casserole with a little salt and pepper and enough water to cover the chicken. Cover and continue simmering until the juices from the chicken run clear when the thigh is pierced with a fork, about 1½ hours. Be sure there is always enough liquid to cover the chicken.

Lift the chicken out of the casserole, letting the juice drain, and let it cool. Remove the string and skin and cut the meat off the bones, reserving the carcass. Cut the meat into strips.

Meanwhile, simmer the cooking liquid with the chicken carcass until it reduces by three-quarters. Strain it and taste it for seasoning. Let it cool, then skim off any surface fat. Pour enough cooking liquid into the terrine mold to make a ¾-inch layer and refrigerate until set.

Strip the parsley sprigs, discarding the stems. Pour boiling water over the parsley leaves, leave 1 minute, and then drain them. (This makes them a bright green.) Arrange a few leaves of parsley on the jellied liquid in the mold and

This terrine of chicken in cider jelly is made with traditional Breton cider. A cool glass of the same dry cider is the perfect accompaniment.

cover with the nicest chicken strips. Add more cooking liquid and chill until it is set. Continue layering the cooking liquid, parsley, and chicken strips until all the ingredients are used. Finish with a layer of cooking liquid. (The terrine can be made up to 3 days ahead and kept in the refrigerator.)

To serve, run a knife around the sides of the mold. Serve directly from the mold, with the cornichons and pickled onions.

MOKA AUX NOIX

COFFEE AND WALNUT CAKE

One of the districts of Saint-Malo still bears the name Moka, a reminder that it was the town from which sailors voyaged to Arabia, to return with coffee and other riches of the East.

8 servings

For the génoise
1 cup ALL-PURPOSE FLOUR
PINCH OF SALT
3 LARGE EGGS
½ cup SUGAR
1 tbsp INSTANT COFFEE DISSOLVED
IN 2 tbsp WATER
3 tbsp UNSALTED BUTTER,
MELTED AND COOLED

For the icing
1½ cups UNSALTED BUTTER,
AT ROOM TEMPERATURE
1½ cups CONFECTIONERS' SUGAR, SIFTED
¼ cup INSTANT COFFEE DISSOLVED
IN ¼ cup WATER
1 cup WALNUT HALVES

8-inch ROUND CAKE PAN; PASTRY BAG AND MEDIUM STAR TUBE (OPTIONAL)

Butter the cake pan and line the bottom with waxed paper. Butter the paper and coat the pan with flour, discarding the excess. Preheat the oven to 350°F.

For the *génoise*, sift the flour with the salt. In a heatproof bowl set over a pan of hot, not boiling, water whisk the eggs with the sugar until the mixture falls from the whisk in a thick ribbon and holds a slowly dissolving trail, about 5 minutes. (An electric mixer can also be used, in which case the pan of hot water is not needed.) Sift the flour over the mixture in three batches and fold together lightly. Add the coffee and melted butter with the last batch.

Pour the batter into the prepared pan and bake in the heated oven until the cake shrinks slightly and the top springs back when lightly pressed with a fingertip, 30 to 40 minutes. Run a knife around the cake and unmold it onto a rack to cool. Peel off the lining paper. (The cake can be kept 1 or 2 days in an airtight container. It freezes well, too.)

To make the icing, cream the butter and gradually beat in the sugar and coffee. Reserve ½ cup of the icing. Finely chop the walnuts, reserving 8 halves for decoration. Beat the chopped nuts into the larger portion of icing.

Cut the cake in half horizontally using a long serrated knife, to make two layers. Spread one cake layer with one-third of the walnut icing. Set the second cake layer on top and press lightly to flatten it. Spread the top and sides of the cake with the remaining walnut icing. Scoop the reserved coffee icing into the pastry bag and decorate the cake with 8 rosettes. Set a reserved walnut half on each rosette. (The cake can be made ahead and refrigerated for a day.)

One of several statues representing the Four Seasons in the garden at Le Bos. The statues are Italian, dating from the 18th century, and were brought back by the corsairs from their trading trips to Genoa. Like many malouinières, the garden at Le Bos overlooks the Rance river.

MANOIR DE VAU-DE-QUIP

VICOMTE MAURICE DE KERVENOAËL IS BRETON BORN AND BRED AND HAS ALWAYS BEEN DETERMINED TO MAINTAIN ROOTS IN THIS ISOLATED WESTERN REGION OF FRANCE. SO IN 1976, HE BOUGHT THE MANOIR DE VAU-DE-QUIP NEAR REDON, IN THE HEART OF BRITTANY. NOT ONLY WAS THE MANOIR IN A SAD STATE OF DISREPAIR, BUT THE PROPERTY HAD BEEN DISMEMBERED INTO HOUSE, FARM, AND WOODLAND, VICTIM OF THE FRENCH INHERITANCE LAWS. LITTLE BY LITTLE THE KERVENOAËLS HAVE PIECED VAU-DE-QUIP TOGETHER AGAIN. NOW THE MANOIR IS AGAIN OWNER OF THE SURROUNDING VALLEY, AND OF WOODS OF WILD CHESTNUT, OAK, AND MARITIME PINE. "YOU COULD SAY WE HAVE RECREATED THE OLD ESTATE," SAYS CATHERINE DE KERVENOAËL. "ALL WE ARE STILL MISSING IS PART OF THE WOODLANDS."

RESTORATION OF THE MANOIR HAS BEEN A PAINSTAKING AFFAIR. FIRST PRIORITY WAS A KITCHEN AND BATHROOM SO THE HOUSE WOULD BE AT LEAST HABITABLE. NEXT WAS TO APPLY FOR AN HISTORIC MONUMENT LISTING — EVENTUALLY THIS ENABLED THE DE KERVENOAËLS TO GET A GOVERNMENT SUBSIDY TO DRY OUT THE NORTH WALL OF VAU-DE-QUIP AND SEAL IT FROM PERVASIVE DAMP. IN SUMMER, STUDENTS CAME ALONG TO HELP THEM PAINT AND HANG WALLPAPER IN THE SEVEN BEDROOMS.

Terraces of huge trees surround Vau-de-Quip, with the nearest towering taller than the three-storied main building. Close by cluster the classic Breton adjuncts to the property – farmhouse, chapel, stables, and outbuildings (right). The stone gateway proudly displays a time-worn family crest (right above). A turret protrudes from the woodland of wild chestnut, oak, and maritime pine (right center).

Now, after 15 years, the dozen ugly T-bars used by the previous owners to prop up the sagging main beams of the ground floor have gone. Finance is on the way for work on the great open fireplaces with their Renaissance carving. Surprisingly, the roof, usually the first source of trouble in an old house like this, has come last. "The most recent roof repairs were 100 years ago, so it certainly needs attention," says the Vicomtesse, "especially the dormer windows, whose stone carvings have been badly eroded by the weather."

Edible mushrooms picked after a light shower from the woods around Vau-de-Quip (top left). The great kitchen-dining room with its dark beams and terra-cotta-tiled floor (top right). Dating from the 15th century, the stone fireplace is decorated with animal motifs.

Central heating is still something of a luxury at Vau-de-Quip, and in winter the family gathers in the great kitchen-dining room with its terra-cotta tiles and overhead beams. At the side of the fireplace is a curious niche – a *"petit four"* for baking small cakes and side dishes. (Most baking would have been done in a bread oven sited away from the main building because of the heat and danger of fire.) The Vicomtesse looks after the cooking and at Christmas turns to simple dishes like a molded dessert made with wild chestnuts from the property. "I notice how much friends appreciate regional dishes, so different from the cooking in restaurants," she says.

The Kervenoaëls told me how lucky they had been to find Vau-de-Quip, since Bretons hold on closely to their land; the property had passed to a new family only three times since the title deeds began in 1488. One owner was the beautiful Louise du Bot du Grég, notorious for her two-faced conduct during the Napoleonic Wars. Married to one of the Royalist Breton leaders fighting against the new Republic, she joined the revolutionaries by engaging in an affair with General Hoche, who had been sent from Paris to suppress the Royalists. Vau-de-Quip was confiscated, but Louise managed to recover her property thanks to her liaison with Hoche. Bold as brass, she hung on to it by marrying a Napoleonic general once Hoche and her husband were out of the way.

Vau-de-Quip lies on the edge of Breton-speaking territory. The land is generously watered by streams – *"vau"* means valley while *"quip"* probably denotes a water spring. It could hardly be more appropriate to its current owners:

Vicomte de Kervenoaël is known teasingly by his friends as "Mr. Mineral Water" because he presides over the company which bottles Evian and Source Badoit.

Tarte au Thon

Warm Tuna Tart

Since the Middle Ages, tuna has been one of the mainstays of Breton fishermen, and boats range hundreds of miles, as far as Senegal, in search of the giant fish.

8 servings

2 tbsp BUTTER
3 SHALLOTS, CHOPPED
4 HARD-BOILED EGGS
6½-ounce CAN OF TUNA IN WATER, DRAINED
½ cup FRESH BREAD CRUMBS SOAKED IN
½ cup MILK AND SQUEEZED DRY
3 tbsp OLIVE OIL
¼ cup CHOPPED FRESH PARSLEY
1 LARGE EGG, BEATEN TO MIX WITH
½ tsp SALT TO GLAZE

For the pie pastry
2½ cups ALL-PURPOSE FLOUR
⅔ cup UNSALTED BUTTER
1 LARGE EGG YOLK
½ tsp SALT
¼ cup WATER

For the sauce
2 tbsp LEMON JUICE, MORE TO TASTE
2 tbsp CHOPPED MIXED FRESH HERBS
SALT AND PEPPER
1 cup CRÈME FRAÎCHE (see page 220) OR HEAVY CREAM

8-inch TART PAN WITH REMOVABLE BOTTOM

Make the pastry dough (see page 221) and chill it at least 30 minutes.

Melt the butter and cook the shallots over low heat until soft, 3 to 5 minutes. Chop the hard-boiled eggs. Flake the tuna with a fork. Mix together the eggs, tuna, soaked bread crumbs, olive oil, shallots, and parsley.

A leaping stone fish adorns the fireplace – a territorial symbol declaring that the châtelain held the right to fish the local seas.

Butter the tart pan. Divide the pastry dough in half. Line the pan with half the dough, overlapping the edges of the pan*. Brush the dough edges with the egg glaze*. Spoon the tuna mixture into the tart shell.

Roll out the remaining dough to a round 2 inches larger than the pan and cover the tart with it. Trim the edges and seal the top and bottom crusts together with a fork or scallop with the back of a knife. Brush the top crust with egg glaze. Using a sharp knife, slash the top every 1 inch so steam can escape. Chill until the pastry dough is firm, about 30 minutes.

Preheat the oven to 425°F and put in a baking sheet to heat.

Bake the tart on the hot baking sheet until the pastry starts to brown, 10 to 15 minutes. Reduce the oven temperature to 350°F and continue baking until the pastry is browned, 15 to 20 minutes longer. (The tart can be baked up to 2 days ahead and refrigerated. Reheat it and serve warm or at room temperature.)

Meanwhile, to make the sauce, mix the lemon juice, herbs, salt, and pepper in a bowl. Gradually whisk in the crème fraîche or cream – the lemon juice will thicken it lightly. Taste and add more salt, pepper, and lemon juice if needed.

Serve the tart hot, with the sauce.

SAUMON EN CRÔUTE DE SEL

SALMON BAKED IN A SALT CRUST

This method of preparing salmon in a salt crust is good with other thick fish fillets – especially cod. The crust is removed before eating.

8 servings

3-pound PIECE OF SALMON FILLET, WITH
THE SKIN, CUT INTO 8 PIECES
8 SPRIGS OF FRESH THYME
1 LARGE EGG, BEATEN TO MIX
1½ pounds UNPEELED BOILING POTATOES
¾ pound SPINACH, WASHED
AND STEMS REMOVED
2 tbsp BUTTER
SALT AND PEPPER

For the salt crust
¾ pound COARSE SALT, PREFERABLY
SEA SALT
2½ cups WHOLE-WHEAT FLOUR
5 LARGE EGG WHITES, MORE IF NEEDED

For the white butter sauce
¼ cup WHITE WINE VINEGAR
¼ cup DRY WHITE WINE
2 SHALLOTS, CHOPPED
1 cup UNSALTED BUTTER
2 tbsp CHOPPED MIXED FRESH HERBS

Saumon en Crôute de Sel – a gutsy taste of the sea. The salt crust is discarded at the table before eating.

For the salt crust, beat together the salt, flour, and egg whites, adding more egg white if necessary to form a dough that holds together. Cover the dough and let it rest at least 15 minutes, and up to 4 hours.

Divide the salt crust dough into 8 equal pieces. Roll out a piece to an 8-inch square. Put a piece of fish, skin-side down, in the center of the dough square. Top with a sprig of thyme. Brush the surrounding dough with beaten egg, then bring up the dough over the fish and seal into a package with the salmon flat inside. Keep it in the refrigerator while preparing the remaining packages. Chill all the fish packages at least 15 minutes, and up to 2 hours.

Preheat the oven to 400°F and put in a baking sheet to heat. Put the fish packages on the hot baking sheet and bake in the heated oven for 12 minutes. Remove the packages and let rest at room temperature for 10 minutes.

While the fish is baking and resting, cook the potatoes in a large pan of boiling salted water until just tender, 15 to 20 minutes. Cook the spinach in a large pan of boiling salted water until tender, 1 to 2 minutes. Drain the spinach and refresh it*. When cool enough to handle, squeeze the spinach by handfuls to remove excess moisture. Make the white butter sauce (see page 55) and stir in the herbs.

Drain the potatoes, peel them, and cut into thick slices. Keep warm. Melt the butter in a frying pan. Add the spinach with a little salt and pepper and cook over medium heat, stirring often, until heated through. Taste for seasoning.

To serve, put the fish, still in the salt crust, on warmed plates with the potatoes and spinach. Pass the sauce separately. Let guests remove the salt crust at the table.

LE REDONNAIS

CHESTNUT LOAF WITH WHIPPED CREAM

The wild chestnut trees around Redon are famous – the locals say they have a special savory taste and will not survive if planted elsewhere. "When I make the cake in Paris with chestnuts bought there," says the Vicomtesse de Kervenoaël, "it simply isn't the same." Though nothing can replace the taste of fresh chestnuts, the results are very good with canned ones.

8 servings

1¾ pounds FRESH CHESTNUTS OR 1 pound
CANNED UNSWEETENED CHESTNUTS
2½ cups MILK, MORE IF NEEDED
1 cup UNSALTED BUTTER,
AT ROOM TEMPERATURE
⅔ cup SUGAR
2 to 3 tsp RUM
¼ pound BITTERSWEET CHOCOLATE,
CHOPPED
½ tsp VEGETABLE OIL

For the Chantilly cream
½ cup HEAVY CREAM
1½ tsp CONFECTIONERS' SUGAR
¼ tsp VANILLA EXTRACT

*9-×5-×4-inch LOAF PAN; PASTRY BAG AND
MEDIUM STAR TUBE (OPTIONAL)*

Lightly butter the loaf pan. Line the bottom with waxed paper, and butter the paper.

If using fresh chestnuts, make a slit at the end of each nut with a small knife. Put them in a pan of cold water and bring just to a boil. Use a slotted spoon to lift out a few nuts at a time and peel them while still hot, removing both the thick outer skin and the thin inner skin. If the chestnuts cool and become difficult to peel, quickly reheat them. Do not let them heat too long, or they will become soft and fall apart. Put the peeled fresh nuts in a saucepan with the milk, cover the pan, and simmer over low heat until tender, 25 to 30 minutes. Drain.

If using canned chestnuts, just drain them. Purée the fresh or canned chestnuts in a food processor or work them through a food mill.

Beat the butter and sugar together until soft. Beat this mixture together with the rum into the nut purée until smooth. Pack the mixture into the prepared pan and smooth the top. Cover and refrigerate overnight, or up to a week.

To finish, unmold the chestnut loaf onto a platter and peel off the lining paper. Melt the chocolate on a heatproof plate set over a pan of hot water. Stir in the oil until the mixture is smooth. Let it cool slightly, then spread the chocolate evenly over the top and sides of the chestnut loaf using a metal spatula. Put it in the refrigerator to set.

Make the Chantilly cream (see page 220) and scoop it into the pastry bag if using. Cut the loaf into thin slices using a knife dipped in hot water and set the slices on individual plates. Decorate with rosettes of Chantilly cream, if using a pastry bag, or spoon the cream onto the slices by hand.

The caretakers of the château cradling two young ducks (left). Both horse chestnuts and sweet chestnuts (the essential ingredient in Le Redonnais) grow around Vau-de-Quip (above).

CHÂTEAU DU VERT-BOIS

THANKS TO THE LOVING CARE OF ANNE PROUVOST AND HER LATE HUSBAND, THE 18TH-CENTURY CHÂTEAU DU VERT-BOIS IS AN OASIS OF BEAUTY IN THE CHILL PLAINS OF NORTHERN FRANCE. THEY INHERITED THE CHÂTEAU WITH ALL ITS ORIGINAL DECORATION, FINE FURNITURE, AND COLLECTION OF DELFT FAÏENCE, TO WHICH MADAME PROUVOST'S FATHER HAD ADDED 19TH- AND 20TH-CENTURY PAINTINGS BY SUCH MASTERS AS RENOIR, BONNARD, DUFY, AND CHAGALL. THE PROUVOSTS THEMSELVES EXPANDED THE COLLECTION WITH MODERN ARTISTS AND ADDED A REMARKABLE GROUP OF RARE MINERALS COLLECTED ON THEIR TRAVELS. IN 1975, THE FONDATION SEPTENTRION (FOUNDATION OF THE NORTH) WAS OPENED AT LE VERT-BOIS TO HELP LOCAL ARTISTS EXHIBIT THEIR WORK. REGULAR CLASSES ARE HELD IN DRAWING, PAINTING, DECORATING FURNITURE, AND BOOKBINDING, WHILE THE APPRAISAL OF ANTIQUES IS PARTICULARLY POPULAR.

The classical, moated Château du Vert-Bois is pure Louis XV, but in miniature. "The building is only one room deep," explains owner Madame Prouvost, "so with floor-to-ceiling windows on both sides we have wonderful light, but few bedrooms." The bridge across the moat – survivor of an earlier fortified farm – is scarcely carriage-width. The gatehouse at Le Vert-Bois (inset above) is almost a century older than the château, and was originally a hunting lodge. It is built in a Flemish style, a striking contrast to the classical lines of the château itself.

Between the two World Wars, when the French textile business was still prosperous, wool merchants like the Prouvosts had close connections with their counterparts in the United States, even opening up mills there. Much of the business was centered on Rhode Island around Woonsocket – as Anne Prouvost told me, "There were plenty of French-speaking Catholics." Very soon the family was at ease in Boston and New York social circles. It was in this company that Madame Prouvost first encountered "the obligatory after-dinner hour of powder room and *crème de menthe* for the ladies while our husbands savored a splendid Cognac." New York memories include filling in as a volunteer waitress at the charity restaurant that is run by the Alliance Française.

Later, in Hollywood, the Prouvosts were entertained by movie mogul Jack Warner – "electronic gates, uniformed guards, fierce dogs,

. . . and a private road peppered with reproduction Greek statues and fountains," recalls Anne Prouvost. Next, the Prouvosts opened a textile mill in South Carolina near Charleston, returning to France with a taste for jambalaya, but "not for that horrible fried chicken."

The Prouvosts were great yachtsmen, regularly taking their children to the Mediterranean. Anne Prouvost was always in charge of the food. "I'm the queen of fish soup and ratatouille," she confesses. "You could always find chicken, however tough, so stewed chicken in sauce is my specialty, too." Back home she has made her cook an expert at *waterzoï*, a Flemish version of *pot-au-feu* which is finished with crème fraîche and huge quantities of chopped parsley. Madame Prouvost also particularly enjoys *flamiche*, a Flemish leek tart baked in rich pie pastry with a topping of creamy custard. "But when I'm alone I simply cook an egg."

The elegant grand salon is presided over by a glittering chandelier and fine impressionist paintings.

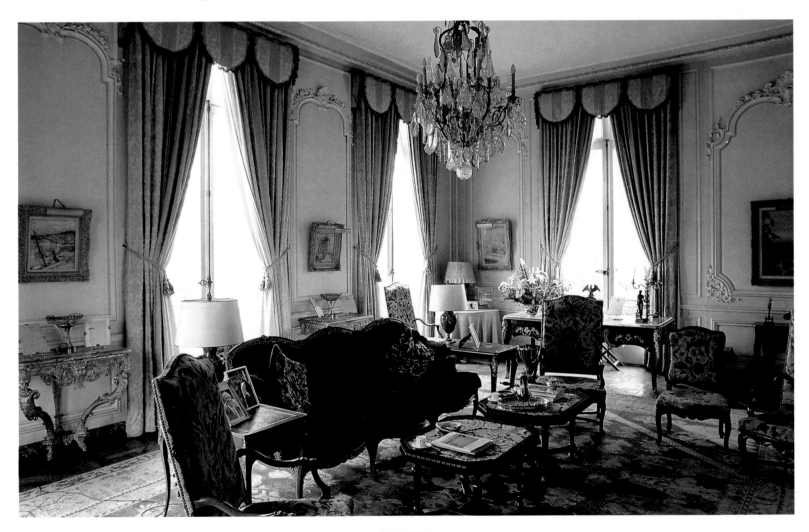

FAISANS EN ESCABÈCHE

OIL AND VINEGAR BRAISED PHEASANTS IN ASPIC

Though only a few miles from the industrial city of Lille, the Château du Vert-Bois is in rustic and idyllic surroundings and aptly lives up to its name of "green woods." Game birds and hare are plentiful here. In this unusual recipe, the musky flavor of wild pheasant is enhanced with vinegar, while oil is used to keep the bird moist. For serving, the halved birds are brushed with a light coating of aspic.

4 servings

2 YOUNG PHEASANTS
(ABOUT 2 pounds EACH)
SALT AND PEPPER
1 ONION, CHOPPED
2 BAY LEAVES
¾ cup WHITE WINE VINEGAR
¼ cup OLIVE OIL
1 quart CLEAR CHICKEN STOCK (see page
221), AT ROOM TEMPERATURE
2 tbsp UNFLAVORED GELATIN
1 SMALL HEAD LEAFY LETTUCE OR
1 BUNCH WATERCRESS

TRUSSING NEEDLE AND STRING

Preheat the oven to 350°F.

Season the cavities of the birds with salt and pepper and truss them*. Put them in a large flameproof casserole with the onion, bay leaves, vinegar, and oil, and season them with salt and pepper. Cover the casserole and bring the liquid just to a boil on top of the stove.

Transfer the casserole to the heated oven and cook the birds until they are tender, about 1½ hours. Baste the birds often and turn them from time to time during the cooking.

Drain the birds and let them cool to room temperature, then cover them and refrigerate until they are well chilled, about 2 hours. Discard the cooking liquid.

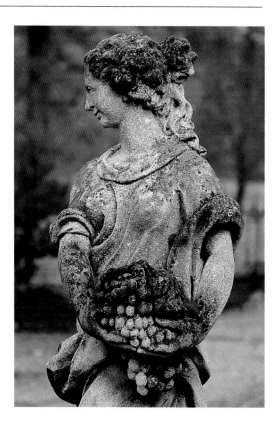

The garden at Le Vert-Bois dates from the mid-18th century and includes a formal French park, an orchard, and the English-style "jardin du curé," designed by Russell Page, the influential English landscape architect.

Remove the string from the birds and pat them dry with paper towels. Halve each bird, cutting along the breastbone and backbone. Set the halves on a rack, skin side up, over a tray to catch the drips, and refrigerate them.

Put 3 or 4 tablespoons of the stock in a small saucepan. Sprinkle the gelatin over and set aside until it swells to a spongy consistency, about 5 minutes. Melt it over low heat, gently shaking the pan. (Do not stir or strings will form.) Add the gelatin mixture to the remaining stock to make aspic. Taste it for seasoning. Let it cool until tepid, stirring occasionally.

Pour about one-quarter of the aspic into a metal bowl set over ice and stir gently until it is very cold, turns syrupy, and starts to set. Working quickly, brush or spoon a thin coating of this aspic over the birds. Chill them until the aspic sets.

Chill more aspic until it is on the point of setting and coat the birds again. Repeat the process twice.

Set the birds on a platter lined with lettuce or decorate the birds with watercress. Cover the birds and refrigerate them up to 24 hours, until ready to serve.

PUDDING DE CABINET

BRIOCHE PUDDING WITH CANDIED FRUIT AND JAM

This extravagant version of bread-and-butter pudding was the specialty of a great-grandmother who left "lasting memories. It was she who preserved the house in its pristine state," says Madame Prouvost. The recipe calls for kramik – *a local brioche – instead of the more usual ladyfingers. If you don't have time to bake the* kramik *(see next recipe), this dessert is quickly made with a store-bought loaf of brioche, weighing about 1 pound, sliced and trimmed to fit the dish.*

10 to 12 servings

¼ cup GOLDEN RAISINS
½ cup MIXED CANDIED FRUITS, CHOPPED
KRAMIK (see opposite), CUT CROSSWISE
INTO 3 LAYERS
1 cup APRICOT JAM
6 LARGE EGGS
1 cup SUGAR
1 quart MILK

For the vanilla custard sauce
2 cups MILK
1 VANILLA BEAN, SPLIT,
OR ½ tsp VANILLA EXTRACT
6 LARGE EGG YOLKS
⅓ cup SUGAR

*2-quart SOUFFLÉ OR OTHER
ROUND BAKING DISH*

Generously butter the soufflé or baking dish. Put it in the freezer until the butter is firm, and then butter it again.

Preheat the oven to 350°F.

Sprinkle some of the raisins and candied fruits over the bottom of the baking dish. Top with a layer of *kramik*. Spread with a thin layer of apricot jam and sprinkle with more raisins and candied fruits.

Whisk the eggs and sugar together until light.

Gradually whisk in the milk. Pour a little of this custard slowly over the bread so it is absorbed.

Put the dish in a water bath* and bring the water to a boil on top of the stove. Transfer it to the heated oven and bake until the custard sets, about 30 minutes. Remove the dish from the oven and layer the remaining bread, jam, raisins and candied fruits in the dish until all the ingredients are used, finishing with a layer of bread. Pour in the remaining custard. If the bread floats, gently press it into the custard. Bring the water bath back to a boil on top of the stove, then return the dish to the oven and bake until the custard sets, 1½ to 2 hours.

Meanwhile, make the vanilla custard sauce (see page 222). Let the pudding cool at least 15 minutes before serving it, or serve it at room temperature. Run a knife around the dish and unmold the pudding onto a platter. Pour a little of the vanilla custard sauce around it and pass the remaining sauce separately.

Exquisite Persian bowls from the prestigious collection of porcelain, sculpture, and fine china displayed at Le Vert-Bois.

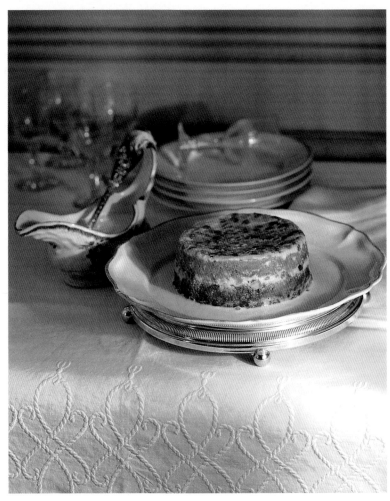

Pudding de Cabinet, the ultimate bread-and-butter pudding.

KRAMIK

BROWN SUGAR BRIOCHE

Some of France's great 19th-century fortunes were made in the northern fields of sugar beet, so, not surprisingly, the local rich yeast bread is sprinkled with brown sugar. Other versions appear throughout Flanders and in Belgium.

⅓ cup MILK
1½ tsp ACTIVE DRY YEAST OR ⅓ oz
COMPRESSED YEAST*
1⅔ cups ALL-PURPOSE FLOUR, MORE IF
NEEDED
PINCH OF SALT
1 tbsp SUGAR
2 LARGE EGGS, BEATEN TO MIX
7 tbsp UNSALTED BUTTER

For the topping
3 tbsp BUTTER, AT ROOM TEMPERATURE
6 tbsp FIRMLY PACKED LIGHT OR DARK
BROWN SUGAR

8-inch ROUND CAKE PAN

Heat the milk in a small saucepan until bubbles form around the edge, then let it cool to lukewarm. Sprinkle or crumble the yeast on top and set aside to dissolve, about 5 minutes.

Sift the flour with the salt into a bowl and make a well in the center. Add the yeast mixture, granulated sugar, and eggs to the well. With your fingertips, stir the ingredients in the well, gradually drawing in the flour to make a smooth dough. It should be very soft. Using your cupped hand, knead the dough by slapping it against the side of the bowl. Continue kneading until the dough is shiny and very smooth, about 10 minutes.

Pound the butter with your fist to soften it first, then work it into the dough until thoroughly incorporated. (Alternatively, you can mix and knead the dough in an electric mixer fitted with a dough hook.)

Transfer the dough to an oiled bowl, flipping it so the top is oiled. Cover it with a damp cloth and let rise in a warm place until doubled in bulk, 1 to 1½ hours.

Meanwhile, butter the cake pan.

Transfer the dough to a floured work surface and knead it lightly to knock out the air. Shape it into a ball and transfer it to the pan. Flour your hands and flatten the dough into the bottom (not the sides) of the pan. Spread it with the butter for the topping and sprinkle with the brown sugar. Let it rise in a warm place until almost doubled in bulk, 15 to 30 minutes. Preheat the oven to 400°F.

Bake the *kramik* in the oven until it is brown and firm, 25 to 30 minutes. Unmold it onto a rack to cool. It is best eaten warm on the day of baking, but can be stored up to a day.

The elegant rooms at Le Vert-Bois are sumptuously furnished and still retain much of their original decoration.

CHÂTEAU D'ITTENWILLER

EACH YEAR IN OCTOBER, FRANÇOIS-JOSEPH D'ANDLAU-HOMBOURG TAKES TWO WEEKS' VACATION TO PICK HIS OWN GRAPES. THE *VENDANGE* AT THE CHÂTEAU D'ITTENWILLER IN ALSACE HAS BECOME SOMETHING OF A FESTIVAL, WITH THE COMTE, HIS TWO BROTHERS, AND THEIR CHILDREN JOINED BY A BEVY OF FRIENDS. PICKING IS DONE BY HAND IN THE OLD WAY. "THIS MEANS WE CAN CUT THE VINES RIGHT BACK FOR LOWER YIELD AND HIGHER QUALITY. WE ARE ONE OF ONLY TWO *CHÂTEAUX* IN ALSACE THAT PRESS AND BOTTLE WINE ON THE PROPERTY ITSELF," HE RECOUNTS WITH PRIDE. "SO MANY FRIENDS WANT TO HELP, WE HAVE TO TURN AWAY VOLUNTEERS!"

HIS WIFE, CHRISTINE D'ANDLAU-HOMBOURG, IS IN CHARGE OF THE COOKING. "WE'RE EXPECTING ABOUT 50 PEOPLE FOR THE HARVEST WEEKEND THIS YEAR," SHE TOLD ME. "WE TAKE A PICNIC TO THE VINES IN LATE MORNING — HOT ROLLS, HAM AND *PÂTÉ* SANDWICHES WITH CORNICHONS, PLENTY OF WINE AND BEER. EVERYONE MUST BE WELL FED TO BE STRONG AND HAPPY!" AFTER THIS SECOND BREAKFAST, LUNCH BACK HOME DOES NOT START UNTIL LATE AFTERNOON AND IT, TOO, IS GENEROUS. AN ENORMOUS *CHOUCROUTE* IS FOLLOWED BY THE LOCAL MUNSTER CHEESE (MILDER TYPES ARE AVAILABLE FOR THE FAINT-HEARTED) AND A DESSERT OF CHOCOLATE CAKE OR PERHAPS FLOATING ISLAND.

Seventeenth-century Château d'Ittenwiller, a reconstruction of an ancient fortified manor, is busiest in the fall when grape-picking dominates château life. The building is typically Alsatian with ivy-covered turrets, and the presence of antlers around the house and the grounds is explained by the well-stocked deer park in the grounds.

A stone archway above the entrance to the wine cellar is shaded by a magnificent maple tree (above).

Lunch the following day is similarly matched to the exigencies of outdoor life. The main course is the Alsatian meat-and-potato dish called *back-eöfe*, which precedes salad, cheese, and assorted fruit tarts of apples, pears, or plums topped in Alsatian fashion with a creamy custard. As for the evenings, a *quiche lorraine* is always available. The Comtesse's recipe is again a local classic, flavored with ham in a custard of whole eggs and cream, and sprinkled with a little Gruyère cheese for a crisp brown crust.

Good food is but a background for the matter in hand – the harvest itself. The enduring concern is the weather because some sun is vital during the ten days before picking. Heavy rain during picking dilutes the grape juice and encourages rot (but not the "noble rot" so necessary to the luscious sweet wines made from late-picked grapes). Once in cask, a wine can develop unpredictably, particularly in the first few weeks. "We all mess up a barrel from time to time, though no one likes to admit it," the Comte acknowledges with a laugh. He speaks with the authority of experience – Alsace has been home to the Andlau-Hombourg family for more than a millenium.

He is particularly proud of the Château d'It-tenwiller Comte d'Andlau-Hombourg white wine, a blend originally made by the Benedictine monks who planted vineyards at Ittenwiller after displacing a nunnery dating back to 1115. The Benedictine "recipe" is based on four grape varieties: Sylvaner (a typically Alsatian grape valued for its acidity), Pinot Blanc for volume, a small amount of Tokay (known in the rest of France as Pinot Gris), and finally Muscat for fragrance and finesse. "It's a wine to drink throughout the meal, good with all but the richest red meats," says the Comte. Two other white wines are also produced on the property: a Riesling, dry and ideally suited to fish dishes, and a fruity Gewürztraminer, at its best as an aperitif, with dessert, or with a slice of the best Alsatian *foie gras*.

The vines at Château d'Ittenwiller extend over seven acres – just sufficient, says the Comte, "for us to maintain the property and enjoy ourselves at the same time." There is certainly much to take pleasure in, for Ittenwiller is a quintessentially Alsatian cluster of buildings, complete with decorative painted shutters, geranium window boxes, an encircling moat, and the slightly surreal touch of stags' antlers here, there, and everywhere. There is no problem renewing the stock because the Château d'Ittenwiller also has its own deer park!

The Château d'Ittenwiller vineyard on a mellow fall afternoon. It extends over 7 acres.

Wine aged well in oak casks acquires an unmistakable character. The Gewürztraminer in this cask is a favorite aperitif wine.

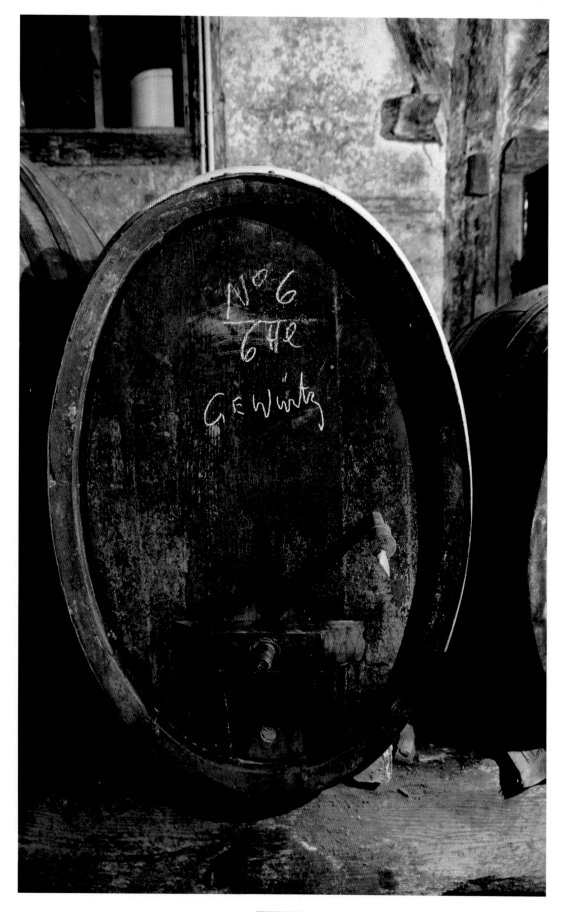

BACKEÖFE

PORK, LAMB, AND BEEF BAKED
WITH POTATOES

This traditional Alsatian stew is commonly prepared and served in oval terrines of the local earthenware pottery. These are still hand-crafted by artisans and painted with country designs. In the old days, housewives carried their terrines filled with backeöfe *to the village communal oven, which was hot from bread-baking. Even today Comte d'Andlau-Hombourg gives old-fashioned instructions. "Cook your* backeöfe *in the baker's oven for 2 to 2½ hours," he writes, "or bake it in your oven at home for 3½ hours."*

8 servings

1 pound STEWING PORK, CUT INTO 2-inch
CUBES
1 pound BONED LAMB SHOULDER, CUT
INTO 2-inch CUBES
1 pound STEWING BEEF, CUT INTO 2-inch
CUBES
2 cups DRY WHITE WINE, PREFERABLY
ALSATIAN
½ pound ONIONS, SLICED

2 CLOVES GARLIC, CHOPPED
A BOUQUET GARNI*
1 tsp CRUSHED PEPPERCORNS
2 pounds BAKING POTATOES,
PEELED AND SLICED
SALT

Combine the pork, lamb, beef, wine, onions, garlic, bouquet garni, and peppercorns in a large nonreactive bowl. Stir well, cover, and refrigerate overnight.

Preheat the oven to 325°F. Line a flameproof casserole with half the potatoes and sprinkle them lightly with salt. Cover the potatoes with all the meats and half the onions and season them. Layer the remaining potatoes and onions in the casserole and add a little more salt. Strain in the wine.

Cover the casserole and bring to a simmer on top of the stove. Transfer to the heated oven and bake until the meats are very tender, 3 to 4 hours. If you like, uncover the casserole during the last 30 minutes, to brown the top.

Taste the cooking liquid for seasoning before serving, in the casserole. (The stew can be refrigerated 1 or 2 days. The flavor mellows with time.)

Bottles of Château d'Ittenwiller white, Riesling, and Gewürztraminer (above).

The local backeöfe, a dish that requires good dry white wine and slow, gentle cooking.

KUGELHOPF

ALSATIAN COFFEECAKE

"Kugelhopf," says Christine d'Andlau-Hombourg, "is a coffeecake flavored with raisins and almonds that we eat for breakfast, for tea, and even at wine tastings." For a crisp brown crust it is best baked in the traditional deep, fluted ring mold made of earthenware.

Makes 2 loaves

¾ cup MILK
1 tbsp ACTIVE DRY YEAST OR
⅔ oz COMPRESSED YEAST*
¾ cup UNSALTED BUTTER
4 cups ALL-PURPOSE FLOUR
PINCH OF SALT
6 tbsp SUGAR
2 LARGE EGGS, BEATEN TO MIX
½ cup DARK RAISINS, SOAKED IN WARM
WATER UNTIL PLUMP, THEN DRAINED
¼ cup WHOLE UNBLANCHED ALMONDS

TWO 1½-quart KUGELHOPF *MOLDS*

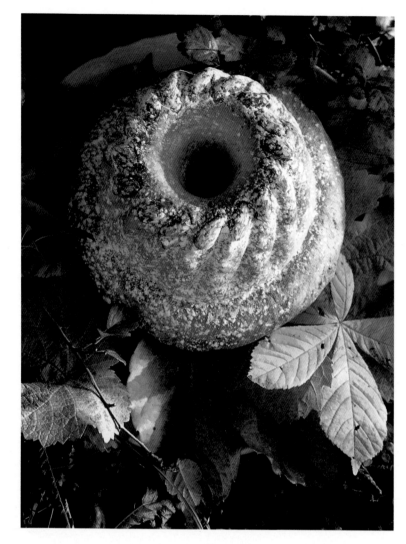

Heat the milk in a small saucepan until bubbles form around the edge. Pour about half of it into a small bowl and let it cool to lukewarm, then sprinkle or crumble the yeast on top and set aside to dissolve, about 5 minutes. Meanwhile, add the butter to the remaining milk in the saucepan and continue heating, stirring, until the butter melts, 2 to 3 minutes. Let it cool to tepid.

Sift the flour with the salt into a large bowl and make a well in the center. Add the butter and yeast mixtures, the sugar, and eggs to the well. With your fingertips, stir the ingredients in the well, gradually drawing in the flour to make a smooth dough. It should be very soft. Using your cupped hand, knead the dough by slapping it against the side of the bowl. Continue kneading until the dough is shiny and very smooth, about 10 minutes. Gently work in the raisins. (Alternatively, you can mix and knead the dough in an electric mixer fitted with a dough hook.)

Oil a large bowl and transfer the dough to it. Cover the bowl with a damp cloth and let the dough rise in a warm place until doubled in bulk, 1 to 1½ hours. Butter the *kugelhopf* molds. Press the whole almonds evenly around the sides and bottom.

When risen, knead the dough lightly to knock out the air. Divide the dough in half and put it in the molds; it should fill them by one-third. Cover with a damp cloth and let rise in a warm place until the dough has almost reached the top of the molds, ¾ to 1 hour. Preheat the oven to 375°F.

Bake the cakes in the heated oven until puffed and brown, 40 to 50 minutes. Unmold them onto a rack to cool.

Kugelhopf is best eaten on the day of baking, but can be stored in an airtight container up to 3 days.

Kugelhopf, sweet yeast cake, is a staple of Alsace and a favorite at breakfast.

PARC DE SCHOPPENWIHR

"ALSACE IS A GARDEN," REMARKS BARON CHRISTIAN DE WATTEVILLE-BERCKHEIM. HIS HOME AT SCHOPPENWIHR IS A SMALL PART OF THIS GARDEN, WITH A PARK WHICH IS A MICROCOSM OF THE PROVINCE ITSELF, A REFLECTION, TOO, OF NATURE'S STRUGGLE TO SURVIVE 20TH-CENTURY PROGRESS. THE PROPERTY INCLUDES TWENTY ACRES OF FOREST, FARMLAND FOR GROWING CORN AND WHEAT, AND A NETWORK OF LAKES AND STREAMS INHABITED BY CARP, PIKE, PERCH, AND OTHER FRESHWATER FISH. "ALAS, FOR THE LAST FEW YEARS THEY'VE BEEN DOING POORLY," LAMENTS THE BARON, "WHAT WITH POLLUTION FROM THE NEARBY PAPER MILL AND TWO YEARS OF DROUGHT."

SCHOPPENWIHR IS AN ANCIENT PROPERTY WHICH HAS BEEN IN THE WATTEVILLE-BERCKHEIM FAMILY SINCE THE 15TH CENTURY. THE PARK IS LANDSCAPED *À L'ANGLAISE*, WITH SPLENDID TREES, INCLUDING AMERICAN AND ASIAN SPECIES, AND ROLLING VISTAS DOTTED WITH SHEEP WHICH ARE KEPT "TO LOOK PRETTY." SADLY, THIS BEAUTIFUL LANDSCAPE IS UNDER DOUBLE THREAT — FROM INCURSION BY ELECTRICAL POWER LINES, AND THE INTRUSION OF YET ANOTHER AUTOROUTE. NOT THAT THE WATTEVILLE-BERCKHEIMS ARE UNACCUSTOMED TO ADVERSITIES — GERMAN, AMERICAN, AND BRITISH SOLDIERS FOUGHT OVER THE GROUND IN JANUARY, 1945, LEAVING THE CHÂTEAU IN RUINS AND AGE-OLD TREES BADLY DAMAGED BY SHRAPNEL.

The landscaped gardens of Schoppenwihr were laid out in a romantic English style in the 19th century and planted with rare and exotic trees.

Intricately carved chair backs add to the grandeur of the great dining room (above).

Now the family lives in a picturesque domain that once housed a vast wine press. It is typically Alsatian, dating largely from the early 1800s, with overhanging eaves, precipitous tiled roofs, and gabled windows.

The Schoppenwihr domain is supplied with game, though as with the fish, stocks are fragile. "With the sweeping expanse of modern fields, birds have nowhere to shelter," explains Christian Watteville-Berckheim, who has memories of a landscape intersected with hedgerows and copses. "Crop-spraying in early June is also to blame since it kills the insects on which game birds feed. This is why so much game is raised on artificial foodstuffs, and can taste unpleasantly of fish when it comes to the table," the Baron adds. As a result, the legendary Auberge de l'Ill, one of the finest restaurants in Alsace, has banned pheasant from its menus for the present.

Fortunately game birds, venison, and even the occasional hare still find their way to the Schoppenwihr table. Young birds are wrapped in grape leaves and barded with fat to roast in classic style, then set on a buttered *croûte* of bread spread with a *pâté* of the liver and heart made piquant with herbs and a thread of Cognac. Older birds may be simmered in wine *en cocotte*, then served in a cream sauce sharpened with horseradish – the Alsatian mustard. "Old birds can be so bland," warns the Baron. He prefers to bake them with sauerkraut until the meat is tender and falls from the bones, soft enough to chop and mix back into the cabbage.

CANARD AU SANG BERCKHEIM

ROAST DUCK WITH MUSTARD SAUCE

This recipe is equally good for other game birds, or for squab. "Serve the bird," says Christian de Watteville-Berckheim, "with a glass of good Alsatian Tokay."

4 servings

2 WILD MALLARD DUCKS (ABOUT 1½ pounds EACH)
¼ cup BUTTER, AT ROOM TEMPERATURE
SALT AND PEPPER

For the sauce
2 tbsp DIJON-STYLE MUSTARD FLAVORED WITH TARRAGON
2 tsp CORNSTARCH
4 tsp OLIVE OIL
½ cup COLD BUTTER, CUT INTO PIECES

TRUSSING NEEDLE AND STRING

Preheat the oven to 500°F.

Truss the birds*. Spread them with the butter and sprinkle with salt and pepper. Set them on one leg in a roasting pan and roast in the heated oven for 8 minutes. Turn them onto the other leg, baste well, and roast 5 minutes longer. Turn the birds onto their backs, baste, and continue roasting until the juice from the center runs pink when a bird is lifted on a two-pronged fork, 5 to 8 minutes. At this point the meat will be rare. If you prefer it well done, continue roasting 5 to 8 minutes longer.

Transfer the birds to a carving board with a well to catch the juices. Cut the birds in half, discarding the backbone. Cover loosely with aluminum foil and set aside to rest. Skim off all the fat from the roasting pan, leaving the cooking juices. Add the juice from the carving board to the roasting pan and heat, stirring to dissolve the browned juices in the pan. Boil to reduce them to about 2 tablespoons.

For the sauce, whisk together the mustard and cornstarch in a saucepan until smooth. Whisk in the oil, a few drops at a time at first, then in a thin stream as for mayonnaise. Warm over low heat for 30 seconds. Whisk in the reduced roasting juices, then whisk in the butter a few pieces at a time, taking the pan on and off the heat so the butter softens and thickens creamily without melting to oil. Taste for seasoning.

Serve the duck on a warmed platter or plates, with the sauce passed separately.

The paneled dining room at Schoppenwihr.

CHOUCROUTE DU BARON

SAUERKRAUT WITH SAUSAGE, BACON, AND PORK LOIN

The Watteville-Berckheims serve this choucroute with Alsatian beer or the same white wine as they use for cooking the choucroute. Note that some cured meats are saltier than others. To remove excess salt, blanch the meat by putting it in a large pan of cold water, bringing it to a boil, and simmering it 5 minutes. Drain it and proceed with the recipe.

8 servings

6 tbsp GOOSE FAT OR LARD

4 LARGE ONIONS, CHOPPED

4 pounds UNCOOKED SAUERKRAUT, RINSED
AND SQUEEZED DRY

1 LARGE APPLE, PEELED, CORED,
AND SLICED

1-pound PIECE OF UNSMOKED BACON

1-pound PIECE OF SMOKED BACON

1 pound SMOKED PORK SAUSAGE

1 pound SMOKED LOIN OF PORK

SALT AND PEPPER

2 BOTTLES (750 ml EACH) WHITE WINE,
PREFERABLY RIESLING

2 tsp JUNIPER BERRIES, TIED IN
CHEESECLOTH

½ cup SCHNAPPS

16 MEDIUM NEW POTATOES

8 CURED PORK CHOPS

8 FRANKFURTERS

DIJON-STYLE MUSTARD FOR SERVING

CHEESECLOTH

Melt ¼ cup of the fat in a large flameproof casserole, add the onions, and cook them over low heat, stirring occasionally, until soft, 6 to 8 minutes. Spread half the sauerkraut over the onions. Place the apple, both kinds of bacon, the smoked sausage, and smoked pork loin on top. Season very lightly. Cover the meat with the rest of the sauerkraut and add the wine. Cut

a piece of waxed paper to fit inside the casserole and press it directly on top of the sauerkraut. Cover and simmer on top of the stove until the sauerkraut is tender, 1½ to 2 hours. Add the juniper berries and schnapps halfway through cooking.

Half an hour before the end of the cooking time, put the potatoes in a pan of salted water, bring to a boil, and cook until tender, 15 to 20 minutes. Drain them and keep warm; peel them just before serving.

Melt the remaining fat in a frying pan and cook the pork chops until well done, 5 to 7 minutes on each side. Add them to the casserole. Cook the frankfurters in very hot water until heated through, about 1 minute. Drain.

To serve, discard the juniper berries and taste the sauerkraut for seasoning. Carve the bacon and pork loin in generous slices. Drain the sauerkraut well and pile it on a large heated platter with the meats, sausage, and potatoes on top. Pass the mustard separately.

"Better too much than too little; choucroute improves when reheated," is an old family saying.

CHÂTEAUX OF THE

Heart of France

CHÂTEAU DU FEŸ

Built around 1640, Château du Feÿ follows the classical style of Louis XIII, with staircases hidden in the wings so as not to interrupt the flow of central rooms, destined for the entertaining of guests. The sturdy towers, linked by a long roof, are typically Burgundian.

RESEARCHING AND WRITING *CHÂTEAU CUISINE* HAS BEEN A PLEASURE ON MANY LEVELS, NOT LEAST BECAUSE IT COMBINES TWO OF MY GREATEST LOVES IN LIFE—WRITING ABOUT FRENCH COOKING AND RESTORING THE CHÂTEAU DU FEŸ IN BURGUNDY, ALONG WITH MY HUSBAND, MARK. WE FIRST BOUGHT LE FEŸ LONG BEFORE WE HAD DECIDED TO OPEN LA VARENNE COOKING SCHOOL THERE, CATCHING OUR INITIAL GLIMPSE OF IT IN MARCH, 1982, IN A SHEETING MIST OF RAIN. I FEARED IT WOULD BE THE TWELFTH IN A SAD SERIES OF BEAUTIFUL HOUSES WRECKED BY NEGLECT AND PREDATORS WHO HAD STRIPPED PANELING AND DRESSED STONE, TAKING ANYTHING PORTABLE OF VALUE. BUT EVEN THROUGH THE DOWNPOUR, THE BEAUTY OF LE FEŸ WAS APPARENT. WE FOUND THAT THE ROOF WAS SOUND, THERE WAS A MODICUM OF BATHROOMS, EVEN SOME CENTRAL HEATING. A WEEK LATER WE HAD OFFERED THE ASKING PRICE AND HAD BEEN ACCEPTED. WE HAD LAUNCHED IRRATIONALLY, IRREVOCABLY, ON THE ADVENTURE THAT THE FRENCH CALL *LA VIE DE CHÂTEAU*.

WE MOVED IN DURING LATE JULY, JUST BEFORE THE FOUR-WEEK AUGUST VACATION WHEN EVERY ARTISAN DISAPPEARS FOR A MONTH. HOWEVER, WE MANAGED TO INSTALL A SMALL FAMILY KITCHEN TO REPLACE THE DERELICT IRON RANGE LEFT OVER FROM THE 19TH CENTURY. NOW, TEN YEARS LATER, THE SAME MAKESHIFT OPEN SHELVES AND CEMENT FLOOR ARE STILL IN PLACE, IN USE TWELVE HOURS A DAY IN THE HOLIDAY SEASON, WHEN FAMILY AND FRIENDS APPEAR FROM NOWHERE. THIS WAS OUR FIRST LESSON IN CHÂTEAU LIFE: THINK AHEAD, BECAUSE TEMPORARY SOLUTIONS TEND TO BECOME PERMANENT.

The entrance to our vegetable garden (right). At Le Feÿ we conduct a running battle with Monsieur Milbert, the 70-year-old gardener who keeps our 2½-acre vegetable garden in apple-pie order. He insists on growing all produce to maximum size, regardless of flavor, whereas we like to gather the first babies of the season as soon as they sprout. His leeks are prodigious, their serried rows a protection against winter hunger.

We were aware the water supply was delicate, dating from the 1940s and pumped under the RN 6 – the old trunk road south – up the hill via half a mile of uncharted private line. It cut out on a public holiday, leaving fifteen of us to wash and cook from the swimming pool. Not long after, the power transformer (also private, uninsured, and even more decrepit than the water system) was struck by lightning. No electricity, no pump, no water – no nothing. The discovery that a chandelier had parachuted to the floor during the storm seemed trivial until we found that the gale was not to blame, but rather a rotten main beam holding up a substantial part of our investment. Lesson number two: Château infrastructure is unique, and expensive.

Inside, Le Feÿ was comfortable but shabby, painted a drab color called "Napoleonic gray" and about as dusty as the Emperor in his tomb. The three reception rooms, leading one from another with mirrors at each end in the classic *enfilade*, were transformed when painted cream. Encouraged, we launched on the bedrooms, then bathrooms, then cast an eye on the three abandoned cottages in the outbuildings. The wall surrounding the two and a half acres of vegetable garden was crumbling dangerously. The immense well, 275 feet deep and dating from the

time of Saint-Vincent de Paul (an early visitor to Le Feÿ), was firmly sealed under a foot of cement. What a shame not to display its ancient masonry! Perhaps lesson number three has never really sunk in: An old property such as Le Feÿ offers limitless possibilities for restoration, at limitless cost.

We quickly took to the culinary treats of château life: garden vegetables and fruits, mis-shapen and bug-ridden but with incomparable flavor; wild strawberries gathered beside the drive in spring; esoteric mushrooms picked under the tutelage of the caretaker's wife, with a quick interview to crosscheck at the pharmacy to be sure they were edible. It was a year before I wandered into a chicken house and discovered the brick bread oven, which now bakes wonder-fully crusty bread and croissants when fired up by the local baker. The old wine and walnut presses stand idle, but the traveling machine comes once a year to crush our apples for cider.

Le Feÿ was bought as a family retreat, but its promise as a culinary haven soon emerged. Starting with a few residential classes, the pro-gram has expanded over nine months of the year, covering French cuisine, cheeses, wines, and professional culinary training. Our son has re-decorated the gamekeeper's cottage in cheery

People often ask us where the name Feÿ comes from. The name "Fay" or "Fays" is common enough in France, probably first used to signal a copse of beeches, but there are no beech trees at Le Feÿ, and the eccentric dots over the "y," indicating two syllables pronounced Fey-ee, have stuck over the centuries. With a little imagination, "Feÿ" might be linked to "Feyturage," a word found in the first French-English dictionary of 1611, meaning "a charme, or inchantment."

citrus yellow and our daughter cooks for summer guests. The twenty-plus beds in the château are constantly overflowing with chefs, students, trainees, college kids, and friends. My husband says the property is busier now than at any time since the French Revolution, and he's probably right. One thing is certain: Like so many château owners, having taken possession of this marvelous property, we have found that it has taken possession of us.

OMELETTE BOURGUIG- NONNE

SNAIL OMELETTE WITH WALNUTS

This omelette can be made with walnuts and no snails, or the snails can be served on their own with a walnut, garlic, and parsley butter. Both are as delicious as the original.

2 servings

½ cup CANNED SNAILS
3 tbsp BUTTER
2 CLOVES GARLIC, CHOPPED
SALT AND PEPPER
3 tbsp COARSELY CHOPPED WALNUTS
2 tbsp CHOPPED FRESH PARSLEY
5 or 6 LARGE EGGS

9-inch OMELETTE PAN

Drain and rinse the snails and cut each into 2 or 3 pieces. Melt half the butter in a frying pan, add the snails, garlic, salt, and pepper, and cook over low heat 4 or 5 minutes. Remove from the heat and stir in the walnuts and parsley. (The snails can be prepared up to 8 hours ahead.)

To make the omelette, whisk the eggs with a little salt and pepper until slightly frothy. If necessary, warm the snail mixture over low heat. Heat the remaining butter in the omelette pan until it stops sputtering. Add the eggs and stir briskly with a fork, pulling the cooked egg from the sides to the center of the pan. After 10 seconds, stir in the prepared snails and continue cooking until the mixture is almost as thick as scrambled eggs, 5 to 10 seconds longer. Leave the omelette on the heat until browned on the base and still soft on top if you like a moist omelette, or almost firm if you prefer it to be well done.

Fold the omelette, tipping the pan away from you and turning the edge with a fork. Slide the omelette onto a warmed platter. Serve it at once, cutting it in half for 2 people.

PAIN AUX NOISETTES

HAZELNUT BREAD

Hazelnut trees grow wild all around Château du Feÿ, a source of the hazelnut oil that is used to moisten the nuts in this bread.

Makes 2 loaves

3 cups WHOLE-WHEAT FLOUR,
MORE FOR SPRINKLING
1 cup ALL-PURPOSE FLOUR
1 tbsp SALT
1½ cups LUKEWARM WATER
½ cup HAZELNUT OIL
1 tbsp HONEY
2 tsp ACTIVE DRY YEAST OR
½ oz COMPRESSED YEAST*
1¼ cups SHELLED HAZELNUTS

TWO 8- or 9-inch CAKE PANS

Pile both types of flour on a work surface. Sprinkle with the salt. Make a well in the center with your hand and pour in 6 tablespoons of the water. Add the hazelnut oil and honey, then sprinkle or crumble the yeast on top and let it set until it dissolves, about 5 minutes. Add the remaining water and work with your fingertips, gradually drawing in the flour to make large crumbs. Press them together to make a ball.

Sprinkle the work surface with flour and knead the dough until smooth and elastic, 5 to 10 minutes. (The dough can also be mixed and kneaded in an electric mixer using the dough hook.) Put the dough in a lightly oiled bowl, turn it over so the top is oiled, and cover with a wet cloth. Let it rise in a warm place until doubled in bulk, 1 to 1½ hours.

Meanwhile, toast the hazelnuts. Preheat the oven to 350°F. Bake the nuts on a baking sheet until browned and the skins are loose, 10 to 15 minutes. Let them cool slightly, then rub with a coarse cloth to remove the skins. Coarsely chop half the nuts in a food processor or crush lightly with the end of a rolling pin.

The entrance to our vegetable garden (right). At Le Feÿ we conduct a running battle with Monsieur Milbert, the 70-year-old gardener who keeps our 2½-acre vegetable garden in apple-pie order. He insists on growing all produce to maximum size, regardless of flavor, whereas we like to gather the first babies of the season as soon as they sprout. His leeks are prodigious, their serried rows a protection against winter hunger.

We were aware the water supply was delicate, dating from the 1940s and pumped under the RN 6 – the old trunk road south – up the hill via half a mile of uncharted private line. It cut out on a public holiday, leaving fifteen of us to wash and cook from the swimming pool. Not long after, the power transformer (also private, uninsured, and even more decrepit than the water system) was struck by lightning. No electricity, no pump, no water – no nothing. The discovery that a chandelier had parachuted to the floor during the storm seemed trivial until we found that the gale was not to blame, but rather a rotten main beam holding up a substantial part of our investment. Lesson number two: Château infrastructure is unique, and expensive.

Inside, Le Feÿ was comfortable but shabby, painted a drab color called "Napoleonic gray" and about as dusty as the Emperor in his tomb. The three reception rooms, leading one from another with mirrors at each end in the classic *enfilade*, were transformed when painted cream. Encouraged, we launched on the bedrooms, then bathrooms, then cast an eye on the three abandoned cottages in the outbuildings. The wall surrounding the two and a half acres of vegetable garden was crumbling dangerously. The immense well, 275 feet deep and dating from the

time of Saint-Vincent de Paul (an early visitor to Le Feÿ), was firmly sealed under a foot of cement. What a shame not to display its ancient masonry! Perhaps lesson number three has never really sunk in: An old property such as Le Feÿ offers limitless possibilities for restoration, at limitless cost.

We quickly took to the culinary treats of château life: garden vegetables and fruits, misshapen and bug-ridden but with incomparable flavor; wild strawberries gathered beside the drive in spring; esoteric mushrooms picked under the tutelage of the caretaker's wife, with a quick interview to crosscheck at the pharmacy to be sure they were edible. It was a year before I wandered into a chicken house and discovered the brick bread oven, which now bakes wonderfully crusty bread and croissants when fired up by the local baker. The old wine and walnut presses stand idle, but the traveling machine comes once a year to crush our apples for cider.

Le Feÿ was bought as a family retreat, but its promise as a culinary haven soon emerged. Starting with a few residential classes, the program has expanded over nine months of the year, covering French cuisine, cheeses, wines, and professional culinary training. Our son has redecorated the gamekeeper's cottage in cheery

Oil the cake pans. Knead the dough lightly to knock out the air, then work in all the hazelnuts. Divide the dough in half and shape it into rounds on a floured surface. Set them, smooth side up, in the prepared pans. Let rise again, uncovered, in a warm place until doubled in bulk, about 1 hour. Preheat the oven to 425°F.

Sprinkle the loaves lightly with whole-wheat flour and slash the top of each two or three times with a knife. Bake in the heated oven 15 minutes. Reduce the oven temperature to 375°F and continue baking until the loaves sound hollow when tipped out of their pans and tapped on the base, 30 to 40 minutes. Transfer them to a rack to cool. The loaves are best eaten the same day.

Omelette Bourguignonne with Pain aux Noisettes. Snails abound in the woods around Le Feÿ after a shower of rain, but we usually resist the temptation and buy them prepared. Wild snails must be kept seven days to purge them of bitterness before you start cooking them – have you ever had snails escape in your cellar?

Le Feÿ is home to a collection of old cookbooks which we both began collecting 25 years ago.

CHÂTEAU DE CHÂTEAU-RENAUD

TO BUY A VAST HALF-RUINED CHÂTEAU IN THE PROVINCE OF BERRY — THE ONCE-ISOLATED CENTER OF FRANCE — WOULD SEEM QUIXOTIC, NOT LEAST FOR YVES AND MICHÈLE HALARD, INTERIOR DESIGNERS FAMED FOR THEIR EXQUISITE FABRICS AND SOPHISTICATED TASTE. YET THIS WAS THE ADVENTURE THEY UNDERTOOK IN 1985. NOT FOR THEM THE GLITTER OF THE MIDI, NOR THE CHIC OF THE LOIRE. "TODAY THE ULTIMATE LUXURY IS UNSPOILED SPACE," EXPLAINS MADAME HALARD. "AFTER THE CONFINES OF LIFE IN PARIS, WE WANTED TO BREATHE."

CHÂTEAURENAUD CERTAINLY OFFERED PLENTY OF SCOPE. SINCE THE REVOLUTION, ITS 17TH-CENTURY STRUCTURE HAD BEEN SCARCELY TOUCHED. THE HALARDS FOUND DOZENS OF GRAY, PEELING ROOMS DETERIORATING FROM DAMP, AND MORE RECENTLY FROM LACK OF INHABITANTS. "THE ORIGINAL AMBIANCE WAS STILL THERE. THAT WAS IMPORTANT FOR US SINCE NO ONE HAD BOTHERED TO INTERFERE," SAYS MICHÈLE HALARD. GRADUALLY SHE AND HER HUSBAND BEGAN RESTORATION, FIRST OF THE ROOF, THEN OF ONE ROOM AFTER THE OTHER (THERE ARE AT LEAST 50 OF THEM). TRANSFORMATION WOULD PERHAPS BE A BETTER TERM, FOR THE HALARD TOUCH IS EVERYWHERE, IN THE FABRICS, THE SUBTLE COLORS OF PAINT MIXED WITH CARE BY YVES HIMSELF, AND IN THE CURIOSITIES COLLECTED IN FORAYS TO NEARBY ANTIQUE FAIRS AND SALE ROOMS. "WE ENJOY A TOUCH OF FANTASY," YVES WHISPERS.

Yves and Michèle Halard have a passion for objets trouvés that fill every room and add to the sense of relaxed informality.

The impressive hallway of Châteaurenaud is dominated by cool, cream stone and decorated very simply with minimal furniture and tapestries in soft, muted colors (right). The library, with its shelves made by the Halards and a distinctive second-hand stepladder, is an enticing place to while away an afternoon (below right).

Michèle Halard brings the same sense of fantasy to the table, often changing the settings with each meal. A collection of Halard napery is about to be launched with a *"Directoire"* theme, full of deep reds, soft yellows, and gray. "I never add flowers, but instead create a still life on the table," she remarks. "It may be rich, sunny, poetic, rustic. And I pick what pleases me – silver, vermeil, vegetables, leaves, baskets. I vary it all the time. Table decoration is unique in that way. How lucky we are – a meal is a celebration three times a day!"

I wondered if Michèle Halard had any time for cooking, and she assured me she is every bit a gourmande. She likes simple country dishes, very much in the current mode, and tries to cut down on the butter and cream. Recipes must be quick to prepare, such as salmon *en papillote*, roast veal with baby onions (the Berry is cattle country), veal *blanquette* ("*très snob*" right now) and a flourless chocolate cake which is delicately spiced with ginger, cinnamon, and powdered coffee. Madame Halard's favorite lunchtime menu is even simpler – two or three choice cheeses from the region, a loaf of good bread, and a glass of wine from Bordeaux.

Châteaurenaud has once more become a living château. What seemed a blind adventure has proved a brilliant stroke. Berry may seem a world removed from Paris, but nowadays the Halards can drive there in two-and-a-half hours. Back at the château, Yves Halard spends a great deal of his time with artisan craftsmen, bringing his brilliant design conceptions to life. "It would be unthinkable to embark on another château adventure. As it is, we will never finish," he declares. "We are here forever," adds Michèle, speaking for them both.

SOUPE CRÈME DE POIS

CREAMED SPLIT PEA SOUP

Ham and split peas are a classic pair, but if you do not have a ham bone, substitute a piece of lean smoked bacon.

6 servings

1¾ cups DRIED GREEN SPLIT PEAS, RINSED
1 HAM BONE WITH
SOME MEAT
3 cups CHICKEN STOCK
(see page 221), MORE IF NEEDED
2½ cups WATER, MORE IF NEEDED
1 LEEK, WHITE PART ONLY,
FINELY CHOPPED
2 ONIONS, FINELY CHOPPED
1 CARROT, FINELY CHOPPED
3 SPRIGS FRESH PARSLEY
½ cup CRÈME FRAÎCHE (see page 220)
OR HEAVY CREAM
SALT AND PEPPER
GRATED NUTMEG

A workroom full of Halard designs and fabric samples, laid out on trestle tables (top left). Pet rabbits in an old outbuilding (above). The light and airy staircase (below) is simply and strikingly decorated.

Combine the peas, ham bone, stock, and water in a large saucepan. Bring to a boil, skimming off the froth occasionally.

Reduce the heat to medium-low, add the chopped vegetables and the parsley, and cover the pan. Simmer until the peas are very tender and well flavored with ham, 1 to 1½ hours, depending on the age of the peas. Stir from time to time during cooking and add more stock and water if the soup starts to stick.

Discard the ham bone. Process the soup in a blender or food processor until smooth. Return the soup to the pan and reheat it. The consistency should be rich but not sticky, so thin it with more stock and water if necessary. (The soup can be refrigerated up to 2 days.)

To finish, reheat the soup if necessary and stir in the crème fraîche or cream. Season to taste with salt, pepper, and nutmeg. Ladle the soup into warmed soup bowls and serve.

ÉPAULE D'AGNEAU FARCIE

LAMB SHOULDER FILLED WITH VEAL KIDNEY, SHALLOTS, AND MUSHROOMS

A rich and aromatic stuffing transforms a roasted shoulder of lamb.

This stuffed lamb recipe combines the simplicity of a large roast with a dramatic presentation. The lamb shoulder is boned, then stuffed with a whole veal kidney and a mixture of mushrooms, shallots, and parsley. With the lamb, serve sautéed scallions and a rich potato gratin.

6 servings

4½-pound SHOULDER OF LAMB, BONED
(RESERVE THE BONES)
SALT AND PEPPER
LEAVES FROM SPRIG FRESH THYME, OR
½ tsp DRIED THYME
2 tbsp VEGETABLE OIL
1 ONION, QUARTERED
1 CARROT, QUARTERED
½ cup WHITE WINE
1 cup BROWN STOCK (see page 221)

For the stuffing
¼ cup BUTTER
2 SHALLOTS, FINELY CHOPPED
1 CLOVE GARLIC, CRUSHED
½ pound MUSHROOMS, FINELY CHOPPED
¼ cup CHOPPED FRESH PARSLEY
1 VEAL KIDNEY (ABOUT ⅔ pound)
3 tbsp COGNAC OR BRANDY
LEAVES FROM SPRIG FRESH THYME, OR
½ tsp DRIED THYME

TRUSSING NEEDLE AND KITCHEN STRING OR POULTRY SKEWERS

Preheat the oven to 475°F and lightly oil a roasting pan.

For the stuffing, melt half the butter in a frying pan and add the shallots. Sauté them over medium heat until just golden, stirring often, about 5 minutes. Add the garlic and stir 1 minute. Add the mushrooms, salt, and pepper and sauté them until they lose all their moisture, about 5 minutes. Stir in the parsley and transfer the stuffing to a bowl. Taste for seasoning.

Skin the kidney, if necessary, and cut out the fat and ducts from the center with a small sharp knife. Put the kidney cut-side down on the work surface. Pressing your hand firmly on top, cut the kidney almost in half lengthwise; leave one side joined. Spread the kidney flat. Melt the remaining butter in the frying pan and brown the kidney over high heat, about 1 minute on each side. Add the Cognac or brandy and heat 20 or 30 seconds, then tip the pan and light the spirit with a match. (Stand back from the flames.) Continue cooking, shaking the pan until the flames subside, about 30 seconds. Remove the pan from the heat and sprinkle the kidney with salt and pepper and the thyme.

Trim the lamb of excess fat. Sprinkle the cut surface of the lamb with salt and pepper and the thyme. Spread the mushroom mixture in the center and cover with the kidney. Sew the openings shut with a trussing needle and string or secure with poultry skewers. Roll up the meat and tie it with string to form a neat roll. Brush with the oil.

Spread the lamb bones, onion, and carrot in the roasting pan and set the lamb on top. Put the pan in the oven and reduce the temperature to 400°F. Roast, basting often, until the meat is medium rare, about 45 minutes: A skewer inserted in the meat should be warm to the touch when withdrawn after 30 seconds, or a meat thermometer should register 130°F.

Transfer the meat to a carving board with a juice catcher, cover loosely with aluminum foil, and let it rest 15 minutes.

To make a gravy, skim off the fat from the roasting pan. Add the wine to the pan and bring it to a boil, scraping to dissolve the browned roasting juices. Add the stock and simmer to concentrate the flavor, 5 to 10 minutes. Strain the gravy into a small saucepan and season.

To finish, remove the string from the roast and carve it into ¼-inch slices. Arrange the meat on a warmed platter. Stir the juice from the meat into the gravy. Serve the gravy separately.

TARTE PAYSANNE AUX POIRES

RUSTIC PEAR TART

Michèle Halard believes a homemade fruit tart is one of life's pleasures. This pear tart is one she makes up quickly for a weekend in the country. You'll find that Bosc and Anjou pears will keep their shapes well during cooking.

8 servings

¾ pound PUFF PASTRY DOUGH
(see page 221)
5 FIRM PEARS (ABOUT 2 pounds
TOTAL WEIGHT)
JUICE OF 1 LEMON
¼ cup UNSALTED BUTTER
¼ cup SUGAR

*10-inch TART PAN WITH A
REMOVABLE BOTTOM*

A simple pear tart –
"one of life's
pleasures," says
Michèle Halard.

Sprinkle the tart pan with water. Roll out the dough to a round about 2 inches larger than the pan and use to line the pan*, leaving about ⅜ inch extending above the rim. Fold over this dough inside the pan, pressing to make a sturdy-sided shell. Chill until firm, about 15 minutes. (The tart shell can be shaped up to 2 days ahead and kept in the refrigerator.)

Preheat the oven to 375°F.

Prick the bottom of the tart shell with a fork. Blind bake the tart shell*.

Meanwhile, peel, halve, and core the pears. Cut each pear half into 6 wedges. Toss them in a bowl with the lemon juice to prevent discoloration. Melt the butter in a large frying pan. Add the pears, sprinkle them with the sugar, and sauté over medium-high heat, tossing often so they caramelize evenly, about 15 minutes.

Spoon the pears into the prepared tart shell. Return to the oven and bake the tart until the pastry is golden and the pears are tender, 15 to 20 minutes.

had trouble with the sugar caramelizing!

BASTION
DES DAMES

"MY HUSBAND SUFFERS FROM RESTORATION FEVER," CONFIDES MONIQUE BOISSEAUX. "HE ALWAYS HAS TO BE BUILDING, OR REBUILDING!" SHE AND HER HUSBAND, ANDRÉ,

The Château de Meursault vineyard, which is 3 miles from Bastion des Dames, is part of André Boisseaux's domain. The vineyard covers 136 acres.

HAVE JUST COMPLETED WORK ON THE DEMEURE SAINT-MARTIN, A CHARMING 18TH-CENTURY TOWNHOUSE IN THE CENTER OF THE BURGUNDIAN WINE TOWN BEAUNE. THEIR FIRST PROJECT, AND THE ONE STILL CLOSEST TO THEIR HEARTS, WAS THE FAMILY HOUSE, THE BASTION DES DAMES DE LA TOUR BUSSIÈRE. THE BASTION IS UNIQUE, BUILT INTO THE MASSIVE RENAISSANCE WALLS OF BEAUNE ITSELF, AND NAMED FOR THE CISTERCIAN NUNS WHO LIVED THERE UNTIL THE REVOLUTION.

AT THE BASE OF THE BASTION IS A GUARD-HOUSE, ITS WALLS 23 FEET THICK — IDEAL INSULATION FOR WINE CELLARS. ABOVE THEM, THE BOISSEAUX HAVE PERCHED A SPACIOUS MODERN HOUSE. "WE LIVE RIGHT ON TOP OF OUR WINES," SAYS MONIQUE BOISSEAUX. AND WHAT WINES! AS A GROWER AND *NÉGOCIANT*, ANDRÉ BOISSEAUX IS A HOUSEHOLD NAME. HIS EMPIRE, LE DOMAINE DU CHÂTEAU DE MEURSAULT, INCLUDES SOME OF THE MOST PRESTIGIOUS NAMES ON THE APTLY NAMED CÔTE-D'OR (SLOPE OF GOLD) — PULIGNY-MONTRACHET, SAVIGNY-LÈS-BEAUNE, VOLNAY, POMMARD, BEAUNE, AND ALOXE-CORTON, AS WELL AS MEURSAULT.

The vineyard is magnificent, but the real showpiece is below ground, where there are 400,000 to 500,000 bottles and 2,000 casks of fine wine.

André Boisseaux told me that he has three passions – hunting, fishing, and fine wine. In the forest of Cîteaux, not far from home, he raises deer, wild boar, and even a few mountain goats. More than once the Boisseaux family has rescued an abandoned baby boar and raised it in the Bastion kitchen. The beasts are notoriously savage, but "Coco" remained tame for several months. He delighted André Boisseaux by roaming the house during parties, to the consternation of guests from countries such as Britain where wild boar is unknown.

Many cooks have access to a vegetable garden, but few have access to home-raised fish and game, and Monique Boisseaux takes full advantage. She enjoys cooking haunch of venison or wild boar, accompanied by whole and puréed chestnuts, apples baked in butter, prunes simmered in red wine, tartlets of cranberry jelly, and of course the best of wine. But no wine is added to the game. "I don't like to marinate game in the old way," she told me. "The sauces are too heavy, masking the flavor of the meat." So Madame Boisseaux uses a dry marinade instead, a mixture of olive oil, chopped carrot and onion, thyme, bay leaf, and rosemary, rubbing it into the meat before letting it stand up to 48 hours. Then it is roasted *à point*, slightly pink, and served with a simple gravy.

Hospitality is a way of life for Burgundian vintners, culminating in the *Paulées*, the feasts held in November during the famous wine auctions at the Hospices de Beaune. On the third Saturday evening in the month, as a curtain raiser, 250 wine-growers and buyers are invited to a grand dinner at Château de Meursault. Sunday brings lunch for over 100 prepared by Madame Boisseaux at the Bastion. She describes the menu as *ultra rapide*, though it hardly sounds like fast food. The first course might be fish *timbales*, or cold poached pike with an herb mayonnaise, followed perhaps by a ham *en croûte* or a Bresse chicken with morel mushrooms, not forgetting the cheese tray and a simple dessert such as fruit tart.

On Monday the *Paulée* itself is held when 600 growers, large and small, gather at Château de Meursault for a banquet which lasts all day. Traditional dishes of the region abound – *gougères* or cheese puffs, versions of *coq au vin* made with both red and white wines, piquant *saupiquet* ham in cream sauce, and, of course, snails whose natural habitat is the grapevine.

Monique Boisseaux unveiled a favorite family recipe to me thus: "The snails are gathered after a shower of rain and left without food to hibernate in the cellar for several weeks. Then they are lined up on a tin tray in a bed of water and cooked gently for 15 minutes or so. Bottles of vintage white Burgundy are enthroned on the table, then the family gathers, forks and *tastevins* in hand, to savor wine and snails *au naturel*. That's the best way, you know," she added, with a hint of despair for those nations that do not share the French appreciation for things that creep and crawl.

TIMBALE DE BROCHET

POACHED PIKE WITH PASTRY IN A VELVETY SAUCE

Traditionally, a "timbale de brochet" would have been served in a timbale or pastry case. Here the delicate puff pastry garnish recalls the original presentation.

The lakes in the forest of Cîteaux are breeding ponds for pike, sandre *(a succulent cousin of pike), carp, and crayfish. Pike or any white-fleshed fish fillets can be used in this recipe.*

6 servings as a main course,
8 to 10 as a first course

½ pound PUFF PASTRY DOUGH (see page 221)
1 LARGE EGG, BEATEN
1½ pounds PIKE FILLET, CUT INTO 3 OR 4
LARGE PIECES
SALT AND PEPPER
2 SHALLOTS, FINELY CHOPPED
¾ cup DRY WHITE WINE
¾ cup WATER
1 tbsp BUTTER
1 tbsp ALL-PURPOSE FLOUR
3 LARGE EGG YOLKS
½ cup CRÈME FRAÎCHE (see page 220)
OR HEAVY CREAM

3-inch COOKIE CUTTER

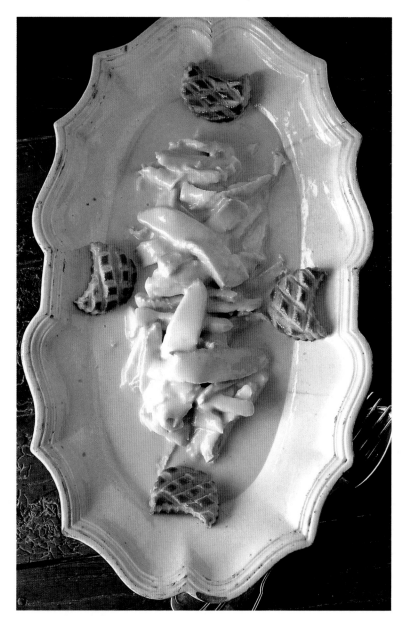

Sprinkle a baking sheet with water. Roll out the puff pastry dough on a floured surface to a sheet ⅛-inch thick. Cut out at least 18 crescents with the cookie cutter. Transfer them to the baking sheet and chill at least 15 minutes.

Preheat the oven to 425°F. Brush the crescents lightly with the beaten egg and bake until puffed and golden, 8 to 12 minutes. (The crescents can be baked a day or two ahead and kept in an airtight container.)

Sprinkle the fish with salt and pepper. Butter a large frying pan and put in the shallots, wine, water, and fish. Press a piece of buttered aluminum foil on top. Bring the liquid just to a simmer on top of the stove, then remove the pan from the heat. Let the fish cool slightly, then transfer it to a platter using a slotted spatula. Keep the fish warm while preparing the sauce.

Strain the cooking liquid and make a sauce: Melt the butter in a saucepan. Whisk in the flour and cook, stirring, until foaming. Whisk in the hot cooking liquid. Bring the sauce to a boil, whisking constantly, then simmer 2 minutes. Mix together the egg yolks and crème fraîche or cream. Whisk in a little of the hot cooking liquid and stir this back into the rest. Cook over low heat, stirring, but do not boil. (The egg yolks will thicken in the heat but if overcooked they will curdle.) Taste for seasoning.

To finish, cut the fish into ⅜-inch diagonal strips. Arrange the fish on a warmed platter and coat with the sauce. Decorate with pastry crescents. Pass the remaining crescents separately.

OEUFS AU VIN DE MEURSAULT

POACHED EGGS IN WHITE WINE SAUCE

Burgundy is famous for poached eggs en meurette, *in a red wine sauce, but Monique Boisseaux prefers this lighter version made with the white wine from her vineyards. A bottle of Chardonnay wine is a less expensive alternative to Burgundian Meursault, but quite acceptable.*

4 servings as a main course, 8 as a first course

2 cups CHICKEN OR WHITE VEAL STOCK
(see page 221)
⅓ cup BUTTER
3 SHALLOTS, FINELY CHOPPED
2 tbsp ALL-PURPOSE FLOUR
2 cups FULL-BODIED WHITE WINE
2 CLOVES GARLIC, CRUSHED
SALT AND PEPPER
A BOUQUET GARNI*
½ pound SMALL MUSHROOMS, QUARTERED
1½ ounces SLAB BACON, CUT INTO
*LARDONS**
2 tbsp VINEGAR
8 LARGE EGGS
12 OR 24 TRIANGULAR *CROÛTES*, FRIED IN
OIL AND BUTTER (see page 220)
2 tbsp CRÈME FRAÎCHE (see page 220) OR
HEAVY CREAM

Bring the stock to a boil. Melt half the butter in a saucepan and add the shallots. Sauté over medium heat until golden, 3 to 5 minutes. Stir in the flour and cook until foaming. Whisk in the boiling stock, the wine, garlic, and a little salt and pepper; add the bouquet garni. Bring the sauce to a boil, whisking constantly. Reduce the heat and simmer, stirring occasionally, until the sauce thickens enough to coat a spoon, ¾ to 1 hour. Strain and set aside.

Melt the remaining butter in a frying pan. Add the mushrooms with salt and pepper. Toss

Oeufs au Vin de Meursault – poached eggs in a white wine and mushroom sauce tempt the diner at Bastion des Dames in Beaune.

them in the butter over medium-high heat until they lose all their moisture, about 5 minutes, then remove. Render the bacon in the pan over low heat, then cook until golden, about 5 minutes. Drain it on paper towels.

Fill a large shallow pan two-thirds full of water, add the vinegar, and bring to a boil. Break 4 eggs, one at a time, into a patch of bubbling water. Regulate the heat so the water barely simmers and poach the eggs until the white sets but the yolk is still soft, 3 to 4 minutes. Remove the eggs with a slotted spoon to a pan of cold water to stop the cooking, then drain them. Poach the remaining eggs.

(The sauce, garnish, and eggs can be cooked up to 2 hours ahead and kept at room temperature. Rub the surface of the sauce with butter to prevent a skin forming.)

To finish, wrap the *croûtes* in aluminum foil and reheat them in a low oven if necessary. Reheat the sauce, stir in the mushrooms, bacon, and crème fraîche or cream, and taste for seasoning. Transfer the eggs to a bowl of very hot water. Leave 2 or 3 minutes to warm, then drain on paper towels and trim off any strings of white.

To serve, put the eggs on warmed plates and spoon the sauce over them. Add the *croûtes* as a final decoration.

LES GOUGÈRES BOURGUIG-NONNES

BURGUNDY CHEESE PUFFS

During the vendanges *at Château de Meursault, the grapes are picked by hand, with the bunches clipped whole so that the juice inside each grape cannot oxidize. Workers take their lunch among the vines, but on the last day of the harvest, long tables laden with food are set up in the old kitchen of the château, and everyone gathers to taste* vin doux, *the first fresh juice pressed from the white grapes. The wine has a rich bouquet and already a light sparkle.*

Makes about 24 3-inch puffs

1 cup WATER
6 tbsp BUTTER, CUT INTO PIECES
¾ tsp SALT
1½ cups ALL-PURPOSE FLOUR
4 LARGE EGGS
1½ cups GRATED GRUYÈRE CHEESE

PASTRY BAG AND ⅜-inch PLAIN TUBE (OPTIONAL)

Light Burgundian gougères are traditionally served with the first wine pressing after the harvest at Château de Meursault.

Preheat the oven to 425°F and butter one or two baking sheets.

Heat the water, butter, and salt in a saucepan until the butter melts. Bring just to a boil and then remove the pan from the heat. Add the flour all at once and beat with a wooden spoon until the mixture is smooth and comes away from the sides of the pan in a ball, about 1 minute. Beat over low heat for 1 minute. Off the heat, beat in 3 of the eggs, one at a time. Whisk the last egg until mixed. Now beat enough of this egg into the mixture to make a dough that is soft and very shiny. Stir in the cheese.

Either put the dough in a pastry bag and pipe 2-inch mounds on a baking sheet, spacing them well apart, or use two spoons to shape the dough. Bake in the heated oven until golden and crisp, 25 to 30 minutes.

CHÂTEAU D'AINAY-LE-VIEIL

THE CHÂTEAU D'AINAY-LE-VIEIL LIES ON THE BORDER OF BERRY, A PROVINCE HOTLY DISPUTED BY THE KINGS OF ENGLAND AND FRANCE DURING THE HUNDRED YEARS WAR.

Princesse Georges-Henri's father, Geraud d'Aligny, was a distinguished poet and wrote of Ainay's walls as "an immutable witness, omnipresent, unchanging."

WITH ITS NINE TURRETS, MOAT, AND CLASSIC DRAWBRIDGE, AINAY WAS A KEY FORTRESS BESIEGED MANY TIMES — IT BELONGED BRIEFLY TO THE CONTROVERSIAL JACQUES COEUR, A MAN OF SUCH POWER AND MEANS IN 15TH-CENTURY FRANCE THAT TODAY IN BERRY YOU CAN VISIT A WHOLE STRING OF IMPOSING *CHÂTEAUX* ALONG THE ROUTE NAMED AFTER HIM.

A SINGLE FAMILY, THE BIGNYS, HAVE OWNED AINAY FOR OVER 500 YEARS AND THEY COUNT JEAN-BAPTISTE COLBERT, LOUIS XIV'S BRILLIANT MINISTER, AMONG THEIR ILLUSTRIOUS FOREBEARS. AN ANCESTOR OF HIS INSTALLED A RENAISSANCE PALACE WITHIN AINAY'S RUGGED WALLS, AND A 19TH-CENTURY DESCENDANT RESTORED ITS GRANDEUR AFTER MANY OF THE ROOMS WERE RANSACKED DURING THE REVOLUTION. TODAY, AINAY IS OWNED BY SIX BROTHERS AND SISTERS IN THE BIGNY LINE OF DESCENT, INCLUDING PRINCESSE GEORGES-HENRI DE LA TOUR D'AUVERGNE, OR MARIE-SOL AS SHE IS KNOWN TO HER FRIENDS.

With her brothers and sisters, Marie-Sol was brought up at Ainay – their remarkable mother, the very soul of the property, turned the château into a refuge for nuns during World War II, then kept the children at home for a while so that she could personally instruct them in the three R's before they left for school. In those days, Ainay was an oasis – not so today to judge by the village soirées held in the vaulted barracks beside the main gate, or the attraction of the folk museum set up with the help of village craftsmen. Ainay is also now famous for its roses – there are over 200 rare varieties, including a new deep pink rose named "Colbert" in honor of the family's heritage.

As a child, Marie-Sol was steeped in country customs and the life that revolves around a château – an education that has proved to be of special value now that she is President of Friends of Vieilles Maisons Françaises. Marie-Sol vividly described to me the activities during the pea season in the two-acre kitchen garden, with the women of the village helping to gather in the harvest. Then, a few weeks later there would be the back-breaking challenge of picking the *haricots verts*. "It is so sad, the disappearance of communal village life," she told me when we first met at Ainay. "Now work is solitary and against the clock. Local farms here used to be proud of their butter, stamping each mound with a distinctive crest such as a rose or thistle. Recently the last dairy near Ainay closed, and now there's only one farm that still supplies unpasteurized milk fresh from the cow."

In the old days at Ainay, fruit picking tended to be a family affair in the *chartreuse* – a formal orchard of espaliered trees which still yields a dozen kinds of fruit, including luscious *pêches de vignes*, the wild purple peaches for which the region is justifiably famous.

There was an elderly gardener in charge of table grapes, Marie-Sol recalls. He would wrap them in sacking to protect them from wasps until ripe, then suspend them in a *fruitière* in the base of a tower. By trimming withered patches from time to time, the bunches could be kept until Christmas. For Marie-Sol, nothing has ever quite taken their place.

The defensive moat at Ainay is purely decorative today. The original wooden drawbridge has been replaced with a stone bridge.

PASTIS

LAYERED FLAKY PASTRY TART
WITH PRUNES AND ARMAGNAC

*Prepared phyllo dough works very well here if
you want to save time. You will need 6 sheets.*

8 servings

4 cups ALL-PURPOSE FLOUR, MORE
IF NEEDED
1 LARGE EGG
$\frac{1}{4}$ tsp SALT
1 cup WATER
$\frac{1}{2}$ tsp LEMON JUICE
$\frac{1}{4}$ cup WALNUT OIL

For the filling

1 cup PRUNES, PITTED
$\frac{1}{3}$ cup ARMAGNAC
$\frac{1}{2}$ cup BUTTER, MELTED
$\frac{1}{2}$ cup SUGAR

*10-inch TART PAN WITH A
REMOVABLE BOTTOM*

*Pastis is traditionally
made by the women
of Quercy. This flaky
tart melts away in
your mouth, leaving a
delicious hint of
prunes, Armagnac,
and butter.*

For the filling, soak the prunes in the Armagnac
for 2 to 3 hours or overnight. Before using,
drain the prunes, reserving the Armagnac.

Sift the flour into a large bowl and make a
well in the center. Add the egg, salt, water,
lemon juice, and oil and work them together
with your fingertips until thoroughly mixed.
Quickly work the flour into the other ingredients to make a pliable, slightly sticky dough.

Flour a work surface and knead the dough,
picking it up and throwing it down, until it is
shiny and very smooth, 5 to 7 minutes. Alternatively, work it in an electric mixer with a dough
hook. Cover the dough with an upturned bowl
to keep it moist and let it rest at least 30
minutes. Meanwhile, preheat the oven to 375°F.
Butter the tart pan.

Cover a table with a sheet and lightly flour it.
Divide the dough into three equal pieces. Roll
out each piece of dough to as large a square as
possible. Cover each one with a damp towel and
let it rest 15 minutes. Flour your hands and

gently insert them under one piece of dough.
Starting at the center and working outward,
carefully stretch the dough with both hands,
making as few holes as possible. It should eventually form a rectangle about 15×30 inches.
Brush the dough with melted butter. Pull,
stretch, and butter the remaining pieces of
dough. Alternatively, butter the sheets of phyllo
dough, if using.

Cut each rectangle of homemade dough into
two rounds 2 inches larger than the tart pan, or
cut each sheet of phyllo dough into one round
of the same size. Press three of the rounds into
the pan, sprinkling each one with sugar and
Armagnac. Arrange the drained prunes in an
even layer on the bottom of the tart shell.
Sprinkle with more sugar. Cover the prunes
with the three remaining dough rounds, again
sprinkling each one with sugar and Armagnac.

Fold the overlapping dough up around the
edges of the tart. Cut the dough trimmings into
2-inch strips and arrange them on top, pleating
them to form ruffles. Sprinkle with sugar,
Armagnac, and melted butter.

Bake the tart in the heated oven until brown
and crisp, 30 to 40 minutes. Serve it lukewarm.

CHÂTEAU DE LA VERRERIE

The *"Pays Fort"* near Sancerre is one of the forgotten parts of the Loire. "It was always a mysterious land of wolves and forests, far off the beaten track," explains Comte Antoine de Vogüé, as he recounts the property's romantic past and its connection with the royal Stuart family of Scotland. First, in the early 15th century, Charles VII of France gave the Stuarts land in recognition of their support during the Hundred Years War against the English. Construction of the present château began then, and was completed in Renaissance style with a magnificent arcaded gallery which still lines one side of the courtyard. A couple of centuries later, La Verrerie reverted to the French Crown, only to be donated once again, this time to Louise de Keroualle, Duchess of Portsmouth and favorite of England's Charles II.

A dreamy and romantic view of La Verrerie across the lake. Construction of the château began in the early 1400s. An elegant Renaissance arcade lines one side of the courtyard (below).

Sixteenth-century frescoes have recently been uncovered in the chapel at La Verrerie.

Since then the château has changed little. It is still tucked away in peaceful woods abundant with game, fronting a placid lake. "It's not a fortress but a *château de plaisance*," says Françoise de Vogüé. "Despite its size, La Verrerie is intimate, full of gaiety and light. In season we hunt wild duck, partridge, and pheasant," the Comtesse continues, "and ride with a couple of dozen hounds in the traditional *chasse à courre* for deer." Visitors are welcome at La Verrerie and can dine with the family in an international atmosphere – the staff must speak at least two languages. "We like to receive our guests as friends," says the Comte, whose son, Béraud, runs Vie de Château, an international agency that receives guests and rents château accommodation throughout France.

In August, when children and grandchildren gather, the Vogüés may be 30 or more at table, with the Comtesse in charge in the kitchen. She often likes to start with a cold first course, using pretty plates and imaginative presentation. A summer favorite is sliced melon interleaved with country ham, decorated with celery and tomatoes from the garden. The main course is likely to be local leg of lamb with garden peas, *haricots verts*, and fried baby potatoes. Unusual sauces are her trademark, such as pan gravy flavored with truffle oil, and fresh English-style mint sauce with cider vinegar and honey.

Françoise de Vogüé cooks with aplomb because for ten years she acted as chef and manager of La Maison d'Hélène, the charming little restaurant in a half-timbered cottage over-looking the lake. Here, too, the cuisine is *du pays*, with Loire salmon served with white butter sauce, and noisettes of venison with apples. The recipes that follow are from her grandmother's collection, a book headed with a typically acid quote from Oscar Wilde: "All men are monsters. The only thing to do is to feed the wretches well. A good cook works wonders!"

SABLÉS AU FROMAGE

BUTTERY CHEESE WAFERS

The Comtesse de Vogüé passes around these crumbly, butter-rich wafers with drinks before dinner. Any well-flavored aged cheese can be used to make sablés *– tangy Cantal from France's Massif Central makes an unusual alternative to Gruyère, if you can find it.*

Makes about 35

2 cups ALL-PURPOSE FLOUR
SALT AND PEPPER
¾ cup UNSALTED BUTTER,
CUT INTO PIECES
1 cup GRATED GRUYÈRE CHEESE
1 LARGE EGG, BEATEN TO MIX WITH
½ tsp SALT TO GLAZE

2-inch COOKIE CUTTER (OPTIONAL)

Sift the flour into a bowl with ¼ tsp salt and a pinch of pepper. Add the butter and rub it in with your fingers until the mixture resembles fine crumbs. Stir in the cheese and press the dough together with your fist. Turn the dough onto a floured surface and knead it, pushing it away with the heel of your hand and gathering it up with your fingers. Wrap the dough and chill it until firm, at least 30 minutes.

Butter one or two baking sheets. Roll out the dough on a floured surface to a sheet about ⅛-inch thick. Cut out rounds with the cookie cutter and put them on the baking sheet. Alternatively, cut the dough into triangles. Brush the *sablés* with egg glaze. Chill them at least 15 minutes before baking.

Preheat the oven to 375°F.

Bake the *sablés* until golden, about 15 minutes. Leave them on the baking sheet for 3 or 4 minutes before carefully removing to a rack to cool completely.

They can be stored in an airtight container for up to a week.

Magnificent frescoes also adorn the cool arcades.

A great fireplace with flaming logs is a welcoming sight for guests at La Verrerie.

OEUFS A LA MIRABEAU

CREAMY MOLDED EGGS WITH TOMATO SAUCE

Named for the family of the Comte de Mirabeau, the 18th-century revolutionary, this unusual recipe is excellent as a first course or for brunch. The eggs are simply whisked with Parmesan cheese, cream, butter, and seasonings, then baked in the oven to a creamy texture. Fresh tomato sauce is the ideal accompaniment.

4 servings

4 LARGE EGGS
3 tbsp HEAVY CREAM
2 tbsp GRATED PARMESAN CHEESE
1 tbsp BUTTER, MELTED
SALT AND PEPPER
GRATED NUTMEG
TOMATO SAUCE (see right)

4 RAMEKINS (¼ cup EACH)

Preheat the oven to 350°F.

Generously butter the ramekins. Put the ramekins in the freezer until the butter is firm, then butter them again.

Break the eggs into a bowl and whisk to mix them. Whisk in the cream, cheese, butter, ¼ tsp salt, a pinch of pepper, and a grating of nutmeg.

Pour the egg mixture into the prepared ramekins. Put them in a water bath* and bring the water to a boil on top of the stove. Transfer them to the oven and bake just until the eggs set and puff slightly, 12 to 15 minutes.

Meanwhile, heat the tomato sauce. Run a knife around the eggs and unmold onto warmed plates. Spoon the tomato sauce in a ribbon around the edge of the plates. Pass the remaining sauce separately.

SAUCE A LA TOMATE

TOMATO SAUCE

The flavor of this tomato sauce is incomparable when made with vine-ripened tomatoes as found in the de Vogüé garden.

Makes about 1 cup

1½ pounds FRESH TOMATOES OR ONE
14-ounce CAN TOMATOES,
WITH THE JUICE
1 ONION, HALVED
4 tbsp BUTTER, CUT INTO PIECES
SALT AND PEPPER

Quarter fresh tomatoes and cook them, covered, in a saucepan over low heat until soft, about 10 minutes. Work fresh tomatoes or canned tomatoes with their juice through a food mill, or purée them in a food processor and then work them through a strainer to remove the seeds.

Combine the puréed tomatoes in a saucepan with the onion and butter, and season. Bring to a boil, then simmer, uncovered, over medium heat until the sauce thickens, about 45 minutes. Stir the sauce occasionally during cooking. Discard the onion. Taste the sauce for seasoning. (This sauce will keep up to 3 days, covered, in the refrigerator. It also freezes well.)

Juicy red raspberries flourish at La Verrerie. Here they are served with "Crottin de Chavignol" – a locally made goat cheese.

GÂTEAU FONDANT AU CHOCOLAT

RICH CHOCOLATE CAKE WITH CARAMEL AND VANILLA CUSTARD SAUCE

Gâteau Fondant au Chocolat is a versatile cake allowing a wide range of cooking times, depending on your taste.

This recipe tolerates a wide range of cooking times. In under an hour you will have a creamy cake which needs to chill at least a day so it's firm enough for slicing. Increase the cooking time to 1¼ or 1½ hours for a drier, firmer result.

10 servings

½ pound BITTERSWEET CHOCOLATE, CHOPPED
1 cup UNSALTED BUTTER, CUT INTO SMALL PIECES
1 cup SUGAR
3 tbsp ALL-PURPOSE FLOUR
3 LARGE EGGS

For the vanilla custard sauce
2 cups MILK
1 VANILLA BEAN, SPLIT, OR ½ tsp VANILLA EXTRACT
5 LARGE EGG YOLKS
⅓ cup SUGAR

For the caramel sauce
¼ cup COLD WATER
½ cup SUGAR
½ cup WARM WATER

9-×5-×4-inch LOAF PAN OR TERRINE MOLD

Line the bottom of the loaf pan with waxed paper and preheat the oven to 350°F.

Melt the chocolate in a heavy saucepan over low heat, stirring constantly. Add the butter and sugar, a little at a time, stirring until the butter is incorporated and the sugar dissolves. Stir in the flour. Heat the mixture until it is very hot, but do not boil. Let cool slightly, then, off the heat, beat in the eggs, one by one. (The heat of the mixture will cook and thicken the eggs.)

Pour the batter into the prepared loaf pan. Set the pan in a water bath* and bring the water to a boil on top of the stove. Transfer to the heated oven and bake the cake until a thin crust forms, 40 to 50 minutes. The cake will rise slightly but will fall again as it cools. Let it cool to room temperature, about 1 hour. Cover and refrigerate the cake at least 24 hours.

Make the vanilla custard sauce (see page 222).

For the caramel sauce, heat the cold water and the sugar until the sugar dissolves, then boil steadily to a golden brown caramel. Remove from the heat and at once add the warm water. (Stand back because the caramel will sputter.) Cook over low heat until the caramel melts, then let it cool. (The caramel sauce can be kept, refrigerated, for a day.)

To finish, run a knife around the cake and unmold it. Peel off the lining paper. Cut the cake into very thin slices. Set the slices on plates and spoon vanilla custard sauce around the edge. Spoon the caramel sauce around the cake, letting the caramel drip into the custard sauce.

LA ROCHE-FROIDE

La Roche-Froide — "Cold Rock" — is aptly named. The house stands in the village of Aixe-sur-Vienne near Limoges, a tall, gray mass dating from the 16th century. This is "*La France profonde*," a region so far from the capital that 18th-century courtiers lived in dread of the word *limoger*, which came to mean banishment (forced retirement or getting laid off in today's jargon). In winter, snow is frequent, icing the roofs and weighing down the surrounding firs, but in summer La Roche-Froide comes to life, thanks to the vivacity of its owners, Robert and Christiane Desproges-Gotteron.

"Entertaining is no bother to me," smiles Christiane Desproges-Gotteron. "I've cooked all my life, first as a child by watching my mother and grandmother." Madame Desproges-Gotteron treasures a turn-of-the-century cookbook, passed down through three generations of women in her family, and once used for instructing young girls at a local convent. Family dinner for 30 is still commonplace. "I like to cook with the seasons," she says. "For example, last weekend we had roast beef, with small tomatoes baked very slowly with olive oil, a bit of sugar, salt, and pepper until they wrinkled and were almost *confit*."

An image of La France profonde. La Roche-Froide is a tall, gray mass dating from the 16th century.

A family wedding is celebrated with a huge cake, decorated with sparklers (below), a celebration echoed 300 years earlier in the dining scene (far right) which hangs on the walls of La Roche-Froide.

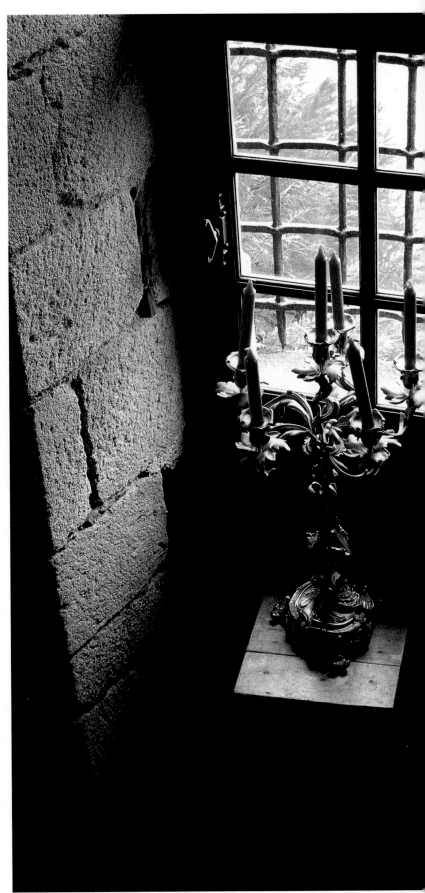

Christiane Desproges-Gotteron also likes to live off the countryside. In the old days, a Limousin farmer's rent was often paid partly in *foie gras*, with the farmer's wife first presenting the fattened birds for family approval. Today, a young woman in the village fattens geese, so a favorite Desproges-Gotteron first course is fresh *foie gras*, served with a contrasting *pâté* of zucchini and onion, briskly flavored with lemon. An alternative might be chicken terrine layered with aspic and baby vegetables, marinated beef *carpaccio*, or perhaps a three-melon soup flavored with mint. All are inspirations of the châtelaine, Christiane Desproges-Gotteron. "I cook by instinct," she says.

She and her husband divide their time between La Roche-Froide and a house nearby at Pompadour, home of the national racehorse stud. Officers from the stud are frequent guests and on August 15, the night of the annual horse trials, the garden is filled with riders in and out of uniform. Robert Desproges-Gotteron traditionally likes to collect his daily newspaper and *baguette* of bread by horse-drawn carriage. "We are still 100 years behind the times," says Madame Desproges-Gotteron.

4 LARGE EGGS
¼ cup CRÈME FRAÎCHE (see page 220) OR
HEAVY CREAM
4 TRUFFLE SLICES
12 BREADSTICKS, FRIED IN OIL AND
BUTTER (see page 220)

4 RAMEKINS (½ cup EACH)

OEUFS AUX TRUFFES

EGGS *EN COCOTTE* WITH TRUFFLES

In her cooking at La Roche-Froide, Madame Desproges-Gotteron mixes richness and simplicity. She may elevate a modest egg to luxury by adding a slice of precious black truffle, but just a pinch of freshly chopped tarragon or chives gives a memorable taste, too.

4 servings

2 tbsp FINELY DICED COOKED HAM
SALT AND PEPPER

Preheat the oven to 375°F.

Butter the ramekins. In each ramekin, put ½ tablespoon of the ham, and a little salt and pepper. Break in an egg and add a tablespoon of crème fraîche or cream. Top with a truffle slice.

If the breadsticks were made ahead of time, wrap them in aluminum foil and reheat them in the oven while cooking the eggs.

Set the ramekins in a water bath* and bring the water to a boil on top of the stove. Transfer the eggs to the heated oven and bake them until the whites are almost set, about 10 minutes; the eggs will continue to cook in the heat of the ramekins after they are removed from the oven.

Serve the eggs at once – the whites should be just set and the yolks soft. Pass the fried breadsticks separately.

POT-AU-FEU A LA ROYALE

BEEF SHORT RIBS, VEAL SHANK, AND CHICKEN SIMMERED WITH VEGETABLES

This pot-au-feu *has been a family recipe for generations and made the reputation of an epicurean great-uncle. Apparently he always returned to the ancestral home after a spell of good eating for a "cure" based on the old cook's special* pot-au-feu. *Christiane Desproges-Gotteron likes to serve her deluxe version with poached duck or goose liver. If you have access to this treat, tie it up in cheesecloth and poach it in the broth, allowing 3 to 4 minutes for the duck liver, 10 to 12 minutes for the goose. To serve, discard the cheesecloth, slice the liver, and arrange with the meats on a platter.*

10 to 12 servings

5 quarts WATER
1 ONION, STUDDED WITH 2 CLOVES
A LARGE BOUQUET GARNI*
SALT
10 BLACK PEPPERCORNS
3 pounds VEAL SHANK,
TIED IN A NEAT BUNDLE
2 pounds BEEF SHORT RIBS,
TIED IN A NEAT BUNDLE
1½ pounds CARROTS, CUT INTO
2-inch PIECES
½ BUNCH CELERY, CUT INTO
2-inch PIECES
1 pound TURNIPS, QUARTERED
2 pounds LEEKS, CUT INTO 2-inch PIECES

For the stuffed chicken
½ cup FRESH BREAD CRUMBS
½ cup MILK
1 tbsp VEGETABLE OIL
4½-pound CHICKEN WITH GIBLETS, GIBLETS
CHOPPED
SALT AND PEPPER
6 ounces CURED HAM, CHOPPED

1 CLOVE GARLIC, FINELY CHOPPED
¼ cup CHOPPED FRESH PARSLEY
1 LARGE EGG, BEATEN
¼ tsp GROUND ALLSPICE

For the garnishes and condiments
1 SMALL LOAF FRENCH BREAD, SLICED
INTO THIN ROUNDS AND TOASTED
COARSE SALT
MUSTARD
CORNICHONS OR GHERKINS

TRUSSING NEEDLE AND KITCHEN STRING

Combine the water, onion, bouquet garni, salt, and peppercorns in a large pot and bring to a boil. Add the veal shank and short ribs to the pot, reduce the heat to low, and simmer, un-covered, skimming occasionally, about 1 hour.

Meanwhile, make the stuffing. Soak the bread crumbs in the milk until soft, then squeeze dry. Heat the oil in a frying pan and add the chopped chicken giblets with salt and pepper. Cook them over medium heat, stirring, until brown, 2 to 3 minutes. Mix them with the soaked bread crumbs, ham, garlic, parsley, and beaten egg, and season with pepper and all-spice. (Salt may not be needed if the ham is salty.) Beat very well until thoroughly mixed. Sauté a small piece of the stuffing and taste it for seasoning. Stuff the chicken and truss the bird*.

Add the stuffed chicken to the pot with enough water to cover all the ingredients. Continue simmering another hour, adding more water as necessary.

Add the carrots, celery, and turnips with more salt if needed, and continue to simmer until the meat, chicken, and vegetables are very tender, about another hour. Add the leeks 20 minutes before the end of cooking. Be sure there is always enough liquid to cover the meats and vegetables. (*Pot-au-feu* can be kept in the refrigerator up to 3 days.)

Reheat the *pot-au-feu* if necessary. Transfer the meats, chicken, and vegetables to a carving board with a juice catcher and discard the string. Boil the broth to reduce it by one-third or until well flavored. Meanwhile, cut the meats into

In pot-au-feu, the cooking liquid is reduced to make a well-flavored broth which can be served as a first course.

The pot-au-feu itself is a delicious assortment of tender meats and vegetables served with a rich stuffing. Madame Desproges-Gotteron also adds a generous slice of foie gras.

medium-thick slices and arrange them on a large warmed platter. Carve the chicken, pile the stuffing on the platter, and arrange the pieces of chicken on top. Arrange the vegetables around the meats and chicken. Cover the platter and keep the meats and vegetables warm.

To serve, strain the broth, taste it for seasoning, and skim off the fat. Put the toasted bread in warmed soup bowls, pour the broth over them, and serve as a first course. Serve the meat platter as a main course, with the salt, mustard, and cornichons as condiments.

Salted and then baked in rich fat, this crisp duck melts in the mouth.

CONFIT DE CANARD CROUSTILLANT

CRISP DUCK *CONFIT*

Madame Desproges-Gotteron likes to serve this tender, crisp-skinned duck with garlic potatoes sautéed in the fat drained from the confit. *Lately,*

when heating the pieces of duck for serving, she has been basting them with a spoonful (or "tear-drop" as she puts it) of honey so it caramelizes on the crisp skin.

4 servings

4-pound DUCK, CUT UP INTO 8
SERVING PIECES*
3 tbsp COARSE SALT
1 tsp GROUND BLACK PEPPER
3 SPRIGS FRESH THYME
3 BAY LEAVES, CRUMBLED
1½ pounds LARD OR GOOSE FAT,
MORE IF NEEDED

Rub each piece of duck with some of the coarse salt and put it in a bowl. Sprinkle with the pepper and the remaining salt and add the thyme and bay leaves. Cover and leave in a cool place for 6 to 12 hours, depending on how strong a flavor you want.

When ready to cook, wipe the excess salt from the duck pieces. Preheat the oven to 300°F. Put the duck pieces, skin side down, in a heavy flameproof casserole and cook over low heat until the fat runs and the duck skin turns golden, 15 to 20 minutes. Add enough melted lard or goose fat to cover the duck, then cover the casserole tightly and transfer it to the heated oven. Cook until the duck is very tender and has rendered all its fat, about 2 hours. Tradition has it the duck should be tender enough to pierce with a straw.

Pour a layer of the rendered fat into the bottom of a terrine or bowl and let it set. Pack the pieces of duck on top and pour over enough fat to cover them completely, adding melted lard if necessary. Cover the bowl and keep it in a cool place at least a week for the flavor to mellow. (If sealed with a cloth sprinkled with salt and then covered with paper, *confit* will keep for several months in a cool place.)

To serve the *confit*, leave it in a warm place until the fat runs. Drain the duck pieces, then fry them in a little of the fat until they are very hot and the skin is crisp and brown. Transfer the *confit* to a warmed platter and serve it very hot. Keep the leftover fat for frying potatoes.

FRAMBOISES A LA MERINGUE ET CHANTILLY

RASPBERRIES WITH BAKED MERINGUE AND WHIPPED CREAM

"The Limousin is raspberry country," notes Christiane Desproges-Gotteron. "All summer they are ridiculously cheap in the market, less than the cost of picking!" When pressed for time, she buys ¼ pound of baked meringues, then layers them with the berries and sauce in a dish. It can even be prepared a day ahead, with the topping of whipped cream added just before serving. "Impossible to bungle!" she says.

4 servings

3 LARGE EGG WHITES
¾ cup SUGAR
SUGAR FOR SPRINKLING
1 pint RASPBERRIES
RASPBERRY SAUCE (see right)

For the Chantilly cream
1 cup HEAVY CREAM
1 tbsp CONFECTIONERS' SUGAR
½ tsp VANILLA EXTRACT

1-quart SOUFFLÉ DISH (OPTIONAL)

Preheat the oven to 250°F. Butter and flour a baking sheet.

Whisk the egg whites until very stiff. Add 3 tablespoons of the sugar and continue whisking until glossy to make a light meringue, about 30 seconds longer. Fold in the remaining sugar using a large metal spoon.

Shape the meringue into ovals with two large spoons, dropping them on the baking sheet. Sprinkle them with sugar and bake in the heated oven until dry and pale beige in color, 1½ to 1¾ hours. Transfer them to a rack and let cool completely. (Baked meringues will keep up to 3 weeks in an airtight container.)

To finish, make the Chantilly cream (see page 220) and chill it. Spoon the berries into the soufflé dish or a serving bowl. Pour in the raspberry sauce and crumble the baked meringues over the top. Spread the Chantilly cream over all.

COULIS DE FRAMBOISES

RASPBERRY SAUCE

Sweet raspberry sauce is a wonderful accompaniment to a variety of desserts and cakes.

Makes 1¼ cups

1 pint RASPBERRIES
2 tbsp SUGAR, MORE IF NEEDED

Purée the raspberries in a food processor or blender with the sugar. Strain the sauce to remove the seeds. Taste it and add more sugar if needed, then chill. The sauce can be kept 1 or 2 days in the refrigerator.

Summer brings a profusion of raspberries to the area around La Roche-Froide.

CHÂTEAU D'ANJONY

THE MEDIEVAL FORTRESS OF ANJONY LOOMS GRIM AND FORBIDDING IN A LOST CORNER OF AUVERGNE. ON THE SUMMER DAY THAT I FIRST INTRODUCED MYSELF TO COMTE AND COMTESSE DE LÉOTOING D'ANJONY, THE TELEPHONE WAS INTERMITTENTLY CUT OFF BY THUNDER AND STORM AND THE RIVER BELOW WAS IN FLOOD. UNLIKE MOST FORTRESSES. ANJONY WAS NEVER INTENDED TO WARD OFF INVADERS. "THE CHÂTEAU WAS BUILT AS A SYMBOL OF POWER." EXPLAINS THE COMTE. "AND THE LÉOTOING D'ANJONYS HAVE LIVED HERE SINCE THE BEGINNING." THE PRESENT CHÂTELAIN IS THE COMTE'S FATHER. THE MARQUIS DE LÉOTOING D'ANJONY.

AS A CLOSE COMPANION TO JOAN OF ARC. LOUIS D'ANJONY WAS GRANTED PERMISSION TO BUILD THIS SIX-STORY. RECTANGULAR KEEP IN 1439. A DIRECT CHALLENGE TO THE LOCAL LORDS OF TOURNEMIRE WHOSE OWN FORT WAS SCARCELY A BOWSHOT DISTANT. SUCH AN AFFRONT COULD NOT PASS UNCHECKED. STARTING WITH A PETTY DISPUTE ABOUT THE RIGHT TO BAKE BREAD IN THE COMMUNAL OVEN. THE QUARREL CLIMAXED A CENTURY LATER IN A DOUBLE MURDER. WITH A CORPSE DISINTERRED FROM HOLY GROUND AND THROWN DOWN BEFORE THE GATES OF THE CHÂTEAU. TO BE FOUND THE NEXT MORNING. HALF EATEN BY DOGS. THE TOURNEMIRES HAD GONE TOO FAR. BOTH KING AND POPE REFUSED TO COUNTENANCE BODY SNATCHING, AND THE FAMILY OF ANJONY TRIUMPHED.

The Château d'Anjony dominates a remote valley in the Auvergne (page 144). Inside, the Salle des Preux, the Warriors' Hall, is a magnificent fresco-covered hall. The murals were painted in the 16th century for a grand wedding, and they feature historical and biblical figures, as well as life-size effigies of the bride and her groom.

The famous Black Virgin in the castle chapel. The 14-inch-high statue, Notre Dame d'Anjony, is thought to date back to the 1400s (above right). The chapel ceiling is decorated with scenes from Christ's life (right). The Anjony crest can be seen in the center of the frescoes.

The fertile Doire valley where Anjony stands majestic on a rocky promontory.

The fruits of their success can be seen in the château, which is a storehouse of treasures – throughout its history, Anjony has never been ransacked. Anjony is home to one of the finest of the medieval black virgins of Auvergne, sculpted in darkened wood, the holy child on her knees clothed in gold. But the virgin is overshadowed by an astonishing gothic chapel, painted with 16th-century biblical scenes stretching right up to the keystone of the vaulted roof. The *"Salle des Preux"* (Warriors' Hall) is equally animated, a Renaissance Hollywood, starring Judas Maccabaeus, Hector of Troy, King David, and Alexander the Great on his elephant gamboling under the gaze of Charlemagne on the opposite wall. At one side of the great fireplace stands Michel d'Anjony, who commissioned the frescoes to honor and impress his wife, Germaine de Foix, cousin of the future King Henri IV. Such grandeur might overwhelm, but not Robert de Léotoing d'Anjony, who adores his cosy study. "In winter these rooms stay wonderfully warm. *Dieu merci* for thick walls!"

I talked with Edith de Léotoing d'Anjony about the countryside surrounding the château, so bleak to a stranger's eye. "We are in the heart of Cantal here," she says. "Fifty years behind the times, from the plumbing upward."

However inhospitable the land may seem, cattle of the sturdy rust-colored Salers breed thrive – 100 or more range on the property. Their milk goes to make cheese: Cantal and Salers, a variation of Cantal made only with the milk from cattle grazed in mountain pastures from May to late September. Both are legally protected with *appellation contrôlée* status. The best resemble an aged Cheddar, smooth but dry with a touch of bite, the result of at least three months of aging at over 3,000 feet. The cheeses are shaped by molds into huge 100-pound disks which can be rolled along like a wheel. Cantal cheese turns up in local dishes like *tourte de Salers*, a cheese pie, and *gannat*, or cheese brioche. Other local specialties include stuffed cabbage and *le pounti*, a meat and vegetable loaf layered with plump prunes. "We get hungry in these climes," remarks the Comtesse.

By no means all of Edith de Léotoing d'Anjony's favorite dishes are Auvergnat. She collects antiquarian cookbooks, and has some that were written nearly 200 years ago by the great chef Antonin Carême. Recently she tried one of his recipes for wild duck with a stuffing of apples and red currants. "Very modern, don't you think?" she remarks. Escoffier's *pudding de cabinet* (layers of ladyfingers and candied fruits baked in custard) is another favorite with an established pedigree (see page 94). Out here in the mountains, fashions change slowly. *Châteaux* like Anjony and the food that is served there are intended to be good for all time.

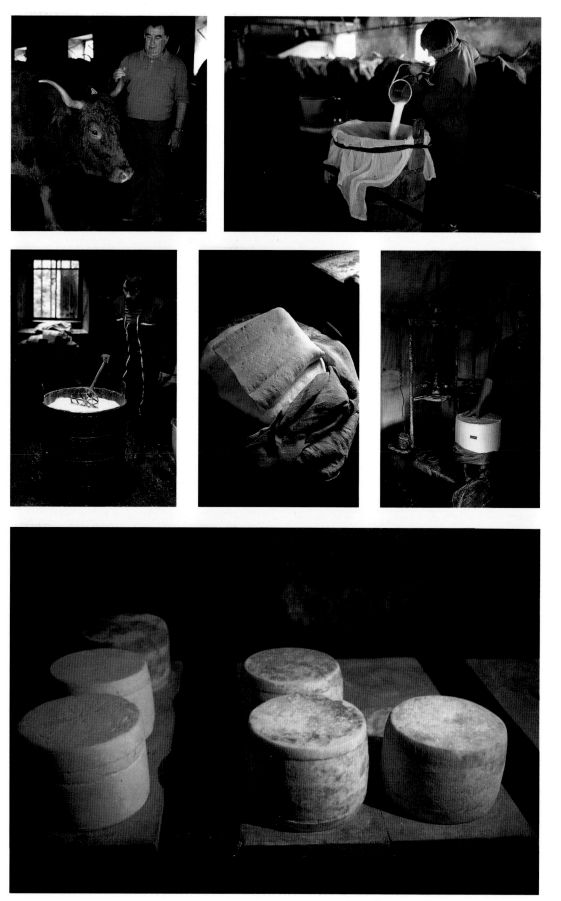

Local cheese being made in Salers from the milk of Salers cows by Henri Rouchy at the Domaine Fouey. This traditional and time-consuming process is increasingly rare today.

The austere towers of Anjony (see page 144) contrast with the charming living quarters and the opulence of the Comtesse's table.

LE POUNTI

MEAT AND VEGETABLE LOAF
WITH PRUNES

Not all château cooking requires truffles and foie gras. *The Comtesse de Léotoing d'Anjony prefers the rustic dishes of the Auvergne highlands such as this traditional loaf layered with prunes. Serve it as a first course or brunch dish. It also makes a good accompaniment to plain roast meat or chicken. "Be sure to add plenty of seasoning,"* says the Comtesse.

8 to 10 servings

12 PITTED PRUNES

3 tbsp COGNAC OR BRANDY

½ pound COOKED HAM OR LEFTOVER ROAST
BEEF OR PORK

½ pound BACON, CUT INTO PIECES

½ pound SWISS CHARD LEAVES OR SPINACH

2 ONIONS, CUT INTO PIECES

3 tbsp CHOPPED MIXED FRESH HERBS,
SUCH AS PARSLEY, TARRAGON,
AND CHIVES

1½ tsp ACTIVE DRY YEAST OR ⅓ oz
COMPRESSED YEAST*

1 cup LUKEWARM MILK

⅓ cup ALL-PURPOSE FLOUR

4 LARGE EGGS

SALT AND PEPPER

1½-quart SHALLOW BAKING DISH

Preheat the oven to 350°F.

Butter the baking dish. Cut the pitted prunes in half and soak them in the Cognac or brandy. Chop together the ham or meat, bacon, Swiss chard, onions, and herbs, either in a food processor or by hand.

Sprinkle or crumble the yeast over the milk and set aside to dissolve, about 5 minutes. Sift the flour into a bowl and gradually stir in the yeast mixture. Whisk in the eggs to make a batter and add a little salt and plenty of pepper.

Stir the batter into the ham mixture. Pour half this batter into the prepared dish. Cover with the soaked prunes and any liquid. Pour the rest of the batter on top of the prunes, spreading it evenly. Bake in the heated oven until browned and a skewer inserted in the center is hot to the touch when withdrawn after 30 seconds, 50 to 60 minutes. Serve lukewarm or at room temperature, cut into slices. (*Pounti* can be kept covered in the refrigerator up to 3 days.)

TRUITES AUX MORILLES

SAUTÉED TROUT WITH MOREL MUSHROOMS

A simple sauce of wine, cream, and mushrooms is the perfect way to enjoy the taste of fresh trout (right).

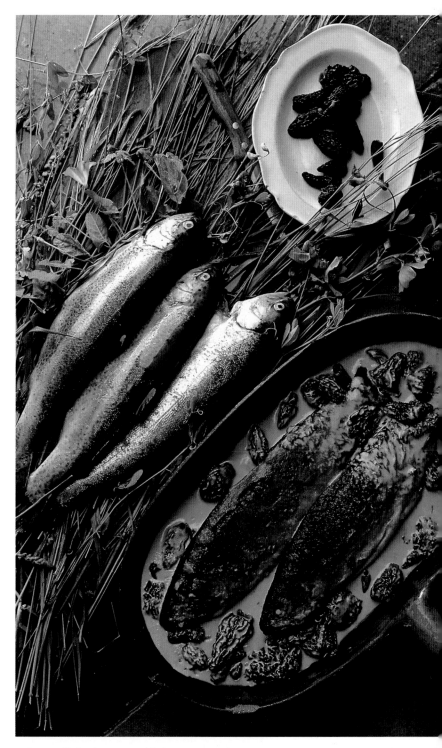

At the foot of Anjony, weekend fishermen sit patiently, rod in hand, hoping to catch the trout that swim through the Doire river. The Comtesse de Léotoing d'Anjony simply panfries the trout with fresh morels during their short season, or otherwise with field mushrooms, stirring in a ladle of cream at the end for a sauce.

4 servings

¼ pound FRESH MORELS OR 1 ounce
DRIED MORELS
4 TROUT (ABOUT ½ pound EACH),
CLEANED AND TRIMMED
SALT AND PEPPER
¾ cup SEASONED ALL-PURPOSE FLOUR
½ cup CLARIFIED BUTTER (see page 220)
¾ cup DRY WHITE WINE
1½ cups CRÈME FRAÎCHE (see page 220)
OR HEAVY CREAM

Pick over fresh morels and trim the stems. Shake and gently brush them to remove any earth, splitting the stems to remove any soil inside. Soak dried morels in warm water to cover until fairly soft, 1 to 2 hours, stirring occasionally to loosen any grit. Rinse the morels in cold running water to remove any remaining grit and pat dry. Cut them into thin slices.

Sprinkle the fish with salt and pepper. Coat them with seasoned flour, shaking off any excess.

Heat the butter in two large frying pans. Add the fish and brown them over medium heat, 2 to 3 minutes on each side. Add the morels to the pans with a little salt and pepper. Continue cooking over fairly low heat until the fresh morels are tender and the flesh of the trout can just be pulled from the bone with a knife, 5 to 7 minutes. Transfer the fish and fresh morels to a warmed platter and keep warm. If using dried morels, leave them in the pans.

Pour off the butter. Add the wine to the pans and bring to a boil, scraping to dissolve the browned pan juices. Simmer until reduced by half. Combine all the juices in one pan. Add the crème fraîche or cream and simmer to concentrate the flavor, 5 to 10 minutes. Taste for seasoning. Pour the sauce over the fish and serve immediately.

CHÂTEAU DE JOZERAND

FOR JOY DE ROHAN-CHABOT, THE CHÂTEAU DE JOZERAND IS BOTH FAMILY HOME AND ARTIST'S *ATELIER*. THE CHÂTEAU HAS BEEN IN HER HUSBAND'S FAMILY SINCE THE EARLY 1700S.

The Château de Jozerand is in a remote spot of northern Auvergne. A ghost is mandatory. In the days of the present Comte's grandfather, the children's tutor complained of a presence that each night shook his bed. A few years later, central heating was installed in the old tower and a skeleton was revealed, buried in the wall. Tests showed the bones to be 15th-century. In the archives it was found that of the three Rochefort d'Ailly brothers who lived in Jozerand at that time, one had disappeared after returning from the wars to claim his inheritance. In 1902, the skeleton was buried in the cemetery, and hauntings ceased.

AND SHE WAS BORN NEARBY. "I ADORE THE COUNTRYSIDE," SHE SAYS, "THE CHANGING SEASONS, THE ICE IN WINTER, THE VIEW OF THE MOUNTAINS FROM MY WINDOW." ICY INDEED, BECAUSE THE CHÂTEAU DE JOZERAND STANDS IN NORTHERN AUVERGNE AT AN ALTITUDE OF 1,600 FEET. "AT CHRISTMAS WE MAY HAVE 20 OR 30 DEGREES OF FROST, OR THE SUN MAY BE SHINING AND WE CAN EAT OUTDOORS."

COMTESSE JOY DE ROHAN-CHABOT IS A NOTED ARTIST, BUT THE LIMITATIONS OF PAINT ON CANVAS ARE NOT FOR HER. SHE LOVES TO EXPERIMENT WITH SURFACES, DECORATING DOORS, FURNITURE, FABRIC, ANYTHING THAT COMES TO HAND. JUST NOW SHE IS DECORATING AN OLD ENAMELED BATH. "IT'S EXCITING. EACH TIME I MUST TO SOME EXTENT INVENT A NEW TECHNIQUE." SHE DRAWS VERY MUCH ON NATURE —"THIS SEEMS TO BE THE YEAR OF SNAILS," SHE CONFIDES. JOY HAS JUST COMPLETED A PORTRAIT OF HER HUSBAND IN A ROCKING CHAIR, SURROUNDED BY A FOREST OF TREES AND POTTED PLANTS.

In the grounds at Jozerand, box hedges and topiary predominate. Joy de Rohan-Chabot has made the old orangery into her studio. Its calm atmosphere and good light make it ideal for working on her painted screens and decorated furniture.

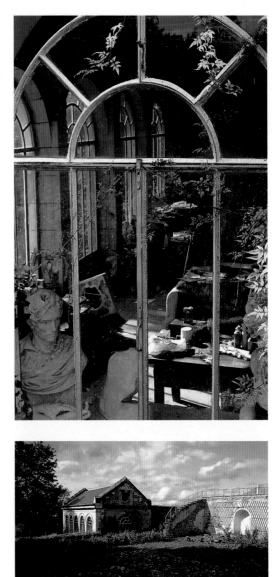

Life at Jozerand revolves around the ancient vaulted kitchen, which does double duty as the family room. "In summer we'll have 30 guests or more, and laughter seems to start at eight in the morning and continue into the small hours." The kitchen is heated from the great open fireplace and the copper pots are put to good use. "I walk for miles from cupboard to cupboard when I am cooking," says the Comtesse. Vegetable soups are her forte, based on leeks, sorrel, or whatever else is in season. In summer, she finds chilled cucumber soup refreshing. The day we talked together she had roast chickens to serve with Chinese black mushrooms and a spicy Oriental sauce. "I love to invent," she says. "I may read a cookbook for ideas, but I never follow it exactly."

Jozerand is an historic monument, but unusually it is listed less for its 14th- and 15th-century shell than as a showcase for its Neo-classical renovations. Today Jozerand blooms with flowered wallpapers and the glowing colors that brought a fresh breeze to salons and bed-chambers over 150 years ago. A modern and individual touch is also in evidence: Joy de Rohan-Chabot loves to decorate screens with collages of roses, trailing vines, and vegetables.

The ambiance at Jozerand is international: Joy's mother was Scottish, and in summer she calls on young British or American cooks to take charge in the kitchen. The current chef is Korean. At any time the language may be English or French, the speaker aged seven to seventy-seven.

The warmth of the Rohan-Chabots, and the relaxed and cosmopolitan atmosphere at their château, are an instant welcome: "Jean is non-conformist, and so am I. Jozerand is a reflection of the two of us."

POTAGE DES COMBRAILLES AUX ORTIES

NETTLE SOUP WITH SORREL

In spring, before the nettles flower, Joy de Rohan-Chabot dons gardening gloves and long trousers to gather nettle tops in the Combraille hills for this special soup. The leaves are simmered with homegrown sorrel in beef stock, and, just before serving, a dollop of fresh cream is added to smooth out the grassy flavors. Nettle soup without the sorrel is good, too.

6 to 8 servings

2 pounds TENDER NETTLE TOPS
¼ cup BUTTER
1 pound SORREL, STEMS REMOVED
1 LARGE ONION, FINELY CHOPPED
3 tbsp ALL-PURPOSE FLOUR
1 quart BEEF STOCK (see page 221)
SALT AND PEPPER
½ cup CRÈME FRAÎCHE (see page 220)
OR HEAVY CREAM

Wash the nettle tops and discard the stems, wearing rubber gloves. Bring a large pan of salted water to a boil. Add the nettle leaves, bring the water back to a boil, and cook, stirring often, until the leaves are very tender, 15 to 30 minutes, depending on the age of the nettles. Drain them.

Process the nettle leaves in a blender or food processor until mostly smooth, then work the purée through a drum sieve or food mill to remove the fibers.

Melt 1 tablespoon of the butter in a big saucepan. Wash the sorrel and cook in the butter over medium heat, stirring often, until it softens to a purée, 3 to 5 minutes. Combine the cooked sorrel with the nettle purée.

Melt the remaining butter in a saucepan and add the onion. Sauté it over medium heat, stirring, until soft, 3 to 5 minutes. Stir in the flour and cook until foaming. Whisk in the stock,

vegetable purées, and a little salt and pepper. Bring the soup to a boil, whisking constantly. Reduce the heat and simmer, stirring occasionally, until the soup is well flavored, about 30 minutes. (The soup can be made ahead and refrigerated up to 2 days.)

To finish, reheat the soup if necessary, stir in half the crème fraîche or cream, and season the soup to taste with salt and pepper. Spoon it into warmed soup bowls and add a spoonful of the remaining crème fraîche or cream to each bowl, swirling to create a marbled effect if you like.

Joy de Rohan-Chabot's nettle soup with sorrel is a delicious and original way to use the first wild plants of spring.

GIGOT BRAYAUDE

SLOW-BRAISED LAMB FROM AUVERGNE

A leg of mature mountain sheep was once traditional for this recipe, braised for 7 hours until the meat began to fall off the bone. Today, the dish is often prepared with younger lamb, but several hours' cooking is still the key. "We eat the meat without a knife, it's so tender," notes Joy de Rohan-Chabot. With the gigot, *the Comtesse serves a tart red currant jelly or blackberry jam, made with berries gathered at Jozerand. Truffade (see page 175) would make a perfect accompaniment.*

8 servings

4½-pound LEG OF LAMB OR MUTTON
2 ONIONS, SLICED
2 CARROTS, SLICED
SPRIG FRESH THYME OR
½ tsp DRIED THYME
1 BAY LEAF

2 cups WATER, MORE IF NEEDED
SALT AND PEPPER
½ cup COGNAC OR BRANDY

KITCHEN STRING

Preheat the oven to 250°F. Trim the meat of all excess fat. Tie the meat tightly with string and put it in a large casserole with the onions, carrots, thyme, bay leaf, water, salt, and pepper. Cover and cook in the heated oven, turning the meat occasionally, about 5 hours. The water should scarcely bubble; if it simmers, reduce the heat. Add more water if necessary so the casserole doesn't dry out during the long cooking. After 5 hours, add the Cognac or brandy, return the casserole to the oven, and continue cooking until the meat is very tender, about 1 hour longer. (The meat can be refrigerated up to 3 days and reheated before proceeding.)

Remove the strings from the meat and carve it into thick slices. Strain the cooking liquid and skim off the fat. This gravy should be rich and concentrated, so boil to reduce it if necessary. Alternatively, add a little water if you do not have enough. Serve the lamb with the unthickened cooking liquid.

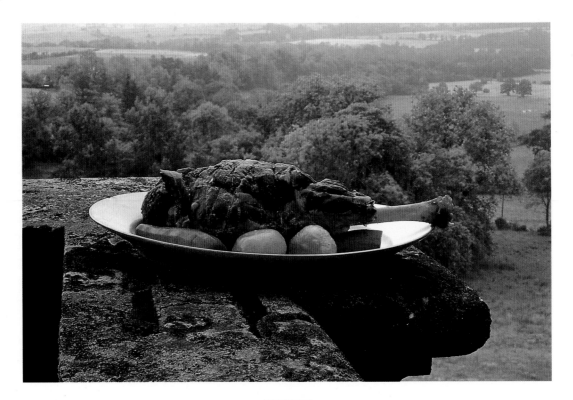

The secret to the perfect Gigot Brayaude is slow cooking at a low temperature.

DAUBE AUX PRUNEAUX

BEEF STEW WITH PRUNES

For Madame de Jenlis, a daube *with beef and prunes spells home cooking, because cattle are a mainstay in Auvergne, raised both for beef and for milk. Auvergnat prunes, though less celebrated than those from the Garonne and Lot river valleys in southwestern France, are still much appreciated locally. With the* daube, *serve boiled potatoes or buttered noodles.*

10 to 12 servings

4½ pounds BEEF CHUCK OR ROUND ROAST,
CUT INTO 2-inch CUBES
1 pound CARROTS, CUT INTO
1½-inch PIECES
1 pound ONIONS, QUARTERED
3 quarts ROBUST RED WINE, MORE
IF NEEDED
1 BAY LEAF

SALT AND PEPPER
¾ pound PITTED PRUNES

Combine the meat, carrots, onions, and wine in a heavy flameproof casserole. Bring the wine to a boil, then reduce the heat and simmer, covered, over very low heat for 3 hours.

Remove the casserole from the heat and add the bay leaf and salt. Add more wine if needed; the wine should barely cover the meat. Let cool to room temperature, then leave to marinate, covered, in the refrigerator for about 24 hours, stirring the meat occasionally.

The next day, add the prunes to the casserole. Bring the wine to a boil, then reduce the heat. Cover the casserole and simmer over very low heat until the meat and prunes are very tender, about 1 hour. (The *daube* can be cooked up to 2 days ahead and refrigerated in the cooking liquid. The flavor mellows on keeping.)

To finish, reheat the *daube* if necessary. If the sauce is thin, remove the solids and boil until it lightly coats a spoon. Season the *daube* with pepper; it should be peppery. As you prefer, skim off the fat, or leave to enrich the meat.

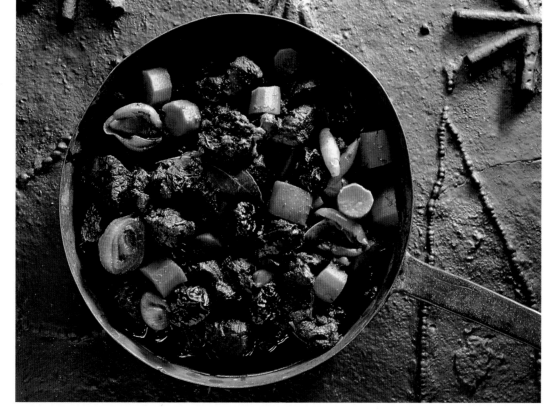

Beef stew is enhanced with dark, mellow prunes, a product of Auvergne.

CHÂTEAU DE VIRIEU

EVER SINCE IT WAS BUILT NEARLY 1,000 YEARS AGO, THE CHÂTEAU DE VIRIEU HAS BEEN A REFUGE. LAST TIME WAS IN THE SECOND WORLD WAR, WHEN VIRIEU WAS A RESISTANCE HIDEOUT. IN 1943, THE GERMANS CONDUCTED A RIGOROUS SEARCH, BUT ALL THEY FOUND IN AN OBSCURE CLOSET WAS A LITTLE BOX OF JADE JEWELRY, MISLAID BY THE MARQUISE DE VIRIEU THREE YEARS EARLIER. "I WAS DELIGHTED IT TURNED UP," SHE SAID. THE INVADERS TOTALLY OVERLOOKED THE MEDIEVAL CACHE UNDER THE TERRACED BATTLEMENT, ORIGINALLY DESIGNED TO STOCK GRAIN IN TIME OF SIEGE. IT WAS FILLED WITH 40 TONS OF GUNS AND AMMUNITION, CRAFTILY CONCEALED BY PLANTINGS OF POTATOES.

DESPITE ITS NAME, THE CHÂTEAU DE VIRIEU HAS NOT ALWAYS BEEN IN THE HANDS OF THE VIRIEU FAMILY. ONE BRANCH BUILT THE CHÂTEAU, BUT AS PART OF A MARRIAGE SETTLEMENT IT PASSED TO ANOTHER FAMILY IN THE 13TH CENTURY. THE PRESENT BRANCH REACQUIRED VIRIEU IN 1874, BUT HAS ONLY MADE A SERIOUS HOME THERE SINCE THE 1920S, WHEN RESTORATION BEGAN. SEVENTY YEARS ON, AND THE WORK STILL CONTINUES. THIS YEAR'S PROJECT, UNDERTAKEN BY AN EXPERT FROM YALE UNIVERSITY, IS THE PRESERVATION AND CATALOGUING OF THE LIBRARY, WHICH INCLUDES MEDIEVAL MANUSCRIPTS AND SOME NOTABLE 16TH- AND 17TH-CENTURY ENGRAVINGS. NEXT YEAR MARIE-FRANÇOISE DE VIRIEU HOPES TO RESTORE THE 16TH-CENTURY DOVECOTE WITH ITS PEPPERPOT ROOF. SHE ALSO SPEAKS WISTFULLY OF PLANS FOR CREATING A MAZE, TO BE PLANTED IN HEDGES OF BOX.

The massive walls of Virieu have withstood assault over the centuries and sheltered arms caches for the Resistance in World War II.

TRUFFADE

CRUSHED POTATOES WITH CHEESE

Hearty truffade *comes from a rugged patch of France, where potatoes and the dependable pig sustain body and soul during the cold winter months. In this variation from the Dauphiné, the Marquise de Virieu uses olive oil, a reminder that sunny Provence is not far away, and the local tomme, a cow's or goat's milk cheese with a musty gray rind. Cantal and Gruyère cheese are also good, especially as they authenticate the mountain origins of the dish.*

4 servings

6 ounces SMOKED SLAB BACON,
CUT INTO *LARDONS**
2 tbsp OLIVE OIL
2 pounds BAKING POTATOES, PEELED
AND THINLY SLICED
SALT AND PEPPER
½ pound TOMME, CANTAL, OR GRUYÈRE
CHEESE, CUT INTO THIN STRIPS

10-inch NONSTICK FRYING PAN

Heat the bacon in the frying pan, stirring, until the fat runs and the bacon is tender; do not brown it. Remove it with a slotted spoon and drain it on paper towels.

Add the oil to the pan and heat it. Add the potatoes and sprinkle them lightly with salt and pepper, remembering the bacon and cheese are salty. Cover and cook over low heat 5 minutes. Return the bacon to the pan. Continue to cook, uncovered, over low heat, stirring the potatoes from time to time and crushing them when they begin to soften, until very tender, 20 to 30 minutes. Stir in the cheese until it melts into threads. Taste for seasoning.

Raise the heat to high and let the mixture cook, without stirring, to brown the base, 5 to 8 minutes. Press on the potato cake occasionally to hold it together. When it is golden on the base, run a spatula around it and turn it out onto a warmed platter. Serve hot.

Truffade, a satisfying dish which is a meal in itself, or try it as a superb accompaniment to Gigot Brayaude (see page 162).

Châteaux of the Sun

CHARTREUSE DE BONPAS

THE CHARTREUSE DE BONPAS WAS ORIGINALLY A CARTHUSIAN FOUNDATION. SET ON THE BANKS OF THE DURANCE RIVER, IT WAS A POPULAR REST HOUSE FOR TRAVELERS ON THE BUSY ROUTE FROM AVIGNON TO AIX-EN-PROVENCE ("*BON PAS*" MEANS "HAPPY STEP" IN FRENCH). THICK STONE WALLS PROVIDED RELIEF FROM THE SEARING SUMMER SUN AS WELL AS PROTECTION FROM BANDITS WHO ROAMED THE COUNTRYSIDE. APPARENTLY THE FOOD WAS ALSO GOOD, BECAUSE AFTER BREAKING HER JOURNEY THERE IN NOVEMBER, 1675, THE DIARIST MADAME DE SÉVIGNÉ QUIPPED THAT THE MONASTERY SHOULD BE CALLED "*BON REPAS*." "YOU WILL RECALL," SHE WROTE TO HER DAUGHTER, "THE FINE REPAST WE ENJOYED THERE WITH THE MONKS."

TODAY BONPAS THRIVES IN THE HANDS OF JÉRÔME AND YVELINE CASALIS, WHOSE FAMILY HAS OWNED IT FOR THREE GENERATIONS. THE PROPERTY IS STILL DEDICATED TO THE PRODUCTION OF WINES AND OLIVE OIL, AS IT WAS UNDER THE MONKS. RED AND WHITE CHARTREUSE DE BONPAS WINES, CLASSIFIED CÔTES-DU-RHÔNE, ARE EXPORTED TO BRITAIN AND THE UNITED STATES. OLIVE OIL PRODUCTION IS MORE MODEST, LIMITED TO A HUNDRED OR SO GALLONS A YEAR AND CONSUMED WITH APPRECIATION ON THE SPOT. "WE LIKE TO FREEZE A SMALL BOWL OF OIL SO IT SETS ALMOST TO A JELLY," MADAME CASALIS TOLD ME, "THEN WE SPREAD IT ON TOAST. DELICIOUS!"

A smiling Madonna welcomes visitors to Bonpas, a haven of refuge for over 600 years. Within the grounds, shady stone gardens and cool ponds provide relief from the intense southern sun (far right).

The walls and chapel of the Chartreuse de Bonpas date back to the time of Pope John XXII in the 14th century.

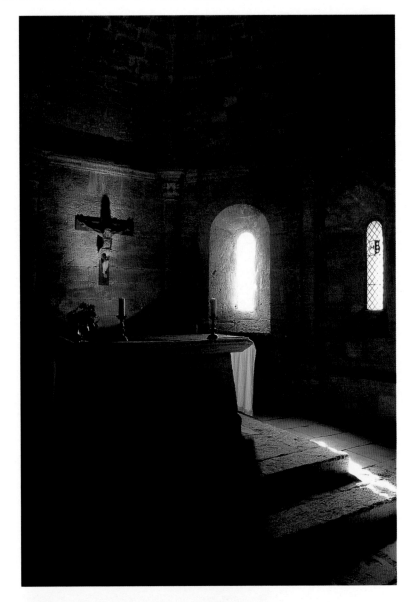

Aïgo boulido, or garlic soup, is a summer favorite with the Casalis family. It is said to assuage colds and high blood pressure. To make it, heads of mild fresh garlic are simmered in salted water with some sprigs of sage, then poured over toasted *croûtes* that have been moistened with olive oil. Other summer dishes include fish terrine and *pistou*, a fresh vegetable soup made with pesto sauce. "We eat according to the seasons," says Yveline Casalis. "No hothouse tomatoes in December or melons in March for us! Just now we're putting up preserves – tomatoes, pears in syrup, and green and purple plums for tarts in the winter."

Winter also brings a robust Provençal *pot-au-feu* with some marrow bones, flavored with garlic, juniper, and "quantities of herbs." Just as *bouillabaisse* is flavored with the garlic mayonnaise *aïoli*, so *pot-au-feu* is served with a light herb mayonnaise. To make it, Madame Casalis crushes a whole hard-boiled egg, mixes it with a raw egg yolk, a chopped shallot, and 2 or 3 tablespoons of chopped fresh herbs, then whisks in a cup or so of her olive oil. The result is light and aromatic, excellent with cold or hot meats.

Add to this culinary abundance the beauties of the Lubéron landscape – picturesque villages tumbling down from pinnacled hillsides, sloping groves of gray-green olive trees, and the fertile orchards of the rich Durance valley. Bonpas was built as a haven, and so it remains.

can also be used in the fricot. *Serve these arti-chokes as a first course, or pair them with a meat dish that doesn't repeat the tomato theme.*

4 servings

8 BABY GLOBE ARTICHOKES OR
4 MEDIUM ARTICHOKES
1 LEMON, HALVED
¼ cup OLIVE OIL
1 ONION, THINLY SLICED
¾ cup WATER, MORE IF NEEDED
1 tsp TOMATO PASTE
2 cups DRY WHITE WINE
1 CARROT, CUT INTO JULIENNE STRIPS*
½ tsp DRIED HERBES DE PROVENCE*
SALT AND PEPPER

For baby artichokes, snap off the tough outer leaves. Trim the stems with a stainless steel knife and cut off the tops of the remaining leaves. Cut the artichokes in half through the stem.

While you're working, rub the cut surfaces of the artichokes with a lemon half. As you finish each artichoke, drop it into a bowl of cold water to which the juice from the remaining lemon half has been added.

For medium artichokes, break off the stems. Using a very sharp stainless steel knife, cut off all large bottom leaves, leaving a cone of small soft leaves in the center. Trim the base to an even round shape, slightly flattened at the base. Quarter the artichokes and cut each quarter into two wedges. Cut out the fuzzy choke, leaving the small soft leaves attached. (If the leaves are tough, cut them all away.)

Blanch* the artichokes in boiling salted water for 10 minutes, then drain them.

Heat the oil in a sauté pan and add the onion. Sauté it over medium heat until soft, 3 to 5 minutes. Stir the water into the tomato paste. Add the tomato water, blanched artichokes, wine, carrot, herbs, salt, and pepper to the pan. Bring the liquid to a boil, then reduce the heat and simmer, covered, until the artichokes are tender and the liquid is almost absorbed, ½ to 1 hour, depending on the age of the artichokes. If the pan becomes dry, add more water during cooking. Taste for seasoning. Serve warm.

Olive oil, white wine, and fresh vegetables, all produced at Bonpas, come together in this Provençal stew (left). The kitchen garden is still enclosed by the monastery's original walls, with its recesses for beehives (above).

FRICOT D'ARTICHAUTS DE PROVENCE

ARTICHOKES SIMMERED IN OLIVE OIL AND WHITE WINE

Little mauve artichokes the size of a child's hand are a specialty of Provence. Those in the Bonpas garden are often eaten raw, leaves and all, à la croque de sel – with sea salt and butter. Or they may be simmered in this fricot, or stew. Common globe artichokes, while too tough to eat uncooked,

SOUPE AU PISTOU

VEGETABLE SOUP WITH GARLIC AND BASIL

The garden at Bonpas provides Yveline Casalis with fresh kidney beans for her soupe au pistou, so she can dispense with the preliminaries of soaking and parboiling, and just simmer the beans with the other vegetables for an easy seasonal treat. (Later in the year, the dried beans must be parboiled first, as here.) In her variation of the time-honored garlic and basil pistou sauce, Madame Casalis blends in tomatoes, adding a fresh bite to her base of long-simmered vegetables and beans.

6 servings

¾ cup DRIED RED KIDNEY BEANS

¾ cup DRIED WHITE KIDNEY BEANS

6 ounces GREEN BEANS, CUT INTO
½-inch PIECES

3 CARROTS, CUT INTO ½-inch PIECES

3 POTATOES, CUT INTO ½-inch PIECES

2 quarts WATER

SALT AND PEPPER

1 MEDIUM ZUCCHINI, CUT INTO
½-inch PIECES

For the pistou

4 CLOVES GARLIC

2 TOMATOES, PEELED AND SEEDED*

2 cups LOOSELY PACKED FRESH
BASIL LEAVES

¾ cup OLIVE OIL

1 tsp SALT

Soak the dried red and white beans separately overnight in cold water; drain. Put them in separate large saucepans and cover them generously with water. Bring the water to a boil, then reduce the heat and simmer the beans until they are tender but still a little firm, 1 to 1½ hours, depending on the age of the beans. Drain the beans thoroughly.

Soupe au Pistou is served throughout the year at Bonpas, using fresh or dried beans as the season dictates.

Combine the red and white beans with all the vegetables, except the zucchini, in a saucepan. Add the water and a little salt and pepper. Bring the water to a boil, then reduce the heat and simmer over low heat until the vegetables are very tender, 1¼ to 1½ hours. Add the zucchini 15 minutes before the end of cooking. (The soup can be made ahead to this point and refrigerated up to 2 days.)

To make the *pistou*, process the garlic, tomatoes, basil, oil, and salt in a food processor or blender until smooth. Taste it for seasoning.

Reheat the soup if necessary and stir in the *pistou*. Taste the soup for seasoning and add salt and pepper if needed. Ladle the soup into warmed soup bowls.

VIN D'ORANGE

FORTIFIED ORANGE WINE

Yveline Casalis always has bottles of homemade orange wine on hand to offer as an aperitif to friends. At the end of July, following the peach harvest, she also prepares a vin de pêche, *made with the peach tree leaves. Forty is the magic number associated with that fortified wine – Madame Casalis computes 40 peach leaves and 40 sugar cubes for every quart of wine and half-quart of* eau-de-vie. *Leave this brew to macerate for 40 days and – voilà! . . . perfection.*

Makes about 2 quarts

1½ quarts WHITE WINE

1 cup NEUTRAL *EAU-DE-VIE*
OR VODKA

1 cup SUGAR

1 LEMON, SLICED

2 ORANGES, SLICED

STRIP DRIED BITTER ORANGE PEEL

½ STICK CINNAMON

2½-quart PRESERVING JAR

Sterilize the preserving jar*. Combine the wine, *eau-de-vie* or vodka, and sugar in the jar and seal it. Leave it in a cool place overnight, shaking the jar thoroughly from time to time or as often as possible during this period.

The next day, add the lemon, oranges, orange peel, and cinnamon to the jar. Seal the jar again and leave it at least 6 weeks, shaking it once a week.

Strain the liquid through cheesecloth into a pitcher. Pour the liquid back into the jar or into four wine bottles and seal.

This wine can be kept 3 or 4 months, stored in a cool, dark place. It is best enjoyed served well chilled.

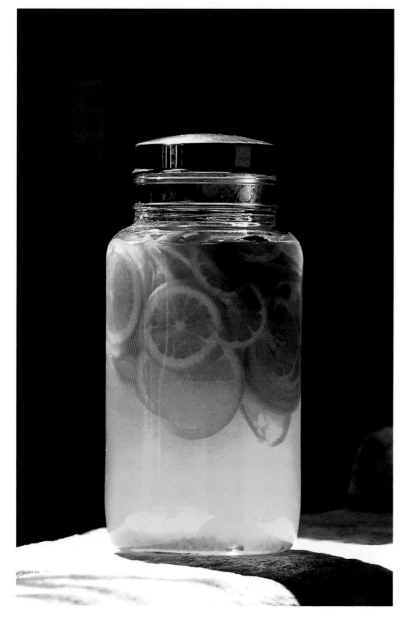

NOUGAT NOIR

HONEY AND ALMOND CANDY

Christmas is a great celebration in the Casalis household, with Provençal customs such as the 13 desserts of Christmas followed with enthusiasm. Desserts are likely to include dried figs, dark and golden raisins, stuffed dates and walnuts, almonds, calissons (almond paste diamonds), candied melon, clementines, oreillettes (pastry fritters), white nougat, and this black nougat, a confection of caramelized honey and toasted almonds.

Makes about 1 pound

⅔ cup HONEY
½ pound WHOLE UNBLANCHED ALMONDS
GRATED ZEST OF 1 ORANGE

*Two 9-×5-×4-inch LOAF PANS;
RICE PAPER OR PARCHMENT
PAPER*

Oil one loaf pan and line the bottom with rice paper or with parchment paper.

Have ready a bowl of cold water. Put the honey in a heavy saucepan and cook over fairly low heat, stirring constantly, until the honey begins to bubble, about 5 minutes. Add the almonds and orange zest and continue to stir until the honey turns deep brown and the almonds make a popping sound, showing they are toasted, about 15 minutes.

Remove the pan from the heat and plunge the base briefly in the bowl of cold water to stop the honey from cooking further. Stir until the nougat cools slightly, about 1 minute, then spoon it into the prepared loaf pan. Flatten the nougat with the back of an oiled spoon. Press a piece of rice paper or parchment paper the size of the inside of the pan on top. Flatten the nougat with the second loaf pan and cans of food or other weights. Refrigerate until firm, about 4 hours.

Peel off parchment paper, but leave on rice paper. Cut the nougat into 1-inch squares. This nougat will keep for several weeks in an airtight container.

Madame Casalis' orange wine is served as part of the Christmas festivities, a reminder of the Mediterranean summer sun.

CHÂTEAU DE SAINT-VINCENT

"A PINE FOREST GLITTERING WITH SUNLIGHT, CASCADING DOWN THE HILLSIDE BEFORE MY VERY EYES. ON THE HORIZON, THE MOUNTAINOUS OUTLINE OF THE ALPILLES . . . NOT A MURMUR, YET FAINTLY, EVER SO FAR AWAY, THE PIPING OF A FLUTE, THE CALL OF A CURLEW IN THE LAVENDER, A TINKLE OF MULE BELLS ON THE ROAD. THIS BEAUTIFUL LANDSCAPE OF PROVENCE LIVES BY THE LIGHT OF THE SUN." SO WROTE THE NOVELIST ALPHONSE DAUDET SHORTLY AFTER HIS FIVE-MONTH STAY AT JONQUIÈRES-SAINT-VINCENT DURING 1866.

THE CHÂTEAU DE SAINT-VINCENT REMAINS UNCHANGED FROM HIS TIME. ITS GOLDEN SANDSTONE TOWERS, VERY PROVENÇAL IN STYLE, STILL GREET THE VISITOR. "SAINT-VINCENT IS A HOUSE OF MANY FACES," EXPLAIN ITS CURRENT OWNERS, THE COMTE AND COMTESSE JEAN DE DEMANDOLX-DEDONS. BEHIND THE 18TH-CENTURY FAÇADE IS HIDDEN THE TRADITIONAL CLOSED COURTYARD, WHOSE CELLARS ARE NOW USED FOR STORING WINE AND AS A *CAVEAU DE DÉGUSTATION.* "THE FOUNDATIONS PROBABLY DATE BACK TO THE 13TH CENTURY," SAYS CHANTAL DE DEMANDOLX-DEDONS. "WE KNOW THAT IN THE 17TH CENTURY THERE WAS ALREADY A SUBSTANTIAL PROVENÇAL *MAS*, OR COUNTRY HOUSE, HERE. YOU CAN SEE THE DATE ON THE LINTEL OVER THE DOOR."

The Provençal property of Saint-Vincent has always been primarily a working farm. The buildings have been modified over the centuries with the earliest dating back to the 1400s and the latest being the gracious 18th-century main house (left). The glass covering the ancient map of the property reflects the sunny gardens (below).

Now, as then, Saint-Vincent remains a flourishing agricultural property, though in extent it is reduced to about ninety acres of vines and cherries, a fraction of the 18th-century domain. The sun so appreciated by Daudet ripens fruit in record time, so that the Muscat table grapes of Saint-Vincent – the prized Hambourg variety – reach the market the first week in August. At the other extreme of the season, in January, the village marks the festival of Saint-Vincent with the usual mass in a chilly 12th-century chapel, followed by a rather more enjoyable lunch which lasts five hours – because, I was told, the congregation mainly comprises local winemakers, who gather together in honor of their patron saint and sample their produce.

The robust red and rosé wines made around Jonquières-Saint-Vincent are classified "Costières de Nîmes." One might describe them as like the wines of Côtes-du-Rhône, but less famous. Likewise the countryside. Just over the Rhône in the Lubéron, second homes abound and tourists proliferate. Here in the Gard, the scene is much as Daudet found it – silent, sun-baked, its own land.

Cherry time – the bright red "Burlat" variety grows on the property and is harvested by migrant workers who come from Algeria every year (right and below).

Firm, juicy cherries are essential for Les Cerises Saint-Vincent so that they keep their shape during cooking.

LES CERISES SAINT-VINCENT

CHERRIES FLAMED WITH KIRSCH

At the Château de Saint-Vincent, May ends in a flurry of activity. The cherry trees begin to droop under the weight of their fruit, and cherry pickers, here for the harvest, work at a feverish pace to gather the ripe Burlat cherries at their peak. The crisp-textured Burlats are perfect for this recipe because they are simmered briefly, before red currant jelly and kirsch are added, but hold their shape well. Juicy cherries and best-quality jelly make all the difference in this dessert. Serve it with vanilla ice cream and you have a cousin to cherries jubilee.

4 servings

2 pounds CHERRIES, PITTED
2 cups WATER
2 tbsp SUGAR, MORE IF NEEDED
1 cup RED CURRANT JELLY
¼ cup KIRSCH OR BRANDY

Combine the cherries, water, and sugar in a large frying pan. Add more sugar if the cherries are sour. Bring to a boil, then reduce the heat and simmer, stirring occasionally, until the cherries are just tender, about 5 minutes.

Remove the pan from the heat and stir in the red currant jelly until melted. Let the cherries cool to lukewarm.

Heat the kirsch or brandy in a small saucepan for 20 or 30 seconds. Tip the pan and light the spirit with a match. (Stand back from the flame.) Pour it flaming over the cherries. Stir lightly to mix and serve at once.

Bourride, the traditional Mediterranean fish stew, is a celebration of Provençal flavors from land and sea.

BOURRIDE

MEDITERRANEAN FISH STEW WITH GARLIC MAYONNAISE

Less famous than its colorful cousin bouillabaisse, bourride *is a white fish stew, always served with the garlic mayonnaise* aïoli. *It is native to western Provence and Languedoc, where fishmongers sell a mixture "for* bourride*" without bothering to detail the different fish. A good* bourride *should contain some white fish such as sea bass, bream, John Dory, and whiting, some firm fish like monkfish and eel, and some richer fish such as mackerel. On the Mediterranean, the bony but full-flavored scorpion fish, or* rascasse, *is always included but it is hard to find elsewhere. Serve the stew with crusty bread for mopping up the wonderful sauce.*

8 to 10 servings

4 pounds SALTWATER FISH,
CLEANED, TRIMMED, AND CUT INTO
THICK STEAKS, WITH THE BONE
1 ONION, SLICED
½ BULB FENNEL, SLICED
SPRIG FRESH THYME
1 BAY LEAF
PARED STRIP ORANGE ZEST
SALT AND PEPPER
1 quart WATER, MORE IF NEEDED
6 LARGE EGG YOLKS

For the aïoli
6 TO 8 CLOVES GARLIC
2 LARGE EGG YOLKS
SALT AND WHITE PEPPER
1 cup OLIVE OIL
JUICE OF 1 LEMON
1 tsp LUKEWARM WATER

For the *aïoli*, purée the garlic, egg yolks, and seasoning in a food processor or blender. With the blades still turning, add the oil in a thin stream. Add the lemon juice and water at the end. Season if needed. (*Aïoli* can be made 3 days ahead and kept refrigerated.)

Prepare the fish up to 4 hours ahead, if you like, and keep it in the refrigerator. However, cook the *bourride* only just before serving.

Pack the firm fish, onion, fennel, thyme, bay leaf, orange zest, salt, and pepper in a large saucepan and add the water. Bring the water to a boil, then simmer briskly for 5 minutes. Add the remaining fish, putting the more delicate, tender pieces on top. The water should just cover the fish, so add more if needed. Simmer until the fish just flakes easily, 8 to 12 minutes.

Transfer the fish to a platter and, if you like, remove bones and skin. Cover with aluminum foil and keep warm. Strain the broth; keep hot.

Whisk the *aïoli* with the egg yolks in a heavy

saucepan. Gradually whisk in the hot broth. Set the pan over low heat and stir constantly until the sauce thickens to the consistency of thin cream. (The heat of the mixture will cook and thicken the egg yolks. Don't boil the sauce or it may curdle.) Taste it for seasoning.

To serve, divide the fish among warmed shallow bowls. Ladle the sauce on top and serve.

GRATIN DE COURGETTES

GOLDEN ZUCCHINI GRATIN

For Chantal de Demandolx-Dedons, Pentecost brings a stream of visitors for the fériade *in Nîmes – the annual festivities inspired by a week of bullfights here – as does the summer music festival at Aix-en-Provence. She looks toward cold dishes, terrines, baked fish, little* tellines, *or cockles, steamed open with garlic, and this gratin of zucchini, which can be served hot or cold.*

6 servings

3 pounds ZUCCHINI, GRATED
SALT AND PEPPER
¼ cup OLIVE OIL
2 LARGE ONIONS, CHOPPED
½ cup CHICKEN STOCK (see page 221)

2 CLOVES GARLIC, POUNDED TO A PASTE
½ cup CRÈME FRAÎCHE (see page 220)
OR HEAVY CREAM
1 cup GRATED GRUYÈRE CHEESE

2-quart GRATIN OR BAKING DISH

Pack a layer of grated zucchini in a colander set over a bowl and sprinkle it generously with salt. Continue layering zucchini and salt until all the zucchini is in the colander, pressing well. Let drain 30 minutes, then rinse and squeeze out all the liquid by handfuls.

Preheat the oven to 375°F and butter the gratin dish.

Heat half the oil in a large frying pan and add the onions. Sauté them over medium heat until soft, 6 to 8 minutes, then remove. Add the remaining oil to the pan and sauté the zucchini in batches over high heat, tossing and stirring constantly, until just tender, 2 to 3 minutes. Add all the zucchini to the pan with the onions and pepper. Stir the stock into the garlic paste, then add it to the zucchini. Cook over high heat, stirring often, until the liquid evaporates, 3 to 4 minutes. Stir in the crème fraîche or cream. Taste for seasoning.

Transfer the zucchini mixture to the prepared dish. Smooth the top and sprinkle the cheese on top. Bake the gratin in the heated oven until hot and golden, 15 to 20 minutes.

"Drippings" from the wine-making process are collected and stored in wooden casks, then eventually transformed into vinegar (above). Tradition is very much alive in Jonquières with Provençal songs, processions, and a lively celebration of the feast of Saint-Vincent, patron saint of vignerons, held in January every year. Local wines, of course, are sampled (below left).

CHÂTEAU DE FLAUGERGUES

THE CHÂTEAU DE FLAUGERGUES WAS BUILT AS A *FOLIE*, A WORD THAT IN FRENCH ALSO CARRIES A HINT OF LEAFY FOLIAGE. AT THE TURN OF THE 17TH CENTURY, THE WEALTHY FINANCIERS OF MONTPELLIER BUILT A STRING OF SUCH WOODED COUNTRY RETREATS, WHERE THEY COULD ESCAPE FROM THE BUSTLE AND HEAT OF THE TOWN. DATING FROM 1696, FLAUGERGUES IS ONE OF THE FIRST AND MOST BEAUTIFUL OF THESE MANSIONS, AND HAS REMAINED SINCE THE BEGINNING WITH DESCENDANTS OF ITS CREATOR, ETIENNE DE FLAUGERGUES.

"WHEN MY HUSBAND INHERITED FLAUGERGUES IN 1973," SAYS BRIGITTE DE COLBERT, "WE HAD LITTLE IDEA HOW MUCH WORK WOULD BE INVOLVED. BUT WE WERE LUCKY, WE WERE YOUNG — I WAS SCARCELY 30. I SUPPOSE YOU COULD SAY IT WAS OUR PERSONAL FOLLY, BUT WE'VE NEVER REGRETTED IT." SHE HERSELF OVERSAW THE RESTORATION OF THE INTERIOR, WITH ITS ANTIQUE CARPETS AND FURNITURE AND NOTABLE COLLECTION OF PAINTINGS. THE WORK DONE IN ONE OF THE BEDROOMS, COMPLETED WITH WALL HANGINGS FEATURING THE TREE OF LIFE, HAS RECENTLY WON A RESTORATION AWARD. WHEN THE MAYOR OF MONTPELLIER ENTERTAINS VIPS, A VISIT TO THE CHÂTEAU DE FLAUGERGUES IS OFTEN PART OF THE PROGRAM.

Italianate in style, the cream stone walls of the Château de Flaugergues rise proudly above a classic balustraded terrace. From the windows a splendid view stretches over the city of Montpellier to the sea. Housing has engulfed the vineyards to the south of the estate, but the château and grounds are now protected as an historic monument.

A glimpse of the superb staircase with its wrought-iron balustrade and vaulted stonework hung with Brussels tapestries (above). The salon with elegant 18th-century furniture (right).

Flaugergues is a wine property of some 100 acres, and the Colberts at once embarked on a program of modernization. Two old-master paintings were sold to the Louvre to finance equipment so that the wine could be bottled in the château cellars instead of being sold in bulk. Gradually all the old vinestock was replaced, until in 1990, the vineyard won *appellation d'origine contrôlée* status as "Coteaux du Languedoc" from the Méjanelle district. Now the Colbert wines are distributed in the United States and Germany, with sales in the rest of the European Community in prospect. "Always better than yesterday, but not as good as tomorrow," is Comte Henri de Colbert's motto. To develop local tourism, he finally won recognition for a signposted "*route historique*" which takes the traveler past the finest *châteaux* and abbeys of Languedoc-Roussillon.

The garden of Flaugergues had been randomly planted with trees by an overzealous 19th-century châtelain, so the Colberts enlisted the help of their four children to recreate the original formal plans, using 10,000 wild box plants culled from the *garrigues*, or scrub, which carpets the Languedoc hillsides.

Olive trees are equally native, and Brigitte de Colbert pickles the green fruit each year, soaking it overnight in a concentrated brine – "It's not easy to find the right balance of salt," she says. "If it is too strong, the olives 'scorch.'" Then they must be rinsed with water twice a day for two weeks before being ready to eat. Locals like to add garlic or some of the *garrigues* herbs such as thyme and rosemary, but the Comtesse leaves hers plain. She makes quince compote too, and lemon jam, all from her own trees. Undaunted by the sight of Montpellier's high-rise buildings on the horizon, Brigitte de Colbert reminds me that "Flaugergues is an agricultural property and we are determined to keep it so."

COQ AU VIN ROUGE DE FLAUGERGUES

CHICKEN IN LANGUEDOC WINE

The mayor of Montpellier sometimes asks the de Colberts to entertain foreign guests. The Comtesse finds that traditional recipes like blanquette de veau *(see page 129) and* coq au vin *made with their own wine are particularly appreciated by these visitors.*

4 servings

4-pound CHICKEN,
CUT UP INTO SERVING PIECES*
1 CARROT, CHOPPED
1 ONION, CHOPPED
2 SHALLOTS, CHOPPED
1 CLOVE GARLIC, CHOPPED
LARGE BUNCH FRESH PARSLEY, TIED
WITH STRING
1 BOTTLE (750 ml) ROBUST RED WINE
2 tbsp RED WINE VINEGAR
3 tbsp VEGETABLE OIL
⅓ cup ALL-PURPOSE FLOUR
3 cups BROWN STOCK (see page 221)
SALT AND PEPPER

For the garnish
5 ounces BABY ONIONS

3 tbsp BUTTER
PINCH OF SUGAR
6 ounces SMALL MUSHROOMS,
CUT INTO QUARTERS
5 ounces SLAB BACON,
CUT INTO *LARDONS*

Combine the chicken pieces, carrot, onion, shallots, garlic, parsley, wine, and vinegar in a large nonreactive bowl. Cover and keep in the refrigerator overnight.

Lift the chicken pieces out of the marinade and pat them dry with paper towels. Heat the oil in a sauté pan or flameproof casserole. Brown the pieces of chicken a few at a time over medium heat. Transfer the marinade vegetables to the pan, using a slotted spoon. Sprinkle the flour over the chicken and vegetables and cook until foaming, 2 or 3 minutes. Stir in the marinade liquid and the stock and bring to a boil. Add the parsley. Reduce the heat to low and simmer, covered, until the chicken is tender, about 40 minutes.

Meanwhile, for the garnish, blanch* the onions in a saucepan of boiling water for 1 minute, then drain and peel them – the skins will strip away easily. Trim the roots and stems of the onions carefully so they will not fall apart during cooking. Put the onions back in the saucepan and add salt, pepper, 1 tablespoon of the butter, the sugar, and water barely to cover. Bring to a boil and simmer until the onions are tender and the liquid has evaporated to a shiny glaze, 10 to 15 minutes.

Melt the remaining butter in a frying pan. Add the mushrooms with salt and pepper. Toss them in the butter over medium-high heat until they lose all their moisture, about 5 minutes. Remove them from the pan. Render the bacon in the pan over low heat until the fat runs, then cook until golden, about 5 minutes. Drain on paper towels.

Transfer the chicken to a warmed serving dish and keep warm. If the sauce is thin, boil it until it lightly coats a spoon; strain it and taste for seasoning. Stir the onions, mushrooms, and bacon into the sauce and taste for seasoning. Pour the sauce over the chicken and serve.

The south-facing gravely slopes are said to be the secret to the flavorsome wines of Flaugergues (above).

PAUPIETTES DE DORADE COLBERT

ROLLED FISH FILLETS WITH SMOKED SALMON AND SHRIMP

"I do all the cooking," says Brigitte de Colbert, *"and I like to experiment – paupiettes Colbert was one of my new recipes this year."*

6 servings as a first course, 3 as a main course

5 ounces THINLY SLICED SMOKED SALMON
¼ cup UNSALTED BUTTER
6 EVEN-SIZED SKINLESS FISH FILLETS
(1½ pounds TOTAL WEIGHT)
PEPPER
¾ pound SMALL SHRIMP, COOKED AND
PEELED
1 BOTTLE (750 ml)
DRY WHITE WINE
2 tsp ARROWROOT OR POTATO STARCH
MIXED WITH
2 tbsp COLD WATER
3 LARGE EGG YOLKS
½ cup CRÈME FRAÎCHE (see page 220) OR
HEAVY CREAM
2 tbsp CHOPPED FRESH PARSLEY

KITCHEN STRING

Process half the smoked salmon in a food processor until smooth. Work in the butter.

Place a fish fillet between two sheets of waxed paper and pound it lightly with the flat side of a large knife. With the tip of the knife, score the fillet lightly in parallel diagonal lines on the side that has been skinned. Repeat with the remaining fillets.

Sprinkle the skinned side of each fillet with pepper and spread it with the salmon butter. Cut the remaining smoked salmon into thin strips. On each fillet, arrange strips of smoked salmon and 3 or 4 shrimp. Set a fillet on a piece of waxed paper 2 inches larger than the fillet. Using the paper to help and starting with a long

side, roll up the fillet into a long roll. Wrap it in the paper and tie the ends with string. Repeat with the remaining fillets.

Pack the fish rolls tightly in a frying pan. Add the wine and press a piece of aluminum foil on top. Bring the wine just to a simmer, then lower the heat and poach the fish just until firm and opaque, 3 to 4 minutes. Transfer the fish rolls to a platter. Keep warm while making the sauce.

Strain the cooking liquid into a saucepan. Bring it to a boil, then simmer until it reduces by two-thirds, to about 1 cup. Whisk the arrowroot or potato starch mixture into the simmering cooking liquid; it will thicken at once. (Add just enough paste to thicken the liquid lightly.) Mix together the egg yolks and cream. Whisk in a little of the hot cooking liquid and stir this back into the rest. Heat gently, stirring, but do not boil. (The heat will cook and thicken the egg yolks but if overcooked they will curdle.) Whisk in the parsley and remaining shrimp. Season.

Remove the paper from the fish rolls and cut each one in half on the diagonal. Arrange the *paupiettes* on warmed plates and coat with the sauce. Serve the remaining sauce separately.

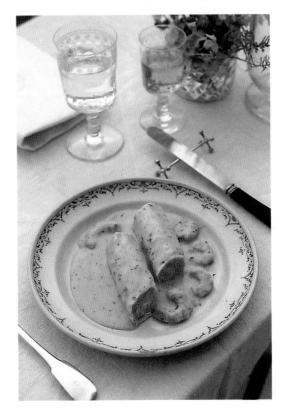

For these stuffed fish rolls, the Comtesse de Colbert favors bream, but any firm white fish such as sole, pompano, or snapper will do. With the fish, she often serves a rice pilaf.

The Colberts grow their own lemons for this jam. Frost is too frequent in Languedoc for citrus trees to grow outside, so at Flaugergues they are planted in tubs and brought into the greenhouse between All Saints' Day and Easter.

CONFITURE DE CITRONS

LEMON JAM

Brigitte de Colbert preserves some of her lemon harvest by making this confiture de citrons *to savor year-round. Somewhat sweeter than lemon curd, the golden jam is a delicious condiment for rich meats like pork and duck, as well as a good spread for breakfast toast.*

Makes about 1½ quarts

4½ pounds LEMONS
2½ cups WATER
7½ cups SUGAR

6 PRESERVING JARS (½ pint EACH)

Scrub the lemons. Cut off the ends and discard them. Cut the lemons into very thin slices. Remove the seeds and tie them in a cheesecloth bag. Put the lemon slices and bag of seeds in a large nonreactive saucepan and add enough cold water to cover. Let stand overnight.

The next day, bring the lemons and water to a boil. Remove from the heat and let stand overnight.

On the third day, drain the lemons and return them to the pan. Add fresh water to cover and again bring the mixture to a boil. Cook the lemons until the peel is tender enough to cut with a spoon. Drain the lemons and set aside.

Heat the measured water and the sugar in the pan, stirring occasionally, until the sugar dissolves, then boil for 5 minutes. Add the lemons and bag of seeds and boil as fast as possible, stirring from time to time, until jell point is reached, about 40 minutes. A candy thermometer should register 220°F. At this temperature, the jam falls from a spoon in a characteristic "sheet" of drips. Alternatively, remove the pan from the heat, pour a few drops of jam onto a cold saucer, and wait a moment to see if the drops begin to set. Push them with your finger – if jell point has been reached, the surface of the jam will wrinkle.

Remove the pan from the heat and discard the bag of lemon seeds. Let the jam cool slightly before pouring it into sterilized jars*. Seal the jars and store in a cool place.

CHÂTEAU DE MALLE

It was in this courtyard, in March, 1814, that the Duke of Wellington camped overnight with his troops. Léontine de Lur-Saluces, an ancestor of the present Comtesse de Bournazel, was age four at the time and clearly recalled the formidable commander taking her on his lap in a rare moment of relaxation. The château is built in a horseshoe shape, with two wings spanning out from the central pavilion, each ending in a round tower.

WITH ITS MANICURED LAWNS, SLEEK TILED ROOFS, AND ACRES OF DISCIPLINED VINES, THE CHÂTEAU DE MALLE RADIATES THE CARE OF A DEDICATED OWNER. THE COMTESSE DE BOURNAZEL CONTINUES THE FAR-SIGHTED PLANS BEGUN BY HER LATE HUSBAND, PIERRE DE BOURNAZEL, ALWAYS FOLLOWING THE STRICT BUDGETING NEEDED FOR A GREAT WINE PROPERTY TO FLOURISH. THE CHÂTEAU DE MALLE HAS LONG BEEN ONE OF THE FINEST GROWTHS OF THE SAUTERNES DISTRICT, BESIDES ENJOYING ONE OF THE MOST BEAUTIFUL SETTINGS IN THE ENTIRE BORDEAUX REGION.

THE CHÂTEAU ITSELF WAS BUILT IN THE EARLY 17TH CENTURY BY AN ANCESTOR, JACQUES DE MALLE. HERE IS THE CLASSIC DESIGN OF THE TIME — THE CENTRAL PAVILION FLANKED BY TOWERS, THE GRAND STAIRCASE, AND PEDIMENTED FAÇADE, IN PERFECTLY BALANCED PROPORTIONS — WITHOUT ANY HINT OF OVERWHELMING GRANDEUR. FOR THE CHÂTEAU DE MALLE WAS CONCEIVED AS A WORKING AGRICULTURAL PROPERTY, AND SO IT REMAINS. THE INTERIOR *BOISERIES* AND FURNISHINGS, STRIKING AS THEY MAY BE, HAVE ALWAYS COME SECOND TO THE REAL WEALTH OF THE ESTATE, WHICH IS IN ITS VINEYARDS, FARM BUILDINGS, AND WINE CELLARS.

Château de Malle is a wine estate with a difference – its 55-acre vineyard spans two wine areas, so the property produces not only the famous sweet white of Sauternes but also the more traditional red and dry white wines of the Graves district. Nancy de Bournazel likes to cook with them all, adding red wine to game dishes, and Sauternes to fish dishes and fruit punch. Her favorite fruit salad combines strawberries, raspberries, melon, grapefruit, and fresh pineapple – "never apple or banana," she decrees – macerated in Sauternes, then piled in a bowl with overlapping slices of kiwi around the edge. "Kiwi has become almost a local fruit now," she tells me.

Châtelaine as well as businesswoman, entertaining is a way of life for Nancy de Bournazel. She is Vice-Grand-Maître of the Commanderie du Bontemps de Sauternes et Barsac, one of the exclusive gastronomic clubs of the Bordeaux region. The yearly feast to celebrate the wine harvest is often held at Château de Malle, bringing as many as 500 "commanders" from all over the world. Last year featured a menu timeless in its simplicity – a salad of lobster and *langoustine*, salmon fillet, and a rack of lamb with spring vegetables – the better to display the half-dozen prestigious Bordeaux vintages that accompanied the feast.

FILETS DE SOLE AU SAUTERNES

POACHED SOLE WITH SAUTERNES WINE SAUCE

It may seem a pity to use a great Sauternes such as Château de Malle for cooking, but vignerons have their privileges, and Nancy de Bournazel does not hesitate to open a bottle and use it to simmer fillets of sole as in this recipe.

6 servings as a main course,
8 to 10 as a first course

3 tbsp BUTTER
3 SHALLOTS, FINELY CHOPPED
½ pound MUSHROOMS, FINELY CHOPPED
SALT AND PEPPER
PINCH OF GRATED NUTMEG
1½ pounds SKINLESS SOLE FILLETS
1 BOTTLE (750 ml) SWEET
WHITE WINE
4 LARGE EGG YOLKS
1 cup CRÈME FRAÎCHE (see page 220)
OR HEAVY CREAM

Melt the butter in a saucepan. Add the shallots and cook, stirring, over medium heat until golden, 3 to 5 minutes. Add the mushrooms, salt, pepper, and nutmeg. Sauté until the mushrooms lose all their moisture, about 5 minutes.

Place a fish fillet between two sheets of waxed paper and pound it lightly with the flat side of a large knife. With the tip of the knife, score the fillet lightly in parallel diagonal lines on the side that has been skinned. Repeat with the remaining fillets. Season the skinned side of each fillet, and spread it with mushroom mixture. Fold it in half, mushrooms inside and tail on top.

The taste of a slightly sweet sauce with fish is unexpected but seems to please everyone who tries Filets de Sole au Sauternes. With it, serve tender spinach sautéed in butter.

Butter a large frying pan or flameproof baking dish. Arrange the fish in the pan, slightly overlapping if necessary, and pour in the wine. Press a piece of buttered aluminum foil on top. Bring the wine just to a simmer, then lower the heat and poach the fish just until firm and opaque, 3 to 5 minutes. Transfer the fish to a platter and keep warm while preparing the sauce.

Strain the cooking liquid into a saucepan. Bring to a boil, then simmer until reduced by half. To thicken the sauce, mix together the egg yolks and crème fraîche or cream. Whisk in a little of the hot cooking liquid and stir this back into the rest. Heat gently, stirring, but do not boil. (The heat will cook and thicken the egg yolks but if overcooked they will curdle.) Season.

Arrange the fish on warmed plates and spoon the sauce over it.

CANARD A LA BOURNAZEL

DUCK WITH PEACHES

There is a secret to the moistness of this duck – double cooking. Giselle, the cook at Château de Malle, begins by steaming the duck, a gentle cooking process that keeps the meat tender, while basting it with the melting fat. She completes the process by roasting the duck in a hot oven so the skin becomes lightly browned. For serving, a simple gravy is suggested along with poached peach halves sautéed in butter. As an accompaniment, serve a golden zucchini gratin (see page 189) or straw potatoes.

6 servings

2 quarts WATER

2 DUCKLINGS (4 to 5 pounds EACH), WITH GIBLETS

SALT AND PEPPER

2 pounds PEACHES

1 ONION, QUARTERED

2 cups BROWN STOCK (see page 221)

¼ cup BUTTER

LARGE KETTLE OR DOUBLE-TIERED STEAMER; TRUSSING NEEDLE AND STRING

Place a rack in the kettle, if using. Bring the water to a boil in the kettle or steamer. Remove the fat from inside the ducklings. Cut off the wing tips and reserve. Season the cavities of the ducklings with salt and pepper. Truss the birds* and prick the skin so the fat can escape during cooking. Lower the birds onto the rack in the kettle or steamer. Cover and steam 30 minutes.

Meanwhile, preheat the oven to 400°F. Peel the peaches by immersing them whole in boiling water, leaving them 10 to 30 seconds, depending on the ripeness of the fruit, and then transferring briefly to ice water. Run a knife around the peaches, following the natural division. Twist the halves and remove the pit. With a knife, gently peel the skin from the flesh. Set the peaches aside.

Lift the ducklings from the kettle, transfer them to abundant paper towels, and pat dry. Set the birds in a roasting pan and surround with the wing tips, necks, gizzards, and onion. Roast in the heated oven, basting often, until the skin is golden and the juice from the center of the birds runs pink when they are lifted on a two-pronged fork, 20 to 30 minutes. The birds will be medium rare. If you prefer the meat well done, roast 10 to 15 minutes longer. Transfer the birds to a carving board, cover with aluminum foil, and let rest 15 minutes.

To make a gravy, skim all the fat from the pan, leaving the cooking juices. Add the chopped duck livers and stock and bring to a boil, scraping to dissolve the browned cooking juices. Simmer to concentrate the flavor until the gravy coats a spoon, 10 to 15 minutes.

Meanwhile, cook the peaches: Melt the butter in a frying pan. Add the peach halves, salt, and pepper and sauté over medium heat, turning often, until they are very hot, 5 to 7 minutes.

To finish, remove the string from the ducklings and set them on a warmed platter. Arrange the peaches around the birds. Strain the gravy and check the seasoning. Add more salt and pepper if necessary. Carve the ducklings at the table and serve the gravy separately.

At Château de Malle, a glass of home-produced Sauternes is the natural accompaniment to Canard à la Bournazel.

CHÂTEAU D'URTUBIE

THE ROBUST WALLS,
SLATE-ROOFED TURRETS,
AND RUSTIC SHUTTERS
OF THE CHÂTEAU
D'URTUBIE ARE SAID TO
HOUSE A GHOST, OWING
TO A 12TH-CENTURY
"CRIME PASSIONNEL."
AT THAT TIME THE CHÂTEAU WAS OCCUPIED BY
JEAN MONTRÉAL AND HIS WIFE, MARIE. JEAN
MADE OFF TO THE COURT OF KING LOUIS XI
WHERE HE REMAINED FOR 30 YEARS. DESERTED
AND DEPENDENT, POOR MARIE TOOK A YEOMAN
AS HER HUSBAND. WHEN JEAN EVENTUALLY
RETURNED TO CLAIM BOTH WIFE AND CHÂTEAU, HE
FOUND HE HAD NEITHER, SO HE TOOK HIS CASE TO
THE JUDGES IN BORDEAUX. MARIE WAS THE LOSER,
BUT NOT FOR LONG. IN DEFIANCE, SHE BURNED A
LARGE PART OF URTUBIE TO THE GROUND, BEFORE
FLEEING WITH HER SUBSTITUTE HUSBAND.

IT IS SAID THAT HER GHOST, IN THE FORM OF A
WHITE GOAT, STILL HAUNTS THE CHÂTEAU. "I REALLY
DON'T KNOW," SMILES THE CURRENT CHÂTELAINE,
NICOLE DE CORAL. "BUT I DO TAKE CARE TO
AVOID THAT STAIRCASE!"

An ancient fortified château, with parts dating back to the 14th century, Urtubie is situated in the heart of the Basque country. Edward III of England is said to have authorized the building of the château in 1341. The small shepherd boy (inset above) is a motif on the large stone fireplace at Urtubie. The Game Room (right) is decorated with Basque furniture and trophies collected by the Comtesse's forebears in Poitou, north of Bordeaux.

Set in France on the fringes of Spain, the Château d'Urtubie has a foot, as it were, in two nations. The Comte and Comtesse de Coral take advantage of Urtubie's unusually cosmopolitan location. The Comtesse speaks fluent Spanish and does her marketing on both sides of the frontier. "The differences are surprising," she says. "The fish in Spanish Irun is excellent, but more expensive than a few miles away in France. In Spain I find the big green sugar melons which are unknown across the border. Also, the Spanish cherries are crisper, with more flavor, and they look different – in France cherries are sold with the stems, but in Spain, without."

In the summer months, Nicole de Coral is a frequent shopper, for not only do her six children bring their offspring to Urtubie, but she welcomes visitors for the night and dinner *en famille*. The cuisine is simple, and very much of the countryside. The menu might begin with a fish mousse, or a zesty *pipérade* of little green bell peppers, tomatoes, and garlic cooked as a purée with scrambled eggs, then continue on to a farm-raised roast chicken, or tuna steaks baked in the oven and topped with a sauce of bell peppers, tomato, and onion.

The ingredients are typically Basque. Signature of Basque cuisine is the *piment d'Espelette*, a chili pepper from the village of Espelette close to Urtubie. Whole, moderately hot green *piments d'Espelette* are added to a dish of spring lamb roasted with garlic and olive oil, while ground hot red peppers add an almost Mexican fire to *ttoro*, the local fish soup. To this day, in the fall, the red-tiled roofs of the village of Espelette are festooned with strings of peppers drying in the sun. Each October a weekend festival is held there to celebrate the pepper harvest, with tastings of the food and wine so characteristic of the region.

PIPÉRADE

BASQUE SCRAMBLED EGGS WITH PEPPERS, TOMATOES, AND CURED HAM

In the Basque country a mildly hot, finger-sized pepper is used for pipérade. *To recreate the dish in Paris, the Comtesse de Coral takes the special pepper with her from Urtubie. When green bell peppers are substituted, as here, the* pipérade *is different, but equally delicious.*

2 servings as a light main course

¼ cup OLIVE OIL
1 ONION, CHOPPED
1 FRESH HOT GREEN PEPPER, CORED, SEEDED, AND CHOPPED
2 GREEN BELL PEPPERS, CORED, SEEDED, AND CHOPPED
2 CLOVES GARLIC, CHOPPED
4 TOMATOES, PEELED, SEEDED, AND CHOPPED*
SALT
6 LARGE EGGS
1 tbsp CHOPPED FRESH PARSLEY
2 THIN SLICES BAYONNE HAM OR SIMILAR SALT-CURED, AIR-DRIED HAM

Heat the oil in a frying pan, add the onion, and sauté over low heat until soft, 3 to 5 minutes. Stir in the hot and bell peppers and garlic and

The Comtesse de Coral often crosses the frontier to buy special varieties for her authentic Basque dishes, such as pipérade (below).

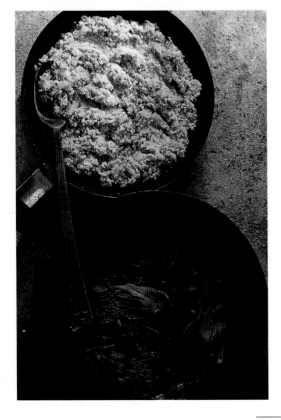

sauté over low heat, stirring often, for 5 minutes. Add the tomatoes and a little salt and cook over medium-low heat, stirring occasionally, until the mixture is very soft and thick, ¾ to 1 hour. Stir often at the end of this time as the mixture thickens. Taste the vegetables for seasoning. (The *pipérade* can be made to this point up to 3 days ahead and refrigerated; reheat the vegetables before proceeding.)

Break the eggs into a bowl, add the parsley and a pinch of salt, and whisk to mix them. Add the egg mixture to the vegetables and stir over very low heat until the mixture thickens but still remains soft and moist. Cooking should take at least 15 minutes so it thickens creamily.

Meanwhile, fry the ham slices in a nonstick frying pan or broil them just until the edges begin to brown, about 15 seconds per side.

Taste the *pipérade* for seasoning, then transfer it to warmed plates. Top each serving with a slice of ham and serve immediately.

GÂTEAU BASQUE

BUTTERY BASQUE CAKE

At the Coral table, the most popular dessert is gâteau basque. *This must be the purest version of this chewy cake as it is flavored simply with lemon zest and rum. Many local versions are filled with black cherry preserves or pastry cream. If you like, press two-thirds of the dough into the prepared pan, spread with ⅔ cup of preserves, and cover with the remaining dough before baking.*

8 servings

3½ cups ALL-PURPOSE FLOUR
1½ cups SUGAR
1 cup BUTTER, CUT INTO PIECES
½ tsp SALT
2 LARGE EGGS
3 LARGE EGG YOLKS
GRATED ZEST OF 2 LEMONS
2 tbsp RUM

1 LARGE EGG, BEATEN WITH ½ tsp SALT TO GLAZE

8-inch ROUND CAKE PAN

Preheat the oven to 375°F. Butter the cake pan, line the bottom with waxed paper, and butter the paper.

Sift the flour onto a work surface and make a large well in the center. Put the sugar, butter, salt, eggs, egg yolks, lemon zest, and rum in the well and work these ingredients together with your fingertips until the mixture is smooth. Gradually incorporate the flour using the fingers and heel of your hand, then work the dough gently until smooth. It will be quite sticky.

Flour your hands and transfer the dough to the prepared pan, smoothing it to an even layer. Brush the top of the dough with the egg glaze and mark a lattice design with a fork.

Bake the cake in the heated oven until firm and golden, 40 to 50 minutes. Unmold it onto a rack, turn right side up, and let cool. Serve at room temperature. The flavor of the cake improves on standing. Store it in an airtight container up to 3 days.

Gâteau Basque – this specialty of the area is easily recognized by the lattice, which is always traced with a fork on the top crust.

CHÂTEAU D'ARCANGUES

THE ARCANGUES DYNASTY HAS NOT ONLY LIVED ON THE SAME PROPERTY SINCE 1150, BUT THE DEEDS OF TITLE HAVE ALWAYS PASSED FROM FATHER TO SON. THE PRESENT MARQUIS, GUY D'ARCANGUES, THINKS THIS MUST BE A RECORD IN FRANCE. HOWEVER, NO FEWER THAN FOUR *CHÂTEAUX* HAVE SUCCEEDED EACH OTHER ON THE SAME SITE, THE LATEST DATING TO 1900 AND FASHIONED IN THE STYLE OF THE SEASIDE PALACES OF NEARBY BIARRITZ.

THE RAMBLING, WISTERIA-COVERED FAÇADE GIVES LITTLE CLUE TO THE GRANDEUR WITHIN. HERE CENTURIES OF FAMILY TREASURES GRACE A GREAT PANELED LIBRARY, AS WELL AS AN 18TH-CENTURY SALON HUNG WITH MAJESTIC GOBELIN TAPESTRIES. ARCANGUES ALSO BOASTS ONE OF THE MOST SPLENDID DINING ROOMS IN PROVINCIAL FRANCE. IT WAS HERE IN THE 1920S THAT THE SEVENTH MARQUIS D'ARCANGUES, CLOSE FRIEND OF KING ALPHONSE XIII OF SPAIN, RECEIVED LUMINARIES SUCH AS MAURICE RAVEL, STRAVINSKY, HEMINGWAY, ANDRÉ GIDE, JEAN COCTEAU, AND SACHA GUITRY. FOLLOWING IN THE STEPS OF HIS FATHER, THE PRESENT MARQUIS HAS MADE HIS MARK ON THE FRENCH ARTISTIC SCENE, AND WISHES TO MAKE THE CHÂTEAU "A CROSSROADS OF THE CULTURAL WORLD." RECENT VISITORS HAVE INCLUDED CATHERINE DENEUVE, SYLVIE VARTAN, AND PRINCE RAINIER OF MONACO.

A portrait of the first Marquis dominates the splendid dining room at Arcangues. The silver coffeepot on display in the center of the table was a gift from the Duke of Wellington when he occupied Arcangues in 1814.

This Baccarat crystal glass is etched with the Marquis d'Arcangues' crown and initial (top left and inset above).

Formal menus for a winter lunch party also bear the Arcangues' coat of arms, and unusual shaded candelabra add intimacy to the grand table (middle left).

The Marquis keeps three wine cellars – one for wine bottled on the estate, one for everyday wine, and one for fine vintages such as these (bottom left).

The kitchen at Arcangues boasts a fine array of graduated copper pots (above).

As a prominent landmark on one of the historic routes to Spain, the Château d'Arcangues has always been at the center of events. The English king, Richard the Lionheart, and later the Black Prince, skirted the property when warring in their province of Aquitaine. The Spaniards destroyed the second Château d'Arcangues in the 1630s. Arcangues was again the scene of fierce battle during the Peninsular Wars, and the Duke of Wellington made it his headquarters for several weeks. He left a silver coffeepot in thanks to Nicolas-François-Xavier, Marquis of the day. The Duke was impressed by French soldiers and the conscription system "which calls out a share of every class – no matter whether your son or my son – all must march." British soldiers, on the other hand, "were the scum of the earth and could not resist wine."

Today Guy d'Arcangues opens the château for concerts and receptions. Guests dine under the resplendent gaze of the 18th-century portrait of the first Marquis, using the rare ancestral silver and the Baccarat crystal engraved with the Arcangues coat of arms. Downstairs, the surroundings are equally lavish. Arcangues boasts no fewer than three cellars, one for everyday wines, a second for fine wines, and a third for the wines that used to be made on the estate. Cooking still takes place in an old Basque-style kitchen with wooden cabinets, open fireplace, and copper pots lining the walls. *"Hurrup eta klik!"* – "drain your cup" – reads the Basque motto on the chimney beam. Guy d'Arcangues prefers to quote the inscription on the chimney in his dining room which translates as "A sharp tooth for all set on the table, and a soft tongue for those who sit around it." He and his forebears have certainly followed this injunction.

Rôti de Boeuf Jardinière, a traditional dish of roast beef and garden vegetables. The corn croquettes add a distinctively Basque flavor to the dish. Corn croquettes are also good as an hors d'oeuvre with drinks.

RÔTI DE BOEUF JARDINIÈRE

ROAST BEEF WITH GARDEN VEGETABLES

Menus at the Château d'Arcangues tend toward the classic – roast beef with garden vegetables and corn croquettes is a favorite – but oddities creep in like the chicken pie featured at a grand dinner for Yves Saint-Laurent recently.

10 servings

2 tbsp VEGETABLE OIL
4½-pound TRIMMED BEEF TENDERLOIN, TIED
SALT AND PEPPER
½ cup WHITE WINE
1 cup BEEF STOCK (see page 221)

For the garnish
1½ pounds BABY OR MEDIUM CARROTS
1½ pounds BABY ONIONS
SUGAR FOR SPRINKLING
1 pound GREEN BEANS, TRIMMED AND CUT INTO 2-inch LENGTHS
¼ cup BUTTER
CORN CROQUETTES (see opposite)

For the garnish, scrub or peel baby carrots, leaving on a little of the green tops. Peel and quarter medium carrots, trimming the edges to form miniature carrots. Cook the carrots in boiling salted water until tender, 15 to 20 minutes, then drain them.

Blanch* the onions in boiling water for 1 minute, then drain and peel them – the skins will strip away easily. Trim the roots and stems of the onions carefully so they will not fall apart during cooking. Cook the onions in boiling salted water until tender, 10 to 15 minutes, then drain and sprinkle with a little sugar.

Cook the green beans in boiling salted water until just tender, 8 to 10 minutes, and then drain. Rinse them with cold water and drain

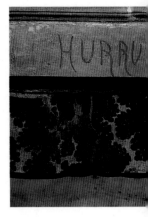

The Basque motto in the kitchen "Hurrup eta klik" – perhaps best translated as "cheers!"

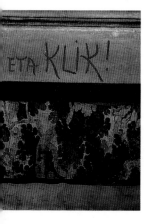

again. (The garnish vegetables can be cooked a day ahead and kept covered and refrigerated.)

Preheat the oven to 500°F.

In a roasting pan, heat the oil on top of the stove and brown the meat all over. Sprinkle the meat with salt and pepper. Roast the meat in the heated oven for about 20 minutes, turning it over every 8 to 10 minutes. A skewer inserted in the center of the meat for 30 seconds should be warm to the touch when withdrawn. For rare meat, a meat thermometer should register 125°F, for medium-done, 140°F. Transfer the meat to a carving board with a juice catcher, cover loosely with aluminum foil, and let it rest 15 minutes.

To make a gravy, skim off the fat from the roasting pan. Add the wine to the pan and bring to a boil, scraping to dissolve the browned roasting juices. Add the stock and simmer to concentrate the flavor, 5 to 10 minutes. Strain the gravy into a small saucepan and season.

To finish the garnish, melt one-third of the butter in each of three saucepans. Add the carrots to one pan, onions to another, and beans to the third. Add a little salt to each pan and cook over medium heat, stirring often, until the vegetables are heated through. Taste for seasoning.

To serve, remove the string from the meat and set it on a warmed platter. Stir the juices from the meat into the gravy. Arrange the vegetables in bouquets, or small heaps, and the corn croquettes around the meat. At the table, carve the meat into thin slices. Pass the gravy separately.

CROQUETTES DE MAÏS

CORN CROQUETTES

In most parts of France, the ears of corn you see ripening along departmental lanes go to animal fodder. But in the cooking of the Basque country, corn is a venerated staple.

Makes about 25 croquettes

6 EARS FRESH CORN OR 3 cups CANNED CORN KERNELS
2 LARGE EGG YOLKS
SALT AND PEPPER
VEGETABLE OIL FOR DEEP-FRYING

For the white sauce
2 cups MILK
2 SLICES ONION
1 BAY LEAF
1 tsp PEPPERCORNS
¼ cup BUTTER
½ cup ALL-PURPOSE FLOUR

For the coating
¾ cup ALL-PURPOSE FLOUR SEASONED WITH SALT AND PEPPER
3 LARGE EGGS, BEATEN TO MIX WITH ½ tsp SALT AND 1 tbsp VEGETABLE OIL
1½ cups DRY WHITE BREAD CRUMBS

If using fresh corn, cook it in a large pan of boiling salted water until just tender, 5 to 7 minutes. Drain, and cut off the kernels with a sharp knife. Canned corn is already cooked, so it only needs to be drained.

Make the white sauce (see page 222); it should be fairly thick. Mix in the egg yolks, corn, salt, and pepper and simmer until the mixture is thick but still soft enough to fall from a spoon, about 2 minutes. Taste for seasoning. Spread the mixture in a buttered shallow pan and rub the top with butter to prevent a skin from forming. Chill until firm, at least 2 hours.

Turn the mixture onto a floured work surface and roll with your hands into a cylinder about 1 inch in diameter. Cut it into 3-inch cork shapes and coat each piece first with seasoned flour, then beaten egg and finally bread crumbs. (The croquettes can be kept at this point up to 24 hours, uncovered, in the refrigerator.)

Heat about 2 inches oil to 375°F in a deep fryer. Fry the croquettes a few at a time until golden, 1 to 2 minutes. Remove them and drain on paper towels. Keep the first batch of croquettes warm in a low oven, with the door ajar, while you fry the rest. Serve once all are fried.

This fascinating family menu book contains recipes and menus from gala dinners held at the château over 60 years ago.

DOMAINE DE RICHEMONT

The old walls and red-tiled roofs at the Domaine de Richemont bask in the southern sun. Shutters are closed for coolness during the heat of the day (far right).

WHEN I ASKED MADAME JONQUÈRES D'ORIOLA IF SHE MAINTAINED A VEGETABLE GARDEN, SHE PAUSED IN SURPRISE. "BUT OF COURSE! HERE WE LIVE ON THE PROPERTY IN THE OLD WAY. MY HUSBAND'S FAMILY HAS BEEN HERE 200 YEARS. HIS FATHER WAS PROUD THAT HE WAS ABLE TO LEAVE ENOUGH LAND TO LIVE OFF TO EACH OF HIS EIGHT CHILDREN." THE DOMAINE DE RICHEMONT, INHERITED BY JOSEPH JONQUÈRES D'ORIOLA, IS A SIMPLE BRICK AND TILE HOUSE WITH THE WORKING BUILDINGS ATTACHED — BARNS, STABLE, AND, OF COURSE, CELLARS FOR VINIFYING AND STORING WINE. NOT SO LONG AGO, CHICKENS, DUCKS, AND GUINEA HENS USED TO SCRATCH WITHIN THE ENCLOSED COURTYARD. TODAY PIGEONS AND RARE DOVES, MONSIEUR JONQUÈRES D'ORIOLA'S PRIDE, STILL STRUT ON THE ROOFS AROUND THE PIGEONHOUSE.

THE VINEYARD IS LESS ACTIVE NOW, BUT IN ITS DAY IT PRODUCED RED AND AMBER RIVESALTES APERITIF WINE, TOGETHER WITH A SOUGHT-AFTER MUSCAT DE RIVESALTES, A *VIN DOUX NATUREL* OR FORTIFIED WINE. "THE RULES FOR THE PRODUCTION OF MUSCAT DE RIVESALTES ARE STRICT," SAYS MONSIEUR JONQUÈRES D'ORIOLA, "AND DATE BACK TO BEFORE THE REVOLUTION. TO OBTAIN THE RIGHT DEGREE OF ALCOHOL, THE FERMENTATION OF THE WINE MUST BE ARRESTED AT A CERTAIN DENSITY. THIS ALWAYS SEEMS TO HAPPEN IN THE MIDDLE OF THE NIGHT. I WOULD FIND MYSELF GETTING UP SEVERAL TIMES TO CHECK, JUST LIKE A BIRTH." AT ONE STAGE IT WAS MADAME JONQUÈRES D'ORIOLA WHO HELPED WITH BOTTLING, THEN RENTED A TRUCK WITH HER DAUGHTER TO TOUR FRANCE, PUBLICIZING AND SELLING RICHEMONT'S WINE.

The Domaine de Richemont is in Catalonia, with a generous view of the "magic mountain" of Mont Canigou. Monsieur Jonquères d'Oriola himself is Catalan and speaks and reads the language, which resembles Langue d'Oc (or Provençal), which is even closer to Latin than Castilian Spanish. Christine Jonquères d'Oriola is Basque, from the western end of the Pyrénées, and I asked her if there were many similarities in the cooking. "Both use a great many peppers," she says, "and rely a good deal on fish. In the Basque country, as well as in Catalonia, one finds dishes piquant with anchovies, olives, and salty mountain ham. Catalan meals are full of the vegetables and fruits that are the great specialty around here."

Traditionally, the first *primeurs*, or baby spring vegetables, in France come from this sheltered corner of Roussillon. The Jonquères d'Oriola table sees tiny artichokes in early spring – the whole head edible – while cherries arrive in May ("the earliest in France," says Madame Jonquères d'Oriola with pride) and the first pears are ripe in August.

"Catalans are great lovers of sweetmeats and dessert," she adds. In the pastry shops of Perpignan, not far from Richemont, *tourons* of almond paste and honey come in a dozen flavors – dark and light caramel, candied fruit, triangular hazelnut, and pinenut cut in bar shapes. Circular fritters called *bunyols* are a year-round snack, while *bunyetes*, a kind of doughnut for dipping in sweet wine, are an Easter treat. During the wine harvest a curious confection called *rob* is made with grape pressings, sugar, and sliced eggplant. As for betrothals, they used to be celebrated with a *croquignolle* – a long cookie, which each fiancé tackled at one end, meeting in the middle with a kiss.

"Ah, so much of the old life has gone," sighs Monsieur Jonquères d'Oriola. "In October, the sunsets behind Mont Canigou are splendid. This is the time when the sheep used to come down from the mountains in the annual transhumance procession. A flock of over 200 would spend the winter with their shepherd in our vineyards. Then one year they did not reappear. We miss them."

SALADE CATALANE

CURLY ENDIVE WITH PEPPERS, ANCHOVIES, AND RED ONION

Here are the flavors of Catalonia packed into a salad bowl.

4 to 6 servings

1 RED BELL PEPPER
1 pound CURLY ENDIVE
2 CLOVES GARLIC, FINELY CHOPPED
2 tbsp CHOPPED FRESH PARSLEY
2 HALF-GREEN TOMATOES, QUARTERED
1 SMALL RED ONION, SLICED AND
SEPARATED INTO RINGS
½ CUCUMBER, SLICED
1 GREEN BELL PEPPER, CORED, SEEDED,
AND CUT INTO THIN RINGS
⅓ cup OIL-CURED GREEN AND
BLACK OLIVES
6 RADISHES, HALVED LENGTHWISE
4 ANCHOVY FILLETS IN OIL, DRAINED
2 HARD-BOILED EGGS, QUARTERED

For the vinaigrette
2 tbsp VINEGAR
SALT AND PEPPER
2 tbsp DIJON-STYLE MUSTARD
⅓ cup OLIVE OIL

Roast the red bell pepper under the broiler, turning it as needed, until the skin is black and blistered, 10 to 12 minutes. Cover the pepper with a wet cloth or wrap it in a plastic bag and set aside until cool. (The trapped steam helps loosen the skin.) With a small knife, peel off the skin. Rinse the pepper under running water and pat dry. Seed and cut it into thin slices.

Trim the endive, wash it, and tear into bite-size pieces. Dry it thoroughly and put in a bowl. Make the vinaigrette (see page 222) and stir in the garlic and parsley. Add the tomatoes, onion, cucumber, red and green bell peppers, olives, radishes, anchovies, and eggs to the bowl. Add the vinaigrette, toss the salad, and serve.

Crème Catalane, a creamy custard enlivened with the spices and fruits of Catalonia.

CRÈME CATALANE

LEMON, CINNAMON, AND FENNEL-SEED CUSTARD

Madame Jonquères d'Oriola's version of crème brûlée *is spiced in typical Catalan style with fennel, cinnamon, and citrus zest. For authenticity it should be baked in an earthenware dish.*

8 servings

1 quart MILK
PARED ZEST OF 1 LEMON
PARED ZEST OF 1 ORANGE
1 tsp FENNEL SEEDS, CRUSHED
1 CINNAMON STICK
2 LARGE EGGS
4 LARGE EGG YOLKS
3 tbsp ALL-PURPOSE FLOUR
3 tbsp CORNSTARCH
½ cup FIRMLY PACKED DARK BROWN SUGAR

1½-quart SHALLOW BAKING DISH

Bring the milk just to a boil. Add the lemon and orange zest, fennel seeds, and cinnamon stick, cover the pan, and leave over low heat to infuse for 15 minutes.

Meanwhile, whisk the eggs and yolks together until thick and light, then whisk in the flour and the cornstarch.

Strain the milk into the egg mixture and stir it with a whisk until the mixture is smooth. Return it to the pan and bring to a boil, whisking constantly. If lumps form as the custard thickens, take the pan from the heat at once and whisk the custard until smooth. Simmer the custard over low heat, whisking constantly, until it softens slightly, indicating that the flour is completely cooked, 3 to 5 minutes.

Remove the pan from the heat and transfer the custard to the baking dish; it should form a layer about 1 inch thick. Refrigerate it until cool, at least 1 hour and up to a day.

To finish, preheat the broiler. Sift the brown sugar evenly over the top of the custard and glaze it under the broiler for several seconds, until the sugar forms a firm crust, watching carefully so it does not burn.

PRIEURÉ DE MONASTIR DEL CAMP

WHEN I TALKED TO JACQUES MARCEILLE, HE WAS AMONG HIS VINES, SUPERVISING THE HARVEST AS HIS FAMILY HAS DONE EVER SINCE THEY BOUGHT THE DERELICT PRIEURÉ DE MONASTIR FROM THE CROWN JUST BEFORE THE REVOLUTION. MONASTIR IS ANCIENT, EVOCATIVE, ROOTED FOR MORE THAN 1,000 YEARS IN THE HARSH SOIL OF ROUSSILLON. LEGEND HAS IT THAT THE FIRST PRIORY WAS BUILT IN THE NINTH CENTURY AT THE BEHEST OF CHARLEMAGNE, WHO PASSED THROUGH ON HIS WAY TO FIGHT THE MOORS IN SPAIN. HIS ARMY WAS EXHAUSTED BY HEAT AND THIRST BUT, REVIVED BY THE SPRING THAT GUSHED MIRACULOUSLY FROM THE STONES OF MONASTIR, MARCHED ON TO WIN THEIR BATTLE. IN LOCAL DIALECT THE STREAM STILL BEARS THE NAME *"EL RUI DEL MIRACLE."*

THIS PART OF ROUSSILLON, ONLY NINE MILES FROM THE SPANISH BORDER, IS MOUNTAINOUS AND WILD, WITH SOME OF THE AMBIANCE OF A FRONTIER CULTURE. IN THE EARLY 19TH CENTURY, IT ATTRACTED THE NOVELIST PROSPER MÉRIMÉE, WHO KNEW MONASTIR'S OWNER, JAUBERT DE PASSA. PASSA WAS HIMSELF A NOTED INTELLECTUAL AND CONSERVATIONIST WHO WROTE ABOUT IRRIGATION SYSTEMS, THE CATALAN LANGUAGE, ARCHAEOLOGY, SILKWORMS, AND GYPSIES, BUT PERHAPS HIS MOST LASTING ACCOMPLISHMENT WAS TO INTRODUCE MÉRIMÉE TO A GYPSY CALLED PEPITA. SHE INSPIRED HIS NOVEL *CARMEN*, WHICH IN TURN INSPIRED BIZET TO WRITE HIS OPERA.

The early 14th-century cloister (right) forms an oasis of peace within the walls of Monastir del Camp. In the mid-19th century, a cache of gold dinars, struck by the Caliphs of Valencia, was discovered here. The church (far right) has been deserted since Augustinians left in 1786, when Louis XVI sold the whole property to the de Passa family. A memorial plaque for Bertrand de Villalonga, an early pilgrim, dates back to 1196 (inset above).

The stone walls of Monastir (above) are timeless, dating back to the 12th century and resembling a crusader fortress – the Templars were active in the region and carved the white entrance to the chapel. Windows in the outer wall are few, originally for safety but kept as protection against the searing sun in this hot corner of France. "Unlike you in the north, in winter we open wide our windows, but in summer only at night," observes Jacques Marceille.

Huge casks of red wine in the cellars of Monastir del Camp (below right).

Today at Monastir the harsh landscape is softened by woodland, which grows along the miraculous stream and shelters lush pasture. A passion for horses has remained in Jacques Marceille's family for centuries, and now the national stud – begun in 1665 – brings stallions each year to the region, to cover local mares. But Jacques Marceille's enduring concern is his vineyards, which stretch over 225 acres, sufficient to produce about 25,000 cases of wine annually. His production includes Côtes du Roussillon red, rivaling a good Côtes-du-Rhône, plus more modest table wines, and a sizeable amount of fortified aperitif and dessert wine. Jacques Marceille's pride is a sweet white Muscat de Rivesaltes, golden and rich. "I've sold this year's production almost before the grapes are gathered!" he says. "We don't have enough of them!"

The *vendange* lasts more than three weeks, with some of the two or three dozen pickers coming from as far as Poland to earn the equivalent of four to five months' salary. With only four full-time workers, Jacques Marceille devotes himself to the land year round, leaving the marketing of his wines to a wholesaler. He does, however, find time to cook. He likes to dig into the dog-eared family copy of *La Cuisinière Bourgeoise*, the culinary bible of 18th- and 19th-century households, which claimed to be of use "to all those who are concerned with the defense of the home."

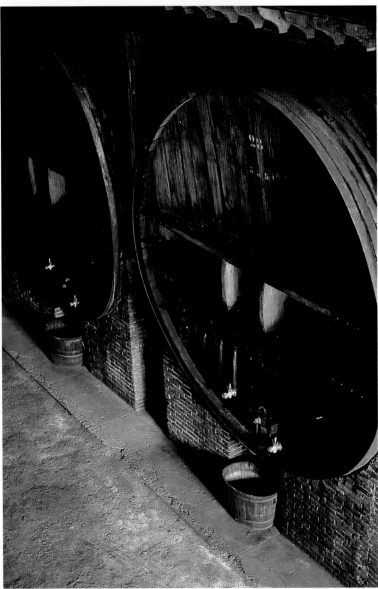

BOULES DE PICOLAT

CATALAN MEATBALLS WITH GREEN OLIVES, HAM, AND TOMATO SAUCE

Jacques Marceille likes to cook Catalan dishes like crème Catalane *(custard flavored with fennel seeds, see page 211) and these meatballs made of pork and beef served with a rust-colored* sauce rousse *of tomato and green olives. At Monastir, boiled potatoes, peeled or in their skins, are the accompaniment.*

4 to 6 servings

1 pound LEAN GROUND BEEF
½ pound GROUND PORK OR FRESH
SAUSAGE MEAT
3 or 4 CLOVES GARLIC, FINELY CHOPPED
1 LARGE EGG
1 LARGE EGG YOLK
SALT AND PEPPER
¼ cup ALL-PURPOSE FLOUR
¼ cup OLIVE OIL, MORE IF NECESSARY
3¼ ounce PIECE SLAB BACON, CUT INTO
*LARDONS**
2 tbsp CHOPPED FRESH PARSLEY

For the sauce rousse
1 ONION, FINELY CHOPPED
1 tbsp ALL-PURPOSE FLOUR
1½ cups WATER
3 tbsp TOMATO SAUCE (see page 142)
1½ cups PITTED GREEN OLIVES, BLANCHED*
IF SALTY
2 ounces SALT-CURED, AIR-DRIED HAM,
CUT INTO ⅜-inch DICE
½ tsp GROUND CINNAMON
¼ tsp GROUND CAYENNE PEPPER

Mix together the ground meats, garlic, egg, and egg yolk with a little salt and pepper. Beat the mixture in a bowl with a wooden spoon until it pulls from the sides of the bowl, 2 to 3 minutes. Sauté a small piece of the mixture and taste it for seasoning. Shape the mixture into 1½-inch

Cured ham hanging in Monsieur Montauzer's renowned charcuterie in the nearby town of Guiche. The salty taste of the meat gives an appetizing edge to the tomato sauce in Boules de Picolat.

balls by rolling it in your hands. Spread the flour on a sheet of waxed paper and season it with salt and pepper. Roll the meatballs, a few at a time, in the flour until they are well coated.

Heat the oil in a large frying pan. Render the bacon over low heat until the fat runs, then cook until golden, about 5 minutes. Remove it with a slotted spoon.

Add the meatballs, without crowding the pan, and brown them over medium heat, 5 to 8 minutes, then remove them.

To make the sauce, add the onion to the frying pan and sauté until soft, 3 to 5 minutes. Sprinkle the flour over the onion and cook it until foaming, 1 to 2 minutes. Stir in the water and bring to a boil, stirring to dissolve the pan juices. Stir in the tomato sauce, olives, ham, black pepper, cinnamon, and cayenne pepper. Taste for seasoning; salt may not be needed.

Reduce the heat to low and return the meatballs and bacon to the pan. Simmer them, covered, until the meatballs are no longer pink in the center, 20 to 25 minutes. The sauce should be thick and rich. Serve hot, with the chopped parsley sprinkled on top.

The cool flagstones in the hall provide relief from the midday sun.

PIGEONS A LA MARIANNE

BRAISED SQUAB WITH ANCHOVIES AND CAPERS

Jacques Marceille also recommends this recipe from La Cuisinière Bourgeoise, *which originally called for cooking the squab very, very gently in the ashes of a fireplace. It's no wonder they love this pungent dish at Monastir, with its sauce – almost a relish – flavored with anchovy, caper, and shallot, all local staples. Quail can take the place of squab and you will need two per person. "Serve the birds," counsels Monsieur Marceille, "with a Côtes du Roussillon."*

4 servings

4 SQUAB or 8 QUAIL,
GIBLETS REMOVED
¾ cup CHICKEN STOCK
(see page 221)
2 tbsp VEGETABLE OIL
2 BAY LEAVES
PINCH OF GRATED NUTMEG
SALT AND PEPPER
6 ANCHOVY FILLETS IN OIL,
DRAINED AND CHOPPED
3 SHALLOTS, FINELY CHOPPED

1 tbsp CAPERS,
DRAINED AND CHOPPED
1 tbsp BUTTER
1 tbsp ALL-PURPOSE FLOUR

KITCHEN STRING

Flatten the squab slightly by pressing firmly on the breastbone. Tie the birds with string and put them in a sauté pan or small flameproof casserole in which they fit quite tightly. Add the stock, oil, bay leaves, nutmeg, and a little salt and pepper. Cover and simmer over low heat, skimming occasionally, until the juice from the center of the birds runs clear when they are lifted on a two-pronged fork, 35 to 45 minutes. Quail will take about 30 minutes. Turn the birds twice during cooking. (The birds can be cooked up to a day ahead and refrigerated in the cooking liquid; reheat before proceeding.)

Transfer the birds to a warmed serving dish, cover tightly with aluminum foil, and keep warm. Skim any fat from the cooking liquid and discard the bay leaves. Add the anchovies, shallots, and capers to the pan and bring the sauce to a boil. Cream the butter and, with a fork, work in the flour to a smooth paste. Drop just enough pieces of this kneaded butter into the boiling sauce, whisking rapidly, until it thickens enough to coat a spoon. Taste it for seasoning.

Remove the string from the birds. Coat the birds with a little sauce and serve immediately, with the remaining sauce.

CHOU EN SURPRISE

SAUSAGE AND CHESTNUT STUFFED CABBAGE

One 19th-century châtelaine, Madame Jaubert de Passa, was particularly fond of this recipe from La Cuisinière Bourgeoise.

6 to 8 servings

1 MEDIUM HEAD SAVOY CABBAGE
(2 to 3 pounds)
1¾ pounds FRESH CHESTNUTS, PEELED AND
COOKED (see page 89), or 1 pound CANNED
UNSWEETENED CHESTNUTS
1 pound FRESH SAUSAGE MEAT, CRUMBLED
SALT AND PEPPER
1 ONION, CHOPPED
1 CARROT, CHOPPED
A BOUQUET GARNI*
1 quart BEEF STOCK (see page 221), MORE
IF NEEDED
¼ cup BUTTER
2 tbsp ALL-PURPOSE FLOUR

Discard any damaged outer leaves from the cabbage and trim the stem. Immerse it in a large pan of boiling salted water and cook until the outer leaves can easily be bent, 15 to 20 minutes. Refresh* the cabbage with cold water. Peel back the outer leaves to reveal the heart. Carefully cut out the cabbage heart and reserve it, leaving a pocket for stuffing.

Break the chestnuts into two or three pieces. Combine the chestnuts, crumbled sausage meat, and a little salt and pepper. Fry a small piece of this mixture and taste it. Adjust the seasoning.

Drape a scalded dish towel in a colander. Set the cabbage in the colander, stem side down. Stuff the cabbage with the chestnut mixture and wrap the leaf ends over to form a parcel. Gather the towel over and tie it with string to make a tight ball. Put it in a large saucepan.

Add the onion, carrot, bouquet garni, and a little salt and pepper to the saucepan. Add enough stock to half cover the cabbage. Bring the stock to a boil and simmer, covered, until a skewer inserted in the center of the cabbage is hot to the touch, 1 to 1¼ hours. Add more stock during cooking if it evaporates rapidly. (The cabbage can be cooked up to a day ahead and refrigerated in the cooking liquid; reheat it before proceeding.)

Shred the reserved cabbage, discarding the core. Melt half the butter in a large frying pan. Add the shredded cabbage with salt and pepper and cook over low heat, stirring often, until tender, 10 to 15 minutes.

Meanwhile, lift the stuffed cabbage out of the cooking liquid and keep it warm. Boil the cooking liquid until reduced by half. Strain it into a small saucepan and bring again to a boil. Cream the remaining butter and, with a fork, work in the flour to a smooth paste. Drop just enough pieces of this kneaded butter into the boiling liquid, whisking rapidly, until the sauce thickens enough to coat a spoon lightly.

Arrange a bed of shredded cabbage on a warmed platter. Unwrap the stuffed cabbage and set it on the platter. Pour some of the sauce around the cabbage. Serve the remaining sauce and shredded cabbage separately.

Chou en Surprise. The outer leaves of a cabbage are stuffed with sausage and chestnuts and reassembled to look intriguingly like the whole vegetable.

Le Vert-Bois

Lille

Miromesnil

Rouen

Creullet

Canon-les-Bonnes-Gens

Anet

Paris

Dampierre
Saint-Jean-de-Beauregard

Le Marais
Courances

Ittenwiller

Le Bos

Le Feÿ

Schoppenwihr

Vau-de-Quip

La Ferté-Saint-Aubin

Tours

Beauregard
La Verrerie

Nantes

Châteaurenaud

Bastion
des Dames

Ainay-le-Vieil

Jozerand

La Roche-Froide

Lyon

Virieu

Anjony
Chassan

Bordeaux

Malle

Caïx

Saint-Vincent
Bonpas

Flaugergues

Toulouse

Marseille

Arcangues

Urtubie

Monastir del Camp

Richemont

ADDRESSES AND OPENING TIMES

Many of the *châteaux* owners featured welcome visitors to their homes. Some offer guided tours, wine tastings, cooking classes, bed and breakfast, annual festivals, or other activities.

CHÂTEAUX OF LEISURE

CHÂTEAU DU MARAIS
91530 Saint-Chéron
40 km (25 miles) south of Paris.
Open Sunday and holidays 2 p.m. to 6:30 p.m., March 15 to November 15. Open to groups year round by written appointment.

CHÂTEAU DE COURANCES
91490 Milly-la-Forêt
Tel: 45 50 34 24.
50 km (31 miles) south of Paris.
Open weekends and holidays 2 p.m. to 6 p.m., April 1 to November 1. Open weekdays by appointment.

CHÂTEAU DE SAINT-JEAN-DE-BEAUREGARD
91940 Les Ulis
Tel: 60 12 00 01.
28 km (17¼ miles) southwest of Paris.
Open Sunday and holidays 2 p.m. to 6 p.m., March 15 to November 15. Open to groups year round by appointment. Plant festival, mid-April. Fruit and vegetable festival, mid-November.

CHÂTEAU D'ANET
28260 Anet
16 km (10 miles) north of Dreux.
Open daily 2:30 p.m. to 6:30 p.m., Sunday and holidays 10 a.m. to 11:30 a.m. and 2:30 p.m. to 6:30 p.m., April 1 to October 31. Closed Tuesday. Open 10 a.m. to 2 p.m., November 1 and 11:30 a.m. to 5 p.m., March 31.

CHÂTEAU DE DAMPIERRE
78720 Dampierre
35 km (21¾ miles) southwest of Paris.
Open daily 2 p.m. to 6:30 p.m., April 1 to October 15. Open to groups in the morning by written appointment.

CHÂTEAU DE LA FERTÉ-SAINT-AUBIN
45240 La Ferté-Saint-Aubin
18 km (11 miles) south of Orléans.
Tel: 38 76 52 72.

Open daily 10 a.m. to 9 p.m., March 15 to November 11. Open off-season by appointment. Hunting festival, second Sunday in September. Garden festival, first weekend in May.

CHÂTEAU DE BEAUREGARD
Cellettes 41120 Les Montils
6 km (3¾ miles) southeast of Blois.
Open daily 9:30 a.m. to noon and 2:30 p.m. to 6:30 p.m., April 1 to October 1. Open daily 9:30 a.m. to 6:30 p.m., July 1 to August 31. Open daily 2 p.m. to 5 p.m., October 1 to April 1. Closed January.

CHÂTEAUX OF MIST AND SEA

CHÂTEAU DE CANON-LES-BONNES-GENS
14270 Mézidon-Canon
25 km (15½ miles) southeast of Caen.
Open weekends and holidays 2 p.m. to 7 p.m., Easter to July 1. Open daily 2 p.m. to 7 p.m., July 1 to October 1. Closed Tuesday.

CHÂTEAU DE MIROMESNIL
Tourville-sur-Arques 76550 Offranville
6 km (3¾ miles) south of Dieppe.
Open Easter weekend 2 p.m. to 6 p.m. Open daily 2 p.m. to 6 p.m., May 1 to October 15. Closed Tuesday.

MALOUINIÈRE DU BOS
Quelmer 35400 Saint-Malo
Daily tours 3:30 p.m. and 5 p.m., July 1 to August 31. Open to groups in May and June by written appointment two months ahead.

MANOIR DE VAU-DE-QUIP
56350 Allaire
10 km (6 miles) west of Redon.
Open to groups July 15 to August 31 by written appointment.

CHÂTEAU DU VERT-BOIS
59910 Bondues
8.5 km (5¼ miles) north of Lille.
Tel: 20 46 26 37.
Open Sunday and holidays 2:30 p.m. to 6 p.m., March 15 to October 15. Closed August. Open to groups year round by written appointment.

PARC DE SCHOPPENWIHR
68000 Colmar
Park open daily 10 a.m. to 6 p.m., April 15 to November 15.

CHÂTEAUX OF THE HEART OF FRANCE

CHÂTEAU DU FEŸ
89300 Villecien
5 km (3 miles) north of Joigny.
Tel: 86 63 18 34.
Home to La Varenne's gastronomic and culinary programs. Write or call for information.

BASTION DES DAMES
21190 Meursault
8 km (5 miles) south of Beaune.
Open daily 9:30 a.m. to noon and 2:30 p.m. to 6 p.m., March 1 to November 31.

CHÂTEAU D'AINAY-LE-VIEIL
18200 Saint-Amand-Montrond
44 km (27½ miles) south of Bourges.
Open daily 10 a.m. to noon and 2 p.m. to 7 p.m., February 5 to November 30. Open 10 a.m. to 7 p.m., July and August. Closed Tuesday February, March, and November.

CHÂTEAU DE CAÏX
46140 Luzech
20 km (12½ miles) west of Cahors.
Wine cellar open daily for wine tasting and buying 9 a.m. to noon and 2 p.m. to 6 p.m.

CHÂTEAU DE LA VERRERIE
Oizon 18700 Aubigny-sur-Nère
46 km (28½ miles) north of Bourges.
Open daily 10 a.m. to noon and 2 p.m. to 7 p.m., March 1 to November 15.

CHÂTEAUX OF THE MOUNTAINS

CHÂTEAU D'ANJONY
Tournemire 15310 Saint-Cernin
22 km (13½ miles) north of Aurillac.
Open daily 2 p.m. to 6:30 p.m., Easter to November 1. Open to groups year round by written appointment.

CHÂTEAU DU CHASSAN
Faverolles 15390 Louaresse
18 km (11 miles) southeast of Saint-Flour.
Open daily 2 p.m. to 6 p.m., June 15 to September 15. Open April 1 to June 15 and September 15 to October 15 by appointment.

CHÂTEAU DE VIRIEU
38730 Virieu-sur-Bourbre
17 km (10½ miles) southwest of La Tour-du-Pin.
Open Sunday 2 p.m. to 6 p.m. June and October. Open daily 2 p.m. to 6 p.m., July 1 to September 30. Closed Monday.

CHÂTEAUX OF THE SUN

CHARTREUSE DE BONPAS
84150 Caumont-sur-Durance
12 km (7½ miles) south of Avignon.
Gardens and wine cellar open daily 9 a.m. to noon and 2 p.m. to 6 p.m.
Open to groups by written appointment. Wine cellar closed Sunday.

CHÂTEAU DE SAINT-VINCENT
30300 Jonquières Saint-Vincent
12 km (7½ miles) southeast of Nîmes.
Wine cellar open daily.

CHÂTEAU DE FLAUGERGUES
34000 Montpellier
3 km (1¾ miles) east of Montpellier.
Tel: 67 65 51 72.
Open daily 2:30 p.m. to 6:30 p.m., July and August or by appointment.

CHÂTEAU DE MALLE
33210 Preignac
7 km (4½ miles) northwest of Langon.
Open daily 10 a.m. to noon and 2 p.m. to 7 p.m., March 21 to November 3. Open daily 10 a.m. to 7 p.m., July 1 to September 30.

CHÂTEAU D'URTUBIE
64122 Urrugne
22 km (13½ miles) south of Biarritz.
Open daily 3 p.m. to 7 p.m., July 13 to September 2. Bed and breakfast available July 1 to September 15.

CHÂTEAU D'ARCANGUES
Arcangues 64200 Biarritz
Tel: 59 43 04 82.
Open for seminars of 30 to 120 people by appointment. Eighteen-hole golf course.

PRIEURÉ DE MONASTIR-DEL-CAMP
66300 Thuir
13 km (8 miles) south of Perpignan.
Tel: 68 38 80 71.
Open daily 10 a.m. to noon and 2 p.m. to 6 p.m., October to Easter. Open 9 a.m. to noon and 3 p.m. to 8 p.m., Easter to October. Closed Thursday and January 15 to 30. Open to groups by appointment.

GLOSSARY

ARROWROOT
Arrowroot (or potato starch) is used to thicken sauces lightly at the end of cooking. Mix the arrowroot in a cup with water, allowing about 1 tablespoon of water per teaspoon of arrowroot. It will make a thin, opaque mixture, which separates on standing but can easily be recombined. Whisk this mixture into a boiling liquid, adding just enough to thicken the sauce to the desired consistency. Do not boil the sauce more than 2 to 3 minutes or it may become thin again.

ARTICHOKE BOTTOMS, PREPARING AND COOKING
Canned or frozen prepared artichoke bottoms can be used to save the time needed to prepare fresh ones. To prepare from fresh, choose large artichokes to make a generous cup shape. Add the juice of ½ lemon to a bowl of cold water. Working with one artichoke at a time, break off the stem. With a sharp knife held against the side of the artichoke, cut off all large bottom leaves, leaving a cone of small soft leaves in the center. Trim the cone level with the top of the artichoke bottom. Rub the artichoke well with cut lemon to prevent discoloration. Cut off the leaves under the bottom and trim it smooth, flattening the base. Rub it again with cut lemon and drop into the cold lemon water. Repeat with the remaining artichokes. To cook the artichoke bottoms, drain them, put them in boiling salted water, and cover with a colander or heatproof plate to keep them submerged. Simmer them until tender, 20 to 25 minutes. To serve the artichokes hot, drain them and scoop out the choke with a teaspoon. To serve them cold, let them cool to tepid in the cooking liquid, drain, and remove the choke.

BARDING FAT
Barding fat is thinly sliced pork fat available at most butchers. Barding fat is often wrapped around meat and game when it has little or no natural fat. It is also used for lining terrine molds, where it is important to enclose meat to maintain a consistent level of moisture. Fat bacon can be substituted.

BLANCHING
Blanching is a preliminary to cooking. Generally, the food is put into cold unsalted water, brought slowly to a boil, skimmed, and then simmered 3 to 5 minutes. The term "to blanch" is misleading, because as well as whitening, the process also removes salt and other strong flavors, for example from salted nuts, bacon, and olives; it cleans and firms meats like calves' feet, sweetbreads, and brains; it sets the brilliant color of green vegetables and herbs, which often do not need further cooking; it loosens the skins of nuts, vegetables, and fruits like chestnuts, tomatoes, and peaches; and it rids rice and potatoes of excess starch.

BLIND BAKING
Pastry shells are blind baked before a filling is added. This procedure is used if the filling is not to be cooked in the shell, or if the filling is especially moist and might soak the pastry during baking. The dried beans or rice for blind baking can be kept and reused. Preheat the oven to 400°F. Crumple a piece of waxed or parchment paper and use it to line the chilled pastry shell, pressing the paper well into the corners; fill the shell with dried beans or rice. Bake until the edges of the pastry shell are set and lightly browned, about 15 minutes. Remove the paper and beans or rice and continue baking until the bottom of the pastry shell is firm and dry, 4 to 5 minutes if the tart is to be baked again with the filling, or 8 to 10 minutes until well browned, to bake the shell completely.

BOUQUET GARNI
A bundle of aromatic herbs used for flavoring braises, ragoûts, and sauces. It should include a sprig of fresh thyme, a bay leaf and several parsley stems, tied together with string. Leek greens and celery tops may also be included.

BREADSTICKS, FRIED
Discard crusts of white bread and cut into ⅜-inch sticks. Fry as for *croûtes*.

BROWN STOCK, see Stock, Brown.

BUTTER
Most French butter is unsalted, but *beurre demi-sel* is lightly salted and *beurre salé* has quite a strong salty flavor. You can use either unsalted or lightly salted butter for recipes except where unsalted butter is specified, e.g. for puff pastry.

BUTTER, CLARIFIED
Melt the butter over low heat, skim the froth from the surface, and let cool to tepid. Pour the butter into a bowl, leaving the milky sediment at the bottom of the saucepan.

CHANTILLY CREAM
For ingredient measurements, see individual recipes. Put the chilled cream in a bowl set in another bowl containing ice water and whip until stiff. Note: If the cream is not cold it may curdle before it stiffens. Add sugar to taste, with vanilla extract or other flavoring, if using, and continue whipping until the cream stiffens again. Do not overbeat or the cream will curdle. Chantilly cream can be stored in the refrigerator for an hour or two. It will separate slightly on standing, but will recombine if stirred.

CHICKEN, to cut up, see Cutting up a raw bird.

CHICKEN STOCK, see Stock, Chicken.

CRÈME FRAÎCHE
This French cream has a slightly tart flavor which is particularly good in sauces. To make 3 cups of crème fraîche, stir together in a saucepan 2 cups heavy cream and 1 cup buttermilk or sour cream. Heat gently until just below body temperature (75°F). Pour the cream into a container and partly cover it. Keep it in a warm place at this temperature until it thickens and tastes slightly acidic, 6 to 8 hours. The cream will thicken faster on a hot day. Stir it and store in the refrigerator; it will keep up to 2 weeks.

CROÛTES
Croûtes are fried or toasted slices of bread used to add texture or to garnish dishes. If using French bread, cut the loaf into thin diagonal slices; if using sliced white bread, cut the bread into squares, triangles, rounds, or hearts, trimming and discarding the crusts.
For toasted croûtes: Bake the sliced bread in an oven preheated to 350°F for 10 to 15 minutes, turning the *croûtes* over halfway through so they brown evenly on both sides. For a lightly fried effect, brush the sliced bread on both sides with melted butter before baking in the oven.
For fried croûtes: Heat enough oil or butter, or a combination of the two, in a frying pan to coat the bottom generously. Add the slices of bread in a single layer, brown them on both sides over a brisk heat, and drain them on paper towels.
Croûtes can be made a day ahead and kept in an airtight container. Wrap them in aluminum foil and reheat in a low oven if necessary before serving.

CUTTING UP A RAW BIRD IN SERVING PIECES
With a sharp knife, cut between leg and body, following the outline of the thigh until the leg joint is visible. Locate the "oyster" piece of meat lying against the backbone, and cut around it so it remains attached to the thigh. Twist the leg sharply outward to break the thigh joint. Cut forward to detach each leg from the body, including the oyster meat. With a knife or poultry shears, cut away and remove the backbone. Cut along the breastbone to halve the carcass. Cut off the wingtips. The bird is now in four pieces.

To cut into eight pieces, divide each breast in half, cutting diagonally through the meat, then through the breast and rib bones so a portion of breast meat is cut off with the wing. Trim the rib bones. Then, cut the legs in half through the joint, using the white line of fat on the underside as a guide. Trim the drumsticks and any protruding bones with poultry shears.

DEGLAZING
To deglaze a pan, boil the juices to a glaze that sticks to the bottom of the pan (this may happen naturally during cooking). Skim off any fat, then add liquid and boil, stirring constantly to dissolve the glaze. Continue boiling until the liquid is reduced and has plenty of flavor.

DUCK, to cut up, see Cutting up a raw bird.

EGG GLAZE
This is made by whisking a whole egg with a large pinch of salt. A glaze of egg yolk, salt, and 1 to 2 tbsp of water, will give a less shiny, more golden finish.

HERBES DE PROVENCE
A popular commercial mixture of dried herbs including thyme, savory, and an anise-flavored herb such as fennel, perhaps with some sage, rosemary, and bay leaf.

HERBS
Quantities given in the recipes are for fresh herbs. The strength of dried herbs varies, but in general they are two to three times as strong as fresh ones.

ICE CREAMS
Vanilla: For 1 pint of ice cream, make vanilla custard sauce (see page 222) using 1 cup of milk, ½ vanilla bean or few drops vanilla extract, 3 or 4 egg yolks, and ⅓ cup of sugar. Chill the custard sauce until it is very cold. Freeze it in an ice cream maker according to the manufacturer's instructions until slushy. Add ½ cup of heavy cream, lightly whipped, making sure to combine it thoroughly, and continue freezing until the mixture is firm.

Lift out the paddle. Pack the ice cream churn into a chilled freezerproof container, cover it tightly, and store in the freezer. If freezing for more than 12 hours, let the ice cream soften in the refrigerator for 30 minutes before serving.

Strawberry: For 1 pint of ice cream, purée ½ pound of fresh strawberries to make ¾ cup of purée; if you like, strain it to remove the seeds. Stir it into the chilled vanilla custard sauce (see above for method and ingredient measurements) with 1 tbsp of kirsch or lemon juice, or to taste. Sweeten the mixture to taste. Continue as for vanilla ice cream.

JULIENNE STRIPS
Julienne strips are matchstick length but more finely cut. For root vegetables, trim the sides of the peeled vegetable to a square, then slice into 2-inch lengths. Cut the lengths into thin vertical slices. Stack the slices and cut into thin strips. For celery, bell pepper, and similar vegetables, cut lengthwise into thin strips measuring 2 inches.

LARDONS

Lardons are usually cut from a piece of bacon, but other fatty cuts of pork can also be used. To cut the *lardons*, trim any rind from the bacon and slice it $\frac{1}{4}$ inch thick, then cut across the slices to make short strips.

LINING A TART PAN

Either fluted or plain pans are suitable; tart pans with removable bottoms are easiest to use. Plain pie pastry should be rolled out to medium thickness ($\frac{1}{4}$ inch), sweet pie pastry a little thicker, and puff pastry thinner. Lightly butter the pan. Roll out the dough about 2 inches larger than the pan. Lift the dough around the rolling pin and unroll it over the pan, being careful not to stretch it. Gently lift the edges and press the dough well into the corners of the pan, using a small ball of excess dough dipped in flour. Roll the pin across the top of the pan to cut off excess dough. With fingers, press the dough evenly up the edge of the pan to increase the height of the pastry shell. Prick the shell every $\frac{1}{2}$ inch with a fork and chill it until firm.

MAYONNAISE

To make $1\frac{1}{2}$ cups of mayonnaise, whisk 2 egg yolks in a small bowl with a little salt, pepper, 2 tbsp white wine vinegar or 1 tbsp lemon juice, and 1 tsp Dijon-style mustard, if using. This will take a minute (or just under). Note: All ingredients should be at room temperature. Set the bowl on a cloth so that it does not move while you are whisking.

Add $1\frac{1}{4}$ cups of vegetable or olive oil, drop by drop, whisking constantly. After adding 2 tbsp of oil, the mixture should be quite thick. Add the remaining oil more quickly, 1 tbsp at a time, or pour from a pitcher in a very slow stream, whisking constantly. Stir in another $\frac{1}{2}$ tbsp of vinegar or $\frac{1}{2}$ tsp of lemon juice, and add salt, pepper, and mustard to taste.

MERINGUE, SIMPLE

For ingredient measurements, see individual recipes. Whisk egg whites until they are very stiff, then whisk in 1 tbsp of sugar for every egg white used so that the whites turn glossy, forming characteristic short peaks. Fold in the remaining sugar lightly. (The first batch of sugar stabilizes the egg white foam, but if the second, larger batch is mixed in too vigorously, the egg whites will lose their volume and turn to syrup.) Finally, add any flavoring you are using.

PASTRY DOUGHS

Pie Pastry: For ingredient measurements, see individual recipes. Sift the flour onto a work surface and make a large well in the center. Pound the butter with a rolling pin to soften it. Put the butter, eggs or egg yolks, salt, and water in the well with flavorings such as sugar. Work together with your fingertips until partly mixed. Gradually draw in the flour with a pastry scraper or metal spatula, pulling the dough into large crumbs using the fingertips of both hands. If the crumbs are dry, sprinkle with another tablespoon of water. Press the dough together – it should be soft but not sticky. Work small portions of dough, pushing away from you on the work surface with the heel of your hand, then gathering it up with a scraper. Continue until the dough is smooth and pliable. Press the dough into a ball, wrap it, and chill it 30 minutes or until firm. Pie pastry dough can be kept in the refrigerator overnight, or frozen.

Sweet Pie Pastry: For ingredient measurements, see individual recipes. Sift the flour onto a work surface and make a large well in the center. Pound the butter with a rolling pin to soften it. Put the butter, salt, sugar, egg yolks, and vanilla extract, if using, into the well and work with your fingertips until they are well mixed and the sugar is partly dissolved. Draw in the flour, then work the dough, wrap it, and chill as for pie pastry dough.

Puff Pastry: To make 1 pound of puff pastry dough, sift 2 cups of all-purpose flour onto a cold marble slab or board, make a well in the center and add 1 tsp salt, $\frac{1}{2}$ cup of cold water, and 1 tbsp of melted butter. Work together with your fingertips until well mixed, then gradually work in the flour. If the dough is dry, add more water to form a soft but not sticky dough. Note: Do not overwork the dough or it will become elastic. Press the dough into a ball, wrap it, and chill 15 minutes.

Lightly flour 1 cup of cold butter, put it between two sheets of waxed paper, and flatten it with a rolling pin. Fold it, replace between the sheets of paper, and continue pounding and folding it until it is pliable but not sticky; it should be the same consistency as the dough. Shape the butter into a 6-inch square and lightly flour it.

Roll out the dough on a floured marble slab or board to a 12-inch square, thicker in the center than at the sides. Set the square of butter in the center and fold the dough around it like an envelope.

Make sure the work surface is well floured. Place the dough seam-side down and lightly pound it with a rolling pin to flatten it slightly. Roll it out to a rectangle about 7 inches wide and 20 inches long. Fold the rectangle into three, like a business letter. Seal the edges with the rolling pin and turn the dough a quarter turn (90°) to bring the closed seam to your left side so the dough opens like a book. This is called a "turn." Roll it out again and fold it in three. Wrap the dough and chill 15 minutes.

Repeat the rolling process until you have rolled and folded the dough six times, with a 15-minute rest in the refrigerator between every two turns. Chill the puff pastry dough at least 15 minutes before using it.

PRALINE

Praline is made of caramel and toasted almonds and keeps several weeks in an airtight container at room temperature.

Combine equal weights of whole unblanched almonds and sugar in a small saucepan. Cook over low heat until the sugar melts, stirring occasionally. Continue cooking over low heat until the sugar turns a deep golden brown and the almonds make a popping sound, showing they are toasted.

Pour the mixture onto a lightly oiled baking sheet, spread out the praline with an oiled wooden spoon, and leave until cool and crisp.

Crack the praline into pieces and grind to a powder in a food processor, blender, or rotary grater.

RABBIT, TO CUT UP IN SERVING PIECES

Trim and discard flaps of skin, tips of forelegs, and any excess bone. Using a heavy knife or cleaver, divide the rabbit crosswise into three sections: Back legs, back, and forelegs including rib cage. Cut between the back legs to separate them; trim the end of the backbone. Chop the front of the rabbit in two to separate forelegs. Cut the back crosswise into two or three pieces, depending on the size, giving six or seven pieces. Leave the kidneys attached to the ribs. For eight or nine pieces, cut each leg in two crosswise.

REFRESHING

After blanching (see page 220), some foods are rinsed under cold running water to stop the cooking and, if it is a brightly colored vegetable, to set the color. Drain the food well and pat it dry with paper towels to rid it of all water.

STERILIZING PRESERVING JARS

It is best to use only special preserving jars with metal or glass tops (check for any cracks or misshapen lids). Some have rubber seals that can be used only once and should be replaced each time. Wash jars and seals and rinse in scalding water; they will be sterilized during the canning process. Keep jars in a low oven or submerged in hot water until you are ready to fill them. Avoid using jars with more than 4-cup capacity because the contents might not process completely.

STOCK

Brown: To make about $2\frac{1}{2}$ quarts of stock, roast 5 pounds veal bones (you can use half veal bones and half beef bones, if you prefer) in a very hot oven for 20 minutes. Add 2 quartered carrots and 2 quartered onions and continue roasting until very brown, about 30 minutes longer. Transfer the bones and vegetables to a stock pot or large saucepan, discarding any fat. Add a bouquet garni (see page 220), 1 tsp whole peppercorns, 1 tbsp tomato paste, and about 5 quarts water. Bring slowly to a boil, then simmer uncovered for 4 to 5 hours, skimming occasionally. Strain the stock, taste it, and, if the flavor is not concentrated, boil it until well reduced. Chill the stock and skim off any fat before using. Stock can be kept in the refrigerator up to 3 days, or frozen.

Chicken: Duck and other poultry bones can be substituted for the chicken. To make about $2\frac{1}{2}$ quarts stock, combine 3 pounds chicken backs, necks, and bones, 1 quartered onion, 1 quartered carrot, 1 stalk of celery cut into pieces, a bouquet garni (see page 220), 1 tsp peppercorns, and about 4 quarts of water in a large pot. Bring slowly to a boil, skimming often. Simmer uncovered, skimming occasionally, for 2 to 3 hours. Strain, taste, and, if the stock is not concentrated, boil it until well reduced. Refrigerate it and, before using, skim off any solidified fat from the surface. Stock can be kept up to 3 days in the refrigerator, or can be frozen.

White Veal: Proceed as for brown stock, using only veal bones, but do not brown the bones and vegetables and omit the tomato paste. Blanch (see page 220) the bones, then continue as for brown stock.

SUGAR

In recipes "sugar" refers to granulated sugar. If another type is needed, such as confectioners' sugar, this is stated.

TOMATOES, TO PEEL, SEED, AND CHOP

Bring a large pan of water to a boil. With a small knife, cut the core out of each tomato. Turn the tomatoes over and lightly score a cross on the base. Immerse them in the boiling water for 8 to 15 seconds, depending on ripeness, until the skin curls away from the cross. This shows that the skin will peel easily. Lift out each tomato with a slotted spoon, let it cool slightly, and then peel it. Halve each tomato crosswise and squeeze out the seeds; scrape away any remaining seeds with a knife. Cut the tomato halves into slices, then chop them.

TRUSSING A BIRD

Trussing not only keeps in the stuffing, it also holds the bird together so that a sprawling leg does not overcook, and the cooked bird sits neatly for carving. Birds under 1 pound are simply tied.

Thread the trussing needle. Pull out any pieces of fat located around the tail cavity of the bird.

Fold back the neck skin and remove the wishbone (it prevents the breast from being carved in neat slices), using the point of a sharp knife to cut it out. Remove any fat.

Set the bird breast up, and push the legs well back and down so that the ends sit straight up in the air. Insert the trussing needle into the flesh at the knee joint, and push it through the bird and out through the other knee joint. Push the bird over onto its breast and, if the wingtips have not been trimmed, tuck them under the second joint. Pull the neck skin over the neck cavity, and push the needle through both sections of one wing and into the neck skin. Continue under the backbone of the bird to the other side. Now catch the second wing in the same way as the first, pushing the needle through both wing bones and pulling it out the other side.

Turn the bird onto its side, pull the ends of the string (from the leg and wing) firmly together, and tie them securely. Turn the bird breast up.

Tuck the tail into the cavity of the bird and fold the skin over it. Push the needle through the skin. Loop the string around one drumstick and over the other drumstick. Tie the ends of the string firmly together. The bird should sit level on the board.

VANILLA CUSTARD SAUCE

For ingredient measurements, see individual recipes. Put the milk or milk and cream into a heavy saucepan with the vanilla bean, if using, splitting it to extract the seeds for more flavor. Heat until bubbles appear around the edge of the milk, then remove from the heat, cover, and let infuse 10 to 15 minutes. Beat the egg yolks with the sugar until thick and pale. Stir in the hot milk and return the mixture to the pan. Cook over low heat, stirring with a wooden spoon, until the custard thickens enough to leave a clear trail when you draw your finger across the back of the spoon. Note: Do not boil or overcook the custard or it will curdle. Remove the custard at once from the heat and strain it into a bowl. If using vanilla extract, stir it in now. Rinse the vanilla bean to use again.

Custard sauce can easily be flavored. For coffee flavor, infuse the milk with coarsely ground coffee beans in place of the vanilla bean, straining the milk before mixing it with the egg yolk and sugar mixture. Or, you can add melted bittersweet chocolate after the custard sauce has thickened and been removed from the heat.

VINAIGRETTE DRESSING

Vinaigrette dressing can be made with vegetable oil, olive oil, or nut oil. In France, red wine vinegar is most often used, but sometimes lemon juice is substituted (using roughly half of the quantity called for in vinegar). Other vinegars such as white wine, sherry, balsamic, or fruit also make delicious vinaigrette dressings. Flavorings such as chopped onion, shallot, garlic, or fresh herbs should only be added to the dressing just before it is used.

For ingredient measurements, see individual recipes. In a small bowl whisk the vinegar with the salt, pepper, and any other seasonings (such as Dijon-style mustard) until the salt dissolves. Gradually add the oil, whisking constantly so that the dressing emulsifies and thickens slightly. Vinaigrette can be made ahead and kept several days at room temperature; it will separate but will re-emulsify when whisked.

WATER BATH

A water bath (*bain-marie*) is used both for cooking and for keeping food warm. Water diffuses direct heat and ensures food remains moist and does not become too hot.

To cook in a water bath, bring a deep roasting pan of water to a boil and set the dish, mold, or pan of food in it; the water should come at least halfway up the sides of the dish. Bring the water back to a boil on top of the stove, then transfer to an oven preheated to 350°F or continue cooking on top of the stove, according to the recipe. Count the cooking time from the moment the water comes to a boil.

To keep foods hot in a water bath, set the dish in a roasting pan of hot but not boiling water and leave over very low heat. The water should not boil.

WHITE SAUCE

Proportions of flour and butter to milk vary, giving a thinner or thicker sauce as required.

For ingredient measurements, see individual recipes. Heat the milk in a saucepan until bubbles form around the edge. If using aromatic ingredients such as onion, bay leaf, and peppercorns, add them, cover the pan, and remove from the heat. Let infuse 5 to 10 minutes. Melt the butter in a saucepan, whisk in the flour, and cook until foaming but not brown, 1 to 2 minutes; let cool. Strain in the hot milk and bring to a boil, whisking constantly. Add seasoning and simmer 3 to 5 minutes. Taste for seasoning. If not using at once, smear the surface of the sauce with butter to prevent a skin forming on it.

WILD MUSHROOMS, TO CLEAN

All fresh wild mushrooms need the same preparation. Pick them over to remove twigs and grass, then lightly trim the stems. Shake and gently brush to remove any earth; morels are the most gritty, so brush each one well, splitting the stem to remove any soil inside. Rinse with cold water, but never soak fresh mushrooms because they quickly soften to a pulp.

Soak dried mushrooms in warm water until fairly soft, 1 to 2 hours. Morels may need rinsing again, but liquid from other mushrooms adds flavor to a soup or sauce. Strain this liquid to remove any grit before adding to another preparation. The flavor of both fresh and dried mushrooms varies very much in strength, but 2 pounds of fresh mushrooms is the approximate equivalent of 3½ ounces of dried mushrooms.

YEAST

If using active dry yeast, allow half the weight of fresh compressed yeast. Sprinkle dry yeast over the liquid and leave it to dissolve; crumble compressed yeast into the liquid, then stir to dissolve it.

ACKNOWLEDGMENTS

Anne Willan gratefully acknowledges the help of Burks Hamner and Edie Frere in Los Angeles, and Andrew Nurnberg in London, in the planning of this book, and the valuable contributions made, as each chapter developed, of La Varenne associates Jackie Bobrow, Elisabeth Evans, Kate Krader, Craig Laban, Kelly McNabb, Cynthia Nims, Stacy Toporoff, and Chef Claude Vauguet, whether at the desk, in the test kitchen, or on photographic location.

Princesse Georges-Henri de la Tour d'Auvergne would like to extend her warmest thanks to all those who helped with *Château Cuisine*, and most particularly to Simone Monneron, the organizing genius behind the countless on-site visits, meetings, and interviews with *châteaux* owners. It has also been a pleasure to work with Anne Willan and her husband, Mark Cherniavsky, and their associate Jane Sigal. A special thank you, too, to Christopher Baker for his exceptional photography and to Burks Hamner for suggesting the book.

Conran Octopus would like to thank the following shops for their help in supplying props:
A LA MINE D'ARGENT, 108 rue du Bac, 75007 Paris
ALIETTE TEXIER, 41 quai de l'Horloge, 75001 Paris
ARGENTERIE DES FRANCS BOURGEOIS, 17 rue des Francs Bourgeois, 75004 Paris
ART DOMESTIQUE ANCIEN, 231 rue Saint Honoré, 75001 Paris
AU PUCERON CHINEUR, 23 rue Saint Paul, 75004 Paris
DOMINIQUE PARAMYTHIOTI, 172 galerie de Valois, 75001 Paris
ERIC DUBOIS, 9 rue Saint Paul, 75004 Paris
FANETTE, 1 rue d'Alencon, 75015 Paris
FUCHSIA, 2 rue Ave Maria, 75004 Paris
GEORG JENSEN, 239 rue Saint Honoré, 75001 Paris
HUGUETTE BERTRAND, 22 rue Jacob, 75006 Paris
LA PALFERINE, 43 avenue Bosquet, 75007 Paris

INDEX

INDEX OF RECIPES